MW00653891

INTRODUCTION TO BENGALI

PART I

Introduction to Bengali

PART I

EDWARD DIMOCK
SOMDEV BHATTACHARJI
SUHAS CHATTERJEE

MANOHAR
2014

First published 1964
Seventh reprint 2014

© Edward Dimock, Somdev Bhattacharji, Suhas Chatterjee, 1964, 2005

All rights reserved. No part of this publication may be
reproduced or transmitted, in any form or by any means,
without prior permission of the authors and the publisher

ISBN 81-7304-190-3

Published by
Ajay Kumar Jain for
Manohar Publishers & Distributors
4753/23, Ansari Road, Daryaganj
New Delhi 110 002

Printed at
Salasar Imaging Systems
New Delhi 110 035

The following materials for a basic course in spoken Bengali represent a revision of the work first produced by Edward Dimock and Somdev Bhattacharji and dated September, 1959. This revision has been made by Edward Dimock, Somdev Bhattacharji, and Suhas Chatterjee, on the basis of their experience with two years classroom work with the materials, and with the helpful advice and comments of those to whom the first draft was sent for criticism.

Since the first draft of these materials was finished in 1959, the first several units of Spoken Bengali by Ferguson and Satterthwaite, as well as materials for other modern South Asian languages, have become available. While we have profited by these, our materials differ somewhat in emphasis from them. As has often been pointed out, a language with the richness and breadth of Bengali warrants two, or even several, treatments in teaching materials. Our conversations and drills are oriented less toward practical situations than toward cultural concepts, facts of Bengali life and history, and selected grammatical points; to these considerations we have occasionally sacrificed the illusion of reality. This does not mean that we neglect the structure of the language and do not attempt to train people to speak. On the contrary, the heavy emphasis of our basic course is upon speaking and understanding the language. But in our approach we have aimed at a compromise between purely structural and purely cultural orientation. Student aims, as well as teachers' interests and methods, differ.

All except the explanatory materials and translation drills have been taped. The use of this book, in fact, assumes the use of these tapes. Much stress is laid, for example, on intonation, in the early lessons. This obviously cannot be understood properly unless it is heard. The work also assumes a certain amount of effort on the part of the instructor. For example, pattern drills, English to Bengali, are given in the text; Bengali to English drills of the same type are not

(although such drills are included on the tapes). The preparation of
additional types of drills we have left, in this version at least, to
the instructor.

   We are greatful to Mr. Richard B. Martin of the language laboratory,
University of Chicago, for his assistance in the preparation of the
taped drills, to our students, for their patience while these materials
were being developed and for their criticism, to Mrs. Arati John, to
Muzaffar Ahmed and Roushan Jahan of the University of Chicago South
Asian Languages Program, for their help with the preparation of the
tapes, to Professor Punya Sloka Ray of the University of Chicago for
his direct help, advice, and constant encouragement, and to various
scholars who have given us their advice and criticism on previous ver-
sions of this work. Our thanks also go to the Ford Foundation and the
United States Office of Education, to whom the second draft of this work
was submitted in December, 1961, in fulfillment of contract. However,
it goes without saying that neither of these agencies is in any way re-
sponsible for the materials in these pages or for the manner of their
preparation.

Edward C. Dimock, Jr.
Somdev Bhattacharji
Suhas Chatterjee

The University of Chicago
May, 1964

CONTENTS

	Page
Introduction	ix
Part I. Phonology	1
Lesson I	55
Lesson II	71
Lesson III	89
Review I	105
Lesson IV	111
Lesson V	130
Lesson VI	144
Review II	160
Lesson VII	169
Lesson VIII	185
Lesson IX	198
Lesson X	213
Lesson XI	228
Lesson XII	240
Lesson XIII	256
Lesson XIV	266

	Page
Lesson XV	279
Lesson XVI	290
Lesson XVII	303
Lesson XVIII	313
Lesson XIX	329
Lesson XX	342
Lesson XXI	353
Lesson XXII	367

INTRODUCTION

I. THE LANGUAGE

The Bengali language is spoken by upwards of seventy millions of people in the eastern part of the Indian sub-continent; it is a recognized language in both the Republic of India and the Republic of Pakistan.

Bengali is an Indo-European language, and therefore of the same linguistic lineage as English and the other European languages, though of a different branch of the family. The branch of the family to which Bengali belongs is called Indo-Iranian; its sub-branch is called Indic. In the Indic family among the modern languages (of which the direct ancestor is a form of Sanskrit) are Bengali, Hindi, Marathi, Gujarati, Sindhi, Assamese, Oria, Punjabi, Nepali, Sinhalese, and Kashmiri. These languages are closely related to one another, as are, for example, Italian and Spanish of the European Romance branch of the Indo-European family. There are three other major language families in the sub-continent, the Dravidian (including Tamil, Telugu, Malayalam, and Kannada), the Tibeto-Burman languages of the north-east, and the Austric or Munda family (tribal languages of central and eastern India).

The immediate origins of the Bengali language are somewhat obscure.[1] The chances are that it derives directly from an Eastern variety of an Indic language closely related to Sanskrit, perhaps a "dialectical" variety of that language. In any case, in the stages of Indic language development known as Prakrit and Apabhramsa, it seems clear that in the eastern areas of the Indian sub-continent -- those areas now occupied by the states of Bengal, Assam, Orissa, the eastern parts of Bihar, and the Pakistani province of East Bengal -- divergent forms of language were developing. The earliest work in Bengali which has been so far discover-

---

1.   For an extensive study of its history, see S.K. Chatterji, <u>Origin and Development of the Bengali Language</u>, Calcutta University, 2 vols., 1926.

ed is that of the so-called <u>carya-padas</u>, late Buddhist religious verses.[2]
Some scholars date these songs as early as the 8th centruy, though the
10th century would perhaps be more accurate. Interestingly, these songs
have been claimed by the Assamese to be in Old Assamese, by speakers of
Oria to be Old Oria, by speakers of Hindi to be Maithali, and by Bengalis
to be Old Bengali.

Bengali has a very long and a very rich literary tradition. The
high points of Bengali literary accomplishment have been in the periods
of the 14th through the 17th centuries, when a great Vaiṣṇava religious
literature including lyrics, biographies, and theological treatises was
written, and the 19th and 20th centuries, when Bengali literature under-
went a renaissance in contact with Western literary forms. This is the
period in connection with which such names as Rabindranath Tagore and
Bankim-candra Chatterji are heard.

That Bengali literature has had these peaks does not mean that between them things were stagnant. On the contrary, in other periods much
literature of interest and often of outstanding quality was being produced: for example, the <u>Caṇḍī-maṅgal</u> of Mukundarām and the <u>Vidyā-sundar</u>
of Bhāratcandra. The Muslim rulers of Bengal, who held sway from the beginning of the 13th century until their defeat by the British in 1757,
were in large part ardent patrons of Bengali literature. Under their
patronage both Hindu and Muslim writers flourished.[3]

2. TYPE OF LANGUAGE

The language which you are about to begin learning is called "standard colloquial" Bengali. This is the form of the language which is spoken by a very large number of people throughout both West Bengal and East
Pakistan today, though it includes elements peculiar to West Bengali
speech, and originally was probably the language spoken in and around the
city of Calcutta. This does not mean that it is the only form of the
spoken language which exists. Dialectical varieties of Bengali occur,
and the dialects of, say, Burdwan district in West Bengal, and Chittagong

---

2. The <u>caryā-padas</u> were discovered in a manuscript in Nepal by M.M.
Haraprasad Shastri. They have been published several times in Benglai,
and some of them translated into English (Sukumar Sen, <u>Old Bengali Texts
in Indian Linguistics</u>, Calcutta, 1948), and into French (M. Shahidullah,
<u>Les chants mystiques</u>, Adrien-Maisoneuve, Paris, 1928).
3. For full discussions, see Sukumar Sen, <u>History of Bengali Literature</u>,
Sahitya Akademi, New Delhi, 1960; D.C. Sen, <u>History of Bengali Language
and Literature</u>, Calcutta University, 1954; J.C. Ghosh, <u>Bengali Literature</u>,
Oxford University, 1949.

in East Pakistan differ so widely as to be practically unintelligible to one another. And, the form of the language spoken in one of the major dialect areas of East Pakistan, in and around the city of Dacca, differs from that presented here not only in lexicon, but also to a considerable extent in phonology and morphology. But the "standard colloquial", or <u>calit-bhasa</u>, will be spoken and understood by educated people at both extremes.

3.   THE MATERIALS

    a.   <u>Aims</u>

        The title of this book is <u>An Introduction to Bengali</u>. We will not neglect the written language; part of our purpose is to teach you to read Bengali well, and <u>An Introduction to Bengali, Part II</u>, deals with this. But it has seemed to us sound practice to introduce you to the spoken language first. Before we begin to teach you the written language we want you to be able to carry on simple but reasonably fluent conversation in Bengali. Thus Part II of this <u>Introduction</u>, the reader, is designed to follow about five lesson units behind Part I. Our reasons for putting the spoken language first are three. First, it is assumed that you will be using the spoken language sometime in the future, that you will at some time be in Bengal. Secondly, the Bengali writing system is quite as deviant from the pronunciation of the language as is the English one; to learn to spell Bengali words in Bengali script is not the most elementary, and therefore not the first, task. Finally, and perhaps most important, we feel that reading the language will come easier to you if its sentence patterns have become familiar through speech. In other words, when you learn to read you will be able to think of a Bengali sentence or clause as a unit, and not be forced to read "word by word", trying to fit each word into the sentence pattern consciously and slowly. The importance of this will be seen when it is realized that Bengali is a "leftward-branching" language in its clause and sentence structure; the verb comes at the end of the clause or sentence. If you first learn to think of the verb as coming in that position, your eye will go there automatically; good habits are more easily established through speech. Further, Bengali is not a highly inflected language, in which there are many case-endings and other factors to make the relationships of words to each other obvious; on the contrary, Bengali, like English, is a language in which great subtlety is possible through syntactic variation. You would be more puzzled by this if you attempted to go directly to the written language than you will be by mastering the patterns of the spoken Bengali first.

    b. <u>Arrangement of materials</u>.

        The arrangement of each unit or lesson within the book is as follows:

        1. Conversation. "Build-up", translation, and Bengali.
        2. Grammatical points which occur in the conversation materials, and syntax diagrams.
        3. Pattern Drills.
        4. Translation drills: English to Bengali.
        5. Vocabulary.

For the first several lessons, the system of taped drills will be outlined in the written text of the lesson as section 2.

        The student is expected to deal with this material as follows
        1. Conversation.

        The conversations and other drills are recorded on tape. Before each class, the student should spend time listening to the taped drills of the lesson, memorizing the sentences and mutations, and preparing himself to be able to reproduce them flawlessly in class. "Flawlessly" means not only in good grammatical form, but with good pronunciation and intonation as well. In the class, the instructor will move around the room, asking each student to reproduce the sentence, first in English, then in Bengali. As one student repeats, other students should repeat the sentence under their breaths. If a mistake is made, both instructor and student should repeat the sentence in full, with corrections. The sentences can then be used as conversations, with the instructor as A and the student as B, or with two students taking two parts, or with some other arrangement. The conversation is the base of the whole lesson. It is necessary, therefore, that the sentences in it should be perfected before going on.

        2. Grammatical section.

        This section is designed to give variants and to highlight formal types of structure <u>which</u> <u>occur</u> <u>within</u> <u>the</u> <u>basic</u> <u>conversation</u>. The grammatical section is not designed to stand alone, but to extend what has already been memorized. Knowing what is in this section will not enable you to speak the language. But occasionally verbal or other paradigms occur within this section; it will not hurt to memorize these. It is important that you know what is in this section -- read it with care, and drill on it where necessary. For the first several lessons also, there are charts of sentence structure included in the grammar section. Go through these charts carefully, forming possible Bengali sentences. The instructor may also use these charts as a basis for constructing Bengali sentences for comprehension drill. In such a comprehension drill, the instructor should speak the Bengali sentence; after him, the student will repeat the sentence and translate it into English.

   2.1. Taped drills.

   In addition to saturation, repetition, and response drills on the sentences of the basic conversation (which will be described in the text in Lesson 1), there will be on the tapes of each of the first ten lessons a series of "mutation drills". These will be rapid-fire sentences based on the grammar section and designed to fix in your minds the major grammatical concepts of the lesson.

   3. Pattern drills.

   These drills are based upon the sentence patterns which occur within the conversation, with variation first in vocabulary, and later with more elaborate variations. The purpose of these is to fix a sentence pattern in the student's mind, so that he can reproduce the pattern automatically, with his concentration only upon the substituted form or forms. This type of drill is good also for vocabulary. The instructor will move around the class, drilling each student on the pattern. It is to be noted that these pattern drills are designed only as a base; it is expected that the instructor will add variations of his own. It is to be noted also that the pattern drills are vertically constructed, so as to constitute a connected conversational sequence: i.e., 1a, 2a, 3a, etc.; 1b, 2b, 3b, etc. Although the patterns are given only in English in the text, on the tapes they are arranged as follows:

   Bengali

   Space for repetition

   Bengali

   Space for repetition

The student will follow the English with his eye, while listening to and repeating the Bengali.

   4. Translation drills.

   These also are based on the conversation, though they are more deviant than are the pattern drills. It is expected that the student will write these translations out, at first in transliteration and, after it has been learned, in the Bengali script. The vocabulary in the last section of each lesson is designed to go with both the pattern drills and with these translation exercises.

5. Vocabulary cards.

Flash cards, with a single item and its meaning on each card, should be made and kept up to date. These cards should be made out in transliteration and, after it is learned, in Bengali script.

6. It is to be noted that there are other types of drills which can be profitably used -- for example, completion drills, in which a correct but incomplete Bengali sentence is given, to be completed by the student with the appropriate item or items. It is also expected that unprepared conversations will be used, in which the instructor supplies a stimulus in the form of a physical object, or in the form of statements and questions to the students. Students will answer in Bengali, and, when corrected, repeat the complete Bengali sentence.

c. The method.

1. The materials presented here assume that one of the instructing staff will be a native-speaking Bengali. The following points should be remembered about this method of instruction, which may be new to some. First, as will be pointed out again, mimicking the speech of the Bengali speaker is not insulting or impolite in the learning situation. On the contrary, it is flattering to him that you want to learn his language correctly. Try to imitate his speech as closely as possible. It is his native language, and he knows how it should be spoken. Secondly, the speech of one Bengali speaker might differ slightly from that of another, just as an American from Boston will speak differently from one from Texas. But as both Bostonians and Texans speak good American English, so you will speak good Bengali if you imitate the speech of your instructor.

It is always a temptation for American students to trust their analytic ability more than their reflexes, and thus to want to think through each response carefully before making it. This method usually leads to the correct response, but at the expense of speed. The system presented here is based on a somewhat different concept. While in no sense do we discount the value and even the necessity of analysis on the part of the student in language learning (minds trained to reason will automatically seek to categorize and classify phenomena, grammatical and otherwise), we have arranged the material on the theory that by constant repetition and corrected drill on forms and patterns, a correct response becomes a reflex. It will thus be necessary for the student to unlearn certain habits, to learn to trust his reflexes. He will usually, to his surprise, find that his responses are right, even though he might not fully understand why. And do not worry about making mistakes; this also is part of the learning process, and you will have a chance to correct yourself.

2. It is wise to remember that you are about to begin learning a language which is perhaps different in grammatical and other concepts from those European languages with which you are used to dealing. Every language has its unique qualities. Do not try to impose the traditional grammatical concepts which you might have learned in Latin, for instance, on Bengali. In some cases it might work, but in others it might only serve to cloud the issue.

3. Learning a language is work. There are possibilities of easing the strain, and we have tried to help with this as much as possible; but there is a point beyond which nothing but your own effort will suffice. You will need to memorize vocabulary and patterns, you will need to work to perfect your pronunciation; there is no way around this in learning any foreign language by any method.

4. Finally, relax. When they reach the point at which they can read and speak the language with some competence, most people feel amply rewarded for their effort. In reaching that point, however, there might be some periods during which you feel that little progress is being made. All that we can say is that you can be taught the language if you are willing to learn. Do not be discouraged if things do not seem to go at first as fast as you had hoped they would. And do not be discouraged if you cannot read and speak the language like a Bengali at the end of two years, to say nothing of two months, of study. Whatever might be the advantages of modern language teaching methodology, it still falls short of the miraculous. To gain complete fluency in any language one must hear, speak, and read it constantly, and these are requirements which obviously cannot be met in the average American university situation. We can and will give you a good grounding in the language, and with practice you will soon reach the point where you will be able to read and speak; it will only take your cooperation.

AN INTRODUCTION TO BENGALI
PART I. PHONOLOGY

1. The following is a diagram with which you should become familiar. Examine the diagram and locate the parts of your mouth indicated with the help of your tongue and of a mirror. The proper reproduction of Bengali sounds is going to force your articulatory organs into positions which will be unfamiliar to you, unless you already happen to know some other Indo-Aryan language. The more aware you are of the location of the articulatory organs and points of articulation, the more control you will have over them, and the easier it will be for you to learn to put your tongue and other organs in proper position for the reproduction of a par ticular sound.

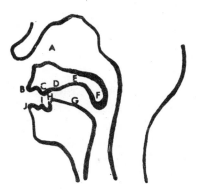

(A -- nasal passage)
B -- upper lip
C -- upper teeth
D -- alveolar ridge
E -- palate
·F -- velum
G -- tongue blade
H -- tongue tip
I -- lower teeth
J -- lower lip

Diagram A.

2. At first, the reproduction of certain Bengali sounds may seem a bit awkward to you. It is important to remember that all people are given the same set of articulatory organs, and that almost any individual can learn to reproduce the sounds of any spoken language. The vocal muscles

2

of some individuals, however, may be more fully developed than those of
others, just as a particular individual may have a more fully developed
and more controllable set of biceps or any other muscles. Therefore some
may find that they can learn to reproduce unfamiliar sounds easily and
rapidly; others may find that they have a little trouble at first. It is
vital for those who do seem to have a little trouble at first to realize
that learning to pronounce Bengali sounds well is a matter of establish-
ing a new set of articulatory habits; these will come with time, effort,
and practice. You will be able to pronounce the language well if you
want to do so enough to work at it.

> The student should be ready to mimic the speakers whom he hears.
> Every inflection, every lip movement, every tongue movement,
> every gesture -- oral and non-oral -- should be repeated by the
> student with as much fidelity as he can attain. He may "feel
> queer" in attempting to mimic but he should remember that he
> has a choice: (1) he may choose to appear queer to himself but
> less queer to the native because of the accurate reproduction
> of the sounds, or (2) he may choose to appear natural to him-
> self but seem to the native speakers of the language to be very
> queer and "foreign" because of his carry-over of English sounds
> to the other language. In adult society within a single language
> group it is likely to appear highly discourteous for one person
> to mimic another, but when different languages are involved the
> speakers of the one are highly pleased when a foreigner attempts
> to speak their language flawlessly. The mimicry of foreign
> speakers with scrupulous attention to detail is socially com-
> mendable rather than rude. The student should take every oppor-
> tunity, therefore, of trying to mimic native speakers, taking
> care to reproduce their sounds as accurately as possible.[1]

3. Symbols.

Since the roman alphabet does not allow for the representation of certain
of the sounds which occur in Bengali, modifications of it have been made
in the romanized transcription in which this part of An Introduction to
Bengali has been partially written. We have tried to use as few unfamiliar symbols as possible, but a few are unavoidable. These will quickly
become familiar to you. Those which may be unfamiliar are the following:

   1. /ṭ/ (subscript dot). There is only one English sound repre-
       sented by the symbol t. In Bengali there are two, "dental"
       and "retroflex". The retroflex sound is represented there-
       fore by a letter with a sub-script dot. The dot will occur
       with the letter symbols ṭ, ṭh, ḍh, and ṛ.

---

1. Kenneth L. Pike, Phonemics, A Technique for Reducing Languages to
Writing. Ann Arbor: University of Michigan Press, 1947. p. 12.

2. /ŋ/. The sound is that represented in English orthography by the letter-sequence _ng_: the final sound in the word "ring" ([riŋ]). The sound is a single one, and therefore is represented by a single symbol in phonemic writing; this also saves orthographic confusion when there is a phone sequence [ŋg], as there sometimes is in Bengali.

3. /th/. This symbol does _not_ represent the sound which it represents in the English words "thin" or then", but symbolizes an aspirated dental stop. For a discussion of aspiration, see below, section 4.1.4.

4. /š/ is one of the common phonetic symbols for the sound represented by the English letter-sequence _sh_. The English word "shin", therefore, would be represented in our transcription as [šin].

5. /æ/ is the symbol for the vowel sound in the English word "cat" ([khæt]).

6. /ɔ/ is the symbol for the vowel which some American dialects have in the word "law" ([lɔ]) or "saw" ([sɔ]); those in whose dialects this sound does not occur will have to learn it as a new sound. See below, section 5.3.2.3.

7. In connected sequences of words, you will also find the signs ' and ". These are intonational signs, ' marking a pause within a sentence, and " the termination of a sentence.

3.1. Since Bengali orthography is quite as deviant from pronunciation as is English orthography, we will not introduce the Bengali script until a fair grasp of pronunciation, vocabulary, and word and sentence patterning has been gained. It is advisable, however, for the student to learn to work in Bengali script as quickly as possible after it has been introduced. Leaning too heavily on the transcription can be dangerous in learning the written language.

4. The Bengali sounds.

4.1. Consonants.
The following is a list of the significant Bengali consonant sounds. The list follows the Bengali alphabetical order: the way in which the consonants are arranged in a Bengali dictionary (consonants as a block follow the vowels as a block). Therefore it will save you trouble in the future

if you learn them this way. The consonants are:

[kɔ, khɔ, gɔ, ghɔ, ŋɔ, cɔ, chɔ, jɔ, jhɔ, ʈɔ, ʈhɔ, ɖɔ, ɖhɔ,
t, th, d, dh, nɔ, pɔ, phɔ, bɔ, bhɔ, mɔ, rɔ, lɔ, śɔ, (sɔ),
hɔ]

4.1.1. A chart of Bengali phonemes (refer to Diagram A) is as follows:

		Labial		Dental		Palatal		Retroflex		Velar		Glottal
		Unaspirated	Aspirated	Unaspirated	Aspirated	Unaspirated	Aspirated	Unaspirated	Aspirated	Unaspirated	Aspirated	
Stops	Voiceless	p	ph	t	th	c	ch	ʈ	ʈh	k	kh	
	Voiced	b	bh	d	dh	j	jh	ɖ	ɖh	g	gh	
Nasals				m		n				ŋ			
Laterals				l								
Flaps				r				ɽ				
Spirants				s		ś						h

4.1.2. A chart of the Bengali sounds, in the traditional Indian arrangement, is as follows:

| | Stops | | | | Other | | | |
| | Voiceless | | Voiced | | | | | Voiceless |
	Unaspirated	Aspirated	Unaspirated	Aspirated	Nasals	Flaps	Laterals	Spirants
Velar	kɔ	khɔ	gɔ	ghɔ	ŋɔ			
Palatal	cɔ	chɔ	jɔ	jhɔ				śɔ
Retroflex	ʈɔ	ʈhɔ	ḍɔ	ḍhɔ				
Dental	tɔ	thɔ	dɔ	dhɔ	nɔ	rɔ	lɔ	sɔ
Labial	pɔ	phɔ	bɔ	bhɔ	mɔ			
Glottal								hɔ

4.1.3. Many of these consonant sounds will be completely familiar to speakers of American English. The familiar sounds are:

kh	as in American English "kit"	[khit]
g	as in American English "get"	[get]
ŋ	as in American English "ring"	[riŋ]
ch	as in American English "chat"	[chæt]
j	as in American English "jam"	[jæm]
ph	as in American English "pan"	[phæn]
b	as in American English "ban"	[bæn]
m	as in American English "man"	[mæn]
l	as in American English "lamb"	[læm]
ś	as in American English "shin"	[śin]
s	as in American English "sin"	[sin]
h	as in American English "ham"	[hæm]

It will be noticed that in some cases the normal English orthography is adequate for the transcription of Bengali. English has no distinction between aspirated (e.g., kh) and unaspirated (e.g., k) stops. Though the the English word is spelled "kit", the sound is actually [khit]. There will be a discussion of aspiration in section 4.1.4., below.

4.1.4. Unfamiliar sounds.

The sounds which will be unfamiliar to most speakers of American English include:

4.1.4.1. The voiceless unaspirated stops. These are [k, c, ṭ, t, p]. (For a discussion of [ṭ, t], see below, section 4.1.4.3.)

The term "unaspirated" means that there is no forcible discharge of breath after the stop has been made and released. The term "stop" means that there is a complete stoppage of breath at some point in the mouth made by a closure of articulator against one of the points of articulation (e.g., the tongue stopping the breath by closing against the alveolar ridge makes an "alveolar stop"); as the breath is stopped completely, a "stop can be held as long as the breath can be held. The **term "voiceless"** means that the vocal cords are kept loose, and that there is therefore no sonorous vibration as there is in "voiced" sounds. The distinction is that between pairs, identical expect for voicing: [k] (voiceless) and [g] (voiced); [p] (voiceless) and [b] (voiced); [c] (voiceless) and [g] (voiced). Say the **pairs aloud** and notice the difference between them.

Aspiration: Most **English** voiceless stops are aspirated, though they are aspirated with less force than are Bengali stops. Aspiration is easy to demonstrate. Take a piece of tissue paper or a lighted match or candle and hold it before your mouth. Then pronounce the following English words:

kit	cat	chat
pit	pat	tat

The tissue paper or the flame will move with the release of the initial stop in each of these words. The breath which moves the paper or flame is the normal English aspiration of an initial voiceless stop of a monosyllabic word or a stressed syllable.

Most English voiced stops are unaspirated. Taking the paper or the flame, pronounce the following English words:

gat	bat	dot
bit	jot	got

The **paper or the flame** will not move with the pronunciation of these words. It is clear, then, that normal American English has both aspirated and unaspirated sounds. However, aspiration in English is connected for the most part with voiceless stops, and non-aspiration with voiced stops. The two series are incomplete. Bengali, on the other hand, has complete series of aspirated and unaspirated stops both voiceless and voiced.

Pronunciation of voiceless unaspirated stops: English does have voiceless unaspirated stops in certain easily defined types of situations. These sounds therefore will not be entirely unfamiliar. Take the tissue paper or flame, and pronounce the following sets of English words:

pit	spit
kit	skit
cat	scat
top	stop

In the pronunciation of the words in the first column, the paper or the
flame should move. In the pronunciation of the words in the second column,
it should not. Voiceless unaspirated stops in English occur when following s, and when final in a word. There is a third stiuation in which
voiceless unaspirated stops occur. Pronounce the following English words:

cóncert	concérted
cóntrast (noun)	contrást (verb)
cónvert (noun)	convért (verb)

In the pronunciation of the words in the first column, the paper or flame
will move on the underlined syllable. In the pronunciation of those in
the second column, it will move less or not at all. This is due to the
stress pattern of English. Voiceless stops are unaspirated or nearly unaspirated in unstressed syllables.

There will be drills on the pronunciation of voiceless unaspirated stops
below, in section 4.3.

4.1.4.2. Voiced aspirated stops.
To repeat, the term "voiced" means that in the pronunciation of the
sound the so-called "vocal cords" are tightened; as the breath passes
through them they vibrate, setting up a resonance, much like that from
the plucked tight string of an instrument. The Bengali voiced unaspirated stops, (e.g., g, j, ḍ, d, b) are approximately the same as in English.
The series of voiced aspirated stops, however, (e.g., gh, jh, dh, bh)
will be less familiar. The closest one can come in English to approxi-
mating a voiced aspirated stop is in such sequences as:

doghouse

cardhouse

In English, however, there is a syllabic break between the d or g and the
the following h, which is not present in the pronunciation of the Bengali sound. Polish and finess in pronouncing voiced aspiratéd stops
are important in speaking the language clearly and well.

4.1.4.3. Dental and retroflex stops.
American English has a set of stops represented by the letters t (voiceless) and d (voiced). Bengali has two sets of stops of this type: dental
and retroflex. Dental stops are those represented symbolically in the
charts and lists above as [t, th, d, and dh]. Retroflex stops are those

represented by [ṭ, ṭh, ḍ, and ḍh]. A great deal of care should be **taken**
in **learning** to hear and to reproduce these two types of sound. As **will**
be seen, a mistake in pronunciation will make a difference in what **you**
say. The distinction between dentals and retroflexes seems to give some
American students trouble at first. There is no reason why it should
long continue to do so -- proper pronunciation is a matter of practice.
Care should be taken form the very beginning to make the contrasts
clear. Otherwise, sloppy pronunciation habits will result.

4.1.4.3.1. Dental stops.

Diagram B.

The English sounds represented by the letters t̲ and d̲ are usually alveolar sounds -- i.e., sounds made by the contact of the tip of the
tongue (A) with the area of the alveolar ridge (B). Pronounce the
English words

tip	dip	tank
top	dim	dank

Notice the area of the alveolar ridge with which the tip of your tongue
comes into contact.

The Bengali sounds represented by the symbols [t, th, d, and dh] are
dental sounds. They are made by contact of the tip of the tongue (A)
with the back of the upper teeth near the gums (B).

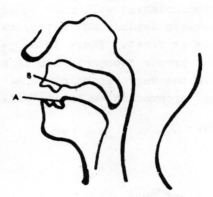

Diagram C.

Practice making dental stops with the tongue in the proper position.
Drill on dental stops will be in sections 4.4.4.ff., below.

4.1.4.3.2. Retroflex stops.
These stops are made with the tongue curled back (retroflexed) toward
the mid-palate. Contact for the stop is made between the tip of the
tongue (A) and the area just behind the alveolar ridge (B).

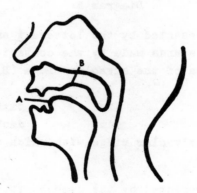

Diagram D.

It is interesting and perhaps instructive to note that the ordinary
English alveolar stop often sounds to a speaker of Bengali like a

retroflex stop. When writing English loan words in Bengali, the symbol
for the retroflexed stop is most often used. This is because the alveolar area is closer to the retroflex region of the palate than to the
dental area. More care, then, will have to be taken with the dental
stops than with the retroflexed ones.

4.1.4.3. Nasals.
As is the case with stops, the ordinary American English nasal represented by n is usually an alveolar or pre-alveolar sound. The Bengali
nasal represented by n is usually, however, a dental sound; it is ar-
ticulated with the tongue in about the same position as it is for the
dental stops.

4.1.4.4. Flaps.
The flap is a type of sound familiar to speakers of British English,
but not to most Americans. If you can say the word "very" as a British-
er would say it, you will be making a flap r (represented as [r]). A
flap is a sound similar in manner of articulation to a stop, the essen-
tial difference between the two types of sounds being the duration of
contact between the articulator and point of articulation. A stop by
definition obstructs the breath completely, and can be held as long as
the breath can be held. A flap, on the other hand, merely taps once
the point of articulation with the tip of the tongue.

There are two types of flaps in Benglai. The first is a dental flap,
made by contact of the tip of the tongue (A) with the post-dental or
pre-alveolar region (B):

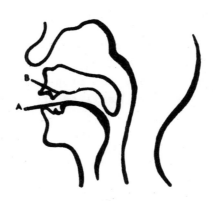

Diagram E.

The second is the retroflex flap, made by contact of the tip of the
tongue (A) with the post-alveolar region (B):

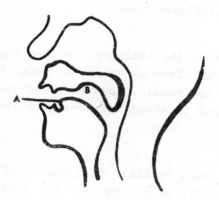

Diagram F.

Neither of these sounds is difficult to make, but **many American students**
have a tendency to use their own r, which is not a flap and quite a different sound from either of the Bengali sounds in question. A good
deal of practice might be necessary with these sounds; drills are given
in section 4.4.3.2., below.

4.2. Consonant drills.
For the time being, the meanings of the words given below are not important. You will read and hear the meanings of the words, and will remember some of them. But our first purpose is not to learn these words; it
is to get their pronunciation correctly.

4.2.1. /kh/ (voiceless aspirated velar stop). Note that in word-final
position, the aspiration tends to be lost. (With some Bengali speakers,
the aspiration tends to be lost when the stop occurs in any position but
syllable-initial.) Using the tape, drill on the pronunciation of the
following Bengali words:

English	Bengali
Initial position:	
envelope	kham
very	khub

canal	khal
empty	khali
ditch	khana
food	khabar
I eat	khai

Medial position:

mix	makha
branch (subdivision)	śakha

Final position:

lakh (unit of 100,000)	lakh (lak - free variant in this position,)
happiness	śukh (suk - f.v.)

Utterances:

I eat food	ami'khabar khai"
This piece (of cloth) is very bad	ekhana'khub kharap"

4.2.2. /g/ (voiced unaspirated velar stop).

English	Bengali

Initial position:

song	gan
cheek	gal
body	ga
tree	gach (gac - f.v.)
round	gol

Medial position:

(to) strike	laga
within reach	nagale
fire	agun
garden	bagan

Final position:

snake (learned word): surname	nag
type of red powder	phag

---

1. hereafter the abbreviation f.v. will be used.

14

Utterances:

>   I sing a song   ami'gan gai"
>   My cheek is red   amar gal'lal"

4.2.3. /ŋ/ (velar nasal). The phone /ŋ/ does not occur in initial position in Bengali.

Medial position:

>   violence (injury, harm)   hiŋśa
>   plough   laŋol
>   world, family   śoŋśar (śoŋśar - f.v.)
>   Bengali (person)   baŋali
>   Bengali (language)   baŋla

Final position:

>   clown   śɔŋ

4.2.3.1. The velar nasal /ŋ/ frequently occurs medially in cluster with /g/ and /k/, thus:

>   with (accompanying)   śɔŋge
>   Ganges River   gɔŋga
>   arithmetic sum   ɔŋko

Utterances:

>   (speak   bɔl-)
>   I speak Bengali   ami'baŋla boli"
>   I eat meat   ami'maŋśo khai"
>   He dresses like a clown   śe'śɔŋ śaje"

4.2.4. /ch/ (voiceless aspirated palatal stop).

Initial position:

>   ashes   chai
>   skin, hide   chal
>   goat   chagol
>   (to) print, stamp   chapa
>   son, boy   chele

Medial position:

>   bed, bedding   bichana (common variant: bisna)

year	bɔchor
child (affectionate)	bacha
I am	achi
false	miche
it is	ache

Final position:

tree	gach (gac - f.v.)
fish	mach (mac - f.v.)

Utterances:

The fire becomes ashes	agun'chai hɔe"
The boy is bad	chele'kharap"
The boy sings a song	chele'gan gae"
(sit	bɔś-)
He sits in the tree	śe'gache bɔśe"

4.2.5. /j/ (voiced unaspirated palatal stop, the point of articulation which is slightly more toward the front of the mouth than is the English sound represented by j).

Initial position:

water	jɔl
net, snare (noun)	jal
(to) know	jana
(to) wake up	jaga
ship	jahaj
who (relative pronoun)	je
that which	ja
I kindle	jalai
shirt	jama

Medial position:

(to) dress, decorate	śaja
(to) sound, ring	baja
I scour	maji

Final position:

easy	śɔhoj
work	kaj

Utterances:

Work is easy	kaj'śohoj"
He goes on a ship	śe'jahaje jae"
There is a fish in the water	jɔle'jal ache"
The net is in the water	jɔle'jal ache"
There is a fish in the net	jale'mach ache"

4.2.6. /ph/ (bilabial voiceless aspirated stop). In lax or rapid speech /ph/ tends tò become a sound very much like the one represented in English by the letter f; some speakers of Bengali have a sound which is bi-labial spirant, made by an expulsion of breath through a narrow aperture in the lips. Note the tendency toward the loss of aspiration in the final position.

Initial position:

flower	phul
fruit	phɔl
whispering	phiś phiś
(to) return	phera
chip, slice	phala
(to) drop	phæla
kind of red powder	phag

Medial position:

(to) jump	laphano
fruitless	biphɔl

Final position:

pardon (noun)	maph (map - f.v.)

Utterances:

(The) boy jumps	chele'laphae"
Flowers are in the garden	phul'bagane ache"
Fruit is on the tree	gache phɔl"

4.2.7. /b/ (bilabial voiced unaspirated stop).

Initial position:

flood	ban
sister	bon

(to) sit	bɔśa
(to) speak, say	bɔla
Bengali (language)	baŋla
(to) sound, ring	baja

Medial position:

father (affectionate)	baba
food	khabar
stupid, foolish	haba

Final position:

very	khub
all	śɔb

Utterances:

He speaks Bengali	śe'baŋla bɔle"
Father eats	baba khan"
He sits with my sister	śe'amar boner śɔŋge bɔśe"
(play	khæl -)
All the boys play in the garden	śɔb chele'bagane khæle"

4.2.8. /m/ (bilabial nasal).

Initial position:

mother	ma
maternal uncle	mama
garland	mala
meat	maŋśo
fair	mæla
name of a month	magh (mag - f.v.)

Medial position:

(to) descend	nama
coat, jacket	jama
long, tall	lɔmba
I	ami

Final position:

name	nam
envelope	kham

mango   am

Utterances:

I am a Bengali.	ami baŋali"
My sister eats mangoes.	amar bon'am khae"
My name is Lal.	amar nam'lal"
My mother is tall.	amar ma'lɔmba"
My uncle sits with me.	amar mama'amar śɔŋge bɔśen"

4.2.9. /l/ (dental lateral).

Initial position:

red	lal
(to) jump	laphano
long, tall	lɔmba
(to) hit, strike	laga
unit of 100,00	lakh (lak - f.v.)
(to) write	lekha

Medial position:

to) play	khæla
(to) drop	phæla
empty	khali
gardener	mali
(to) speak, say	bɔla

Final position:

water	jɔl
cheek	gal
flower	phul
goat	chagol

Utterances:

My gardener is very tall.	amar mali'khub lɔmba"
My sister plays in the garden.	amar bon'bagane khæle"
He throws flowers in the water.	śe'phul jɔle phæle "
All the traps are empty.	śɔb jal'khali"

4.2.10. /ś/ (palatal sibilant). Although very like the English sound, the Bengali /ś/ is made with the tip of the tongue drawn further back from the front of the mouth than is normal in English.

Initial position:

shawl	śal
(to) dress	śaja
easy	śɔhoj
there	śekhane
he, she, it	śe
week	śɔptaho

Medial position:

(to) come	aśa
(to) sit	bɔśa
dwelling-place, nest	baśa

Final position:

| month | maś |
| end | śeś |

Utterances:

All the boys sit in the garden.	śɔb chele'bagane bɔśe"
Next month will be the wedding.	agami maśe'bie hɔbe"
He comes there.	śe'śekhane aśe"

4.2.10.1. The sound represented in English by the letter s, the initial sound in the words "sill" and "sand", also occurs in Bengali, though in certain particular types of circumstances. In Bengali this sound, the dental sibilant, occurs only together with the dental consonants /t, th, n, and r/. It never occurs by itself initially or between vowels, nor does it occur finally together with other consonants except in loan words from English. Note the following pronunciations:

wife	stri (learned)
bath	snan (coll. /can/)
place	sthan (learned)
road	rasta
slowly	aste

head, skull	mɔstok (learned)

4.2.11. /h/ (glottal spirant).

Initial position:

crawling (noun)	hama
violence, malice	hiŋśa
periodic market	hat
hand	hat

/h/ occurs only rarely in medial position, and that primarily in words reborrowed by Bengali from Sanskrit. In most cases in spoken Bengali a medial h̲ has been elided. The phone never occurs in final position, except in heavily Sanskritized Bengali and in monosyllabic interjections.

Utterances:

Mother goes to the market.	ma'haṭe jan"
There are flowers in my hand.	amar hate'phul ache"
The street becomes empty.	rasta'khali hɔe"

4.3. Consonant drills: voiceless unaspirates.

4.3.1. /k/ (voiceless unaspirated velar stop).

Before undertaking the following drills on voiceless unaspirated stops, reread section 4.1.4., and with the help of a piece of tissue or flame, practice the aspirated and unaspirated sounds (represented by the symbols k̲ and k̲h̲), until you are able to pronounce k̲ with little or no aspiration.

Aspirated	Unaspirated
khɔ	kɔ
kha	ka
khi	ki
khu	ku
khæ	kæ
khe	ke
kho	ko

Now pronounce the following Bengali words:

Initial position:

what	ki
who	ke
time	kal
desire	kamona
ear	kan
near	kache
paternal uncle	kaka
crow	kak (kag - f.v.)
paper	kagoj
black	kalo
why	kæno

Medial position:

remainder, balance	baki
type of plant	makal
morning	śɔkal
all	śɔkol
(to) scold	ɔŋka

Final position:

| let it go | ɟak |
| vegetable · | śak (śag - f.v.) |

Utterances:

Who is he?	śe keʰ
In the morning he goes to the garden.	śe śɔkale'bagane jae"
I wake up in the morning.	ami'śɔkale jagi"
The crow is black.	kak kalo"
Kali is black	kali kalo"
She buys vegetables at the market	śe haţe'śak kene"

4.3.1.1. The following are contrasts between /kh/ and /k/. You will see that in all cases the aspiration is all that makes the difference between two separate meanings. It will be clear that in order to understand Bengali and to be understood in it, you will have to learn to make **very** clear distinctions between aspirated and unaspirated stops.

	Aspirated		Unaspirated
English	Bengali	English	Bengali
canal, creek	khal	time	kal
sheath	khap	cup	kap
empty	khali	ink; name of goddess	kali
he (honor.) eats	khan	ear	kan
ditch	khana	blind of one eye	kana
very good	khaśa	(to) cough	kaśa
scalp; I/we open	khuli	porter	kuli

Utterances:

Crows eat mangoes.	kag'am kahe"
Kali is very black.	kali'khub kalo"
The vegetables are very bad .	śak'khub kharap"

4.3.1.2. Sometimes the distinction between Bengali <u>k</u> and <u>g</u> is difficult for a speaker of English to hear. Listen to and then pronounce the following sets of contrasts:

	Voiceless		**Voiced**
English	Bengali	English	Bengali
ear	kan	song	gan
time	kal	cheek	gal
name of goddess	kali	abuse (noun)	gali
crow	kak	let him sing	gak
nose	nak	snake, surname	nag

4.3.2. /c/ (voiceless unaspirated palatal).
Practice the following two sets of sounds until you are able to pronounce <u>c</u> with little or no aspiration:

Aspirated	**Unaspirated**
chɔ	cɔ
cha	ca
chi	ci
chu	cu
chæ	cæ

che	ce
cho	co

Now pronounce the following Bengali words:

Initial position:

tea	ca
I want	cai
he wants	cae
skin, leather	camṛa
wheel	caka
custom, habit, fashion	cal
(to) move, go	cɔla

Medial position:

(to) dance	naca
(to) wash (as clothes)	kaca
below, under	nice
platform	maca
speech	bacon

Final position:

dance (noun)	nac
sound of crunching	kɔckɔc
creaking sound (as of shoes	mɔcmɔc

Utterances:

I want tea.	ami'ca cai"
My sister dances.	amar bon'nace"

4.3.2.1. The following are contrasts between /c/ and /ch/. Again, you will see that distinction of aspiration is vital to the meaning.

Aspirated		Unaspirated	
English	Bengali	English	Bengali
ashes	chai	I want	cai
skin, hide	chal	fashion; rice	cal
big sack	chala	(to) drive. goad	cala
young of an animal	cha	tea	ca

knife	churi	robbery	curi
(to) print	chapa	(to) press	capa
thick rope	kachi	I wash	kaci

Utterances:

I want tea.	ami'ca cai"
I want ashes.	ami'chai cai"
He sits under the tree.	śe'gacher nice bośe

4.3.2.2. Sometimes the distinction between c and j is difficult for a speaker of English to hear. Listen to and then pronounce the following sets of contrasts:

Voiceless		Voiced	
English	**Bengali**	**English**	**Bengali**
let him ask	cak	let it go	jak
tea	ca	go!	ja
fashion	cal	trap, net	jal
he wants	cae	he goes	jae
he (hon.) wants	can	he (hon.) goes	jan
below	nice	one's own, one's self	nije

4.3.3. /ṭ/ and /ṭh/ (retroflex voiceless stops, unaspirated, aspirated) Before beginning to pronounce the following series of stops, practice putting your tongue in the proper position (see section 4.1.4.3.2.); then pronounce the following aspirated set. When the articulatory position seems comfortable to you, try the unaspirated set, checking yourself with the paper or the flame, as before.

Aspirated	Unaspirated
ṭhɔ	ṭɔ
ṭha	ṭa
ṭhi	ṭi
ṭhu	ṭu
ṭhæ	ṭæ
ṭhe	ṭe
ṭho	ṭo

Now pronounce the following Bengali words:

	English	Bengali

Initial position:

English	Bengali
thick	ṭhaś
exactly	ṭhik
tap, knock	ṭhuk
deity; cook	ṭhakur
sacred place	ṭhan

Medial position:

English	Bengali
gum, glue	aṭha
measure of land	kaṭha
stick, club	laṭhi
difficult	koṭhin
(to) rise up	oṭha

Final position:

English	Bengali
wood, fuel	kaṭh (kaṭ – f.v.)
field, meadow	maṭh (maṭ – f.v.)

Utterances:

English	Bengali
I don't exactly know.	ami'ṭhik jani na"
Mother goes to the field.	ma'maṭhe jan"
He has a club.	or'laṭhi ache"

Pronounce the following Bengali words with unaspirated retroflex stops:

	English	Bengali

Initial position:

English	Bengali
commentary (on a book)	ṭika
spindle, reel	ṭaku
tile	ṭali
(to) draw, pull	ṭana
money	ṭaka
hat	ṭupi
aim	ṭik, ṭip

Medial position:

English	Bengali
(to) cut, divide	kaṭa

(to) pound to pulp	baṭa
cup	baṭi
small	choṭo
(to) lick, lap	caṭa

Final position:

matted hair	jɔṭ
sound of footsteps	gɔṭ gɔṭ
periodic market	haṭ

Utterances:

He cuts wood.	śe'kaṭh kaṭe"
He draws water.	śe'jɔl ṭane"
Lila has money.	lilar'ṭaka ache"
The mali is a simple man.	maliṭa'śɔrol lok"

4.3.3.1. The following are contrasts between /ṭ/ and /ṭh/; practice them well. The distinctions are vital.

Aspirated		Unaspirated	
English	Bengali	English	Bengali
deity; cook	ṭhakur	of the spindle	ṭakur
measure of land	kaṭha	(to) cut	kaṭa
you (fam.) send	paṭha	plank	paṭa
exactly	ṭhik	aim	ṭik, ṭip
(to) hammer	ṭhoka	a knock; to copy	ṭoka
be cheated	ṭhoke	becomes sour	ṭoke
on the back; cake	piṭhe	having hammered	piṭe

Utterances:

I want money.	ami'ṭaka cai"
I want a cook.	ami'ṭhakur cai"
There is a tree in the field.	maṭhe'gach ache"
He comes, making a gɔṭ gɔṭ sound.	śe'gɔṭ gɔṭ kore aśe"
Foreigners are cheated.	bideśira ṭhoke"

4.3.3.2. Sometimes the distinction between ṭ and ḍ is difficult for a speaker of English to hear. Listen to and then pronounce the following sets of contrasts:

	Voiceless			Voiced	
English		Bengali	English		Bengali
money, rupee		ţaka	call (verb)		ḍaka
baldness		ţak	call, mail (nouns)		ḍak
draw (verb)		ţana	wing		ḍana
balance		ţal	lentils, branch		dal

4.3.4. /t/ and /th/ (dental voiceless stops, aspirated and unaspirated).
For this set also, first find with your tongue the dental position, and
practice finding that position with your tongue until it feels natural
and comfortable to you (see ante, section 4.1.4.3.1.). Then pronounce
the following series:

Aspirated	Unaspirated
thɔ	tɔ
tha	ta
thi	ti
thu	tu
thæ	tæ
the	te
tho	tc

Now pronounce the following Bengali words with aspirated stops:

English	Bengali

Initial position:

English	Bengali
(to) remain, stay	thaka
station, police station	thana
flat metal dish	thala
kind of borderless cloth	than
bag, sack	tholi
(to) stop	thama

Medial position:

English	Bengali
head	matha
pain	bætha

word, story	kɔtha

Final position:

way, road	pɔth (pɔt - f.v.)
chariot	rɔth (rɔt - f.v.)

Utterances:

ʃay here.	ami'ekhane thaki"
I ʃ.op here.	ami'ekhane thami"
I have pain.	amar'bætha ache"

Pronounce the following Bengali words with unaspirated dental stops:

Initial position:

foundation, base, area	tɔla
shelf	tak
heat, warmth	tap
musical measure	tal
tune	tᴇn
oil	tᴇl
(to) stare	tæka

Medial position:

how much, how many	kɔto
leaf, page	pata

Final position:

hand	hat
seven	ʃat

4.3.4.1. The following are contrasts between /t/ and /th/.

Aspirated		Unaspirated	
English	Bengali	English	Bengali
(to) remain	thaka	(to) stare	taka
piece of cloth	than	tune	tar
let it remain	thak	shelf	tak
head	matha	to be enthusi-astic	mata
ocean	pathar (learned)	of the page	patar

| flat metal dish | thala | lock, padlock | tala |
| bag | thole | picks up | tole |

Utterances:

I remain on the road.	ami'pothe thaki"
I stop in the road.	ami'pothe thami"
I talk with him.	ami'tar śonge'kotha boli"
How many words are on the page?	patae'koto kotha ache"

4.3.4.2. Sometimes the **distinction between** t and d is difficult for a speaker of English to hear. Listen to and then pronounce the following set of contrasts:

Voiceless		Voiced	
English	**Bengali**	**English**	**Bengali**
tune	tan	right, gift	dan
bottom	tol	group	dol
his, her	tar	door	dar
opinion	mot	liquor	mod

4.3.4.3. Contrasts between dentals and retroflexes are as significant as those between aspirates and unaspirates. Note and pronounce the following contrasting pairs:

Aspirates			
Dental		Retroflex	
English	**Bengali**	**English**	**Bengali**
police station	thana	cold	ţhanḍa
stop	tham	posture	ţham (poetic)
(to) remain	thaka	deity; cook	ţhakur

Utterances:

It is cold there.	śekhane ţhanḍa"
There is a police station there.	śekhane'thana ache"
My head is cold.	amar matha'ţhanḍa"

Unaspirates

Dental		Retroflex	
English	Bengali	English	Bengali
you (inf.) stare	taka	money	ṭaka
tune	tan	you (inf.) draw	ṭan
musical measure	tal	balance	ṭal
clapping of hands	tali	tile	ṭali
hand	hat	periodic market	haṭ

Utterances:

There is money in his hand. tar hate'ṭaka ache"
There is money in his market. tar haṭe'ṭaka ache'

4.3.5. /p/ (voiceless unaspirated bilabial stop).
Practice the following sets (the aspirated set will give you no trouble, as /ph/ is pronounced just as p is pronounced before a vowel in English). until you can pronounce /p/ with little or no aspiration:

Aspirated	Unaspirated
phɔ	pɔ
pha	pa
phi	pi
phu	pu
phæ	pæ
phe	pe
pho	po

Now pronounce the following Bengali words:

English	Bengali
Initial position:	
leaf, page	pata
betel	pan
heap (village drama)	pala
ripe	paka
sail; a surname	pal
wing, fan	pakha

Medial position:

term of affectionate address	bapu
(to) print, (stamp)	chapa
(to) measure	mapa
(to) mutter a prayer	jɔpa

Final position:

snake, curse	śap
silence	cup

Utterances:

The snake bites the boy.	śapṭa'cheleke kaṭe "
I eat betel.	ami'pan khai"
He measures the field.	śe'maṭh mape"

4.3.5.1. The following are contrasting pairs of words illustrating bilabial voiceless stops:

Aspirated		Unaspirated	
English	Bengali	English	Bengali
chip, (slice)	phala	heap	pala
flower	phul	bridge	pul
(to) crack	phaṭa	plank	paṭa

4.3.5.2. Sometimes the distinction between p and b is difficult for a speaker of English to hear. Listen to and then pronounce the following sets of contrasts:

Voiceless		Voiced	
English	Bengali	English	Bengali
heap, (village drama)	pala	bangle	bala
betel leaf	pan	flood	ban
sin	pap	father (coll.)[1]	bap
term of affectionate address	bapu	a Bengali Hindu gentleman	babu

4.4. Consonant drills: voiced aspirates.

---

1. The usage of the term is restricted; it is never a form of address.

4.4.1. /gh/ (voiced aspirated velar stop).

The voiced aspirate series is one which will not be familiar to most
speakers of American English. Before attempting the pronunciation of the
Bengali words, try the following series of exercises, first the unaspirated, which will be familiar to you, and then the aspirated voiced stops.
Practice the aspirated series until you can imitate the tape well.

Unaspirated	Aspirated
gɔ	ghɔ
ga	gha
gi	ghi
gu	ghu
gæ	ghæ
ge	ghe
go	gho

Now pronounce the following Bengali words:

	English	Bengali
Initial position:		
	water pot	ghɔṭ
	landing or bathing place	ghaṭ
	sweat	gham
	grass	ghaś
	clarified butter	ghi
	oil-mill	ghani
Medial position:		
	blow	aghat
	fierce (tiger-like)	bagha
	lightness	laghob
Final position:		
	tiger	bagh (bag - f.v.)
	name of a month	magh (mag - f.v.)
Utterances:		
	I go to the ghat.	ami'ghaṭe jai"
	I cut the grass.	ami'ghaś kaṭi"
	I fetch the ghi.	ami'ghi ani"

Is that a tiger?   oṭa ki'bagh"

4.4.1.1. The following are contrasts between /g/ and /gh/:

	Unaspirated		Aspirated	
English	Bengali	English	Bengali
you (fam.) manage	baga	tiger-like	bagha
(to) strike	laga	lightness	laghob
round	gol	buttermilk	ghol
fair colored	gora	(to) roam	ghora
body	ga	sore	gha
within grasp	bage	by the tiger	baghe

4.4.2. /jh/ (voiced aspirated palatal affricate).
Before attempting the pronunciation of Bengali words, try the following
series of exercises, first the unaspirated, then the aspirated. Practice
the aspirated series until you can imitate the sound well.

Unaspirated	Aspirated
jɔ	jhɔ
ja	jha
ji	jhi
ju	jhu
jæ	jhæ
je	jhe
jo	jho

Now pronounce the following Bengali words:

English	Bengali

Initial position:

pungent (hot, as food)	jhal
sharp, clever	jhanu
plunge (jump)	jhup
maid-servant	jhi

Medial position:

| among | majhe |
| (to) understand | bojha |

Final position:

the middle   majh (maj - f.v.)

Utterances:

English	Bengali
The food is hot.	khabarṭa jhal"
The boy is clever.	cheleṭa jhanu"
He sits among the flowers.	śe'phulgulor majhe bɔśe"
I understand what you say.	tumi ja bɔlo'ta ami bujhi"

4.4.2.1. The following are contrasts between /j/ and /jh/:

Unaspirated		Aspirated	
English	**Bengali**	**English**	**Bengali**
he scours	maje	among	majhe
(to) be shut	boja	(to) understand	bojha
respectful suffix	ji	maid-servant	jhi
net	jal	pugent, hot	jhal
shirt	jama	blackened brick	jhama
weave	jola	bag	jhola
I scour	maji	boatman	majhi

4.4.3. /ḍ/ and ḍh/ (retroflexed voiced stops, unaspirated and aspirated). Again, there are two problems for speakers of American English with the voiced retroflexed stops: first, the position in which the stop is made, and, secondly, the aspiration. Refer to sections 4.1.4.2. and 4.1.4.3.2. First practice placing the tongue in the proper position for retroflexed sounds, until that position seems natural and comfortable. Then try the following series, first the unaspirated stops, which will be natural to you, then the aspirated.

Unaspirated	Aspirated
ḍɔ	ḍhɔ
ḍa	ḍha
ḍi	ḍhi
ḍu	ḍhu
ḍæ	ḍhæ
ḍe	ḍhe
ḍo	ḍho

Now pronounce the following set of Bengali words with unaspirated stops:

English	Bengali
Initial position:	
(to) call	ḍaka
dry land	ḍaŋa
branch, lentil	ḍal
small boat.	ḍiŋi
egg	ḍim
(to) sink	ḍoba
stick, staff	ḍaŋḍa
very, very much	bɔḍḍo

The voiced retroflex stop occurs in medial position in a word only as a doubled ("long" or "geminate") consonant or in some other consonant clusters -- see section 4.5.; the sound does not occur finally except in loanwords from English. An example of such a loan word is:

road	roḍ

Utterances:

I sink in the water.	ami'jɔle ḍubi"
There is a staff in his hand.	tar hate'ḍaŋḍa"
The bird sits on the branch.	pakhiṭa'ḍale bɔśe"
The egg is very small.	ḍimṭa'khub choṭo

Now pronounce the following Bengali words with voiced aspirated stops:

English	Bengali
(to) hide, conceal	ḍhaka
shield	ḍhal
(to) pour out	ḍhala
mound	ḍhipi
loose, slack	ḍhil
a kind of drum	ḍhol

The voiced retroflex aspirated stop never occurs medially between vowels or finally.

36

Utterances:

I hide the book.	ami'boiṭa ḍhaki"
The drum sounds.	ḍholṭa baje"
He pours out the water.	śe'jɔl dhale"

4.4.3.1. The following are contrasts between /ḍ/ and /ḍh/:

Unaspirated		Aspirated	
English	Bengali	English	Bengali
(to) call	ḍaka	(to) conceal	ḍhaka
in the egg	ḍime	slow	ḍhime
branch	ḍal	shield	ḍhal

Utterances:

I call the boy.	ami'cheleṭake ḍaki"
I hide the boy.	ami'cheleṭake ḍhaki"

There is also in Bengali a retroflex flap /ṛ/ (see also section 4.4.5.1.).
This sound occurs only medially and finally in Bengali words -- in places,
in other words, where the stop /ḍ/ does not occur except in loans.
Place your tongue in the proper position, practice making flaps, and then
try the following series:

aṛɔ
aṛa
aṛi
aṛu
aṛæ
aṛe
aṛo

Now pronounce the following Bengali words:

English	Bengali
Medial position:	
big	bɔṛo
house	baṛi
(to) fly	oṛa

(to) read, study	pɔɽa
(to) step over, thresh	maɽa
section of a town	paɽa
reply	śaɽa
fence	bæɽa

Final position:

bone	naɽ
feeling, sensation	śaɽ

Utterances:

I read the book.	ami'boiṭa poɽi"
The boy is very big.	cheleṭa'khub bɔɽo'
The bird flies.	pakhiṭa oɽe"
My house is there.	amar baɽi'śekhane"

For contrasts between the retroflex and dental flaps, see section 4.4.5.1

4.4.4. /d/ and /dh/ (voiced dental stops, unaspirated and aspirated).
Again, there are two problems with these sounds: tongue position and
aspiration. Refer to sections 4.1.4.2. and 4.1.4.3. Place your tongue,
as before, in the proper position for dentals, and then pronounce the
following series:

Unaspirated	Aspirated
dɔ	dhɔ
da	dha
di	dhi
du	dhu
dæ	dhæ
de	dhe
do	dho

Now pronounce the following set of Bengali words:

English	Bengali

Initial position:

price	dam
gift	dan
stain (blemish)	dag

38

day	din
chin, beard	daɽi

Medial position:

elder brother	dada
white	śada
river	nodi
first, original	adi

Final position:

omission	**bad**
taste	śad

Utterances.

Elder brother goes home.	dada'baɽite jan"
Giving is good.	dan kɔra'bhalo"
His beard is very long.	tar dari'khub lɔmba"

4.4.4.1. Now pronounce the following set of Bengali words with aspirated dental stops:

English	Bengali

Initial position:

abode	dham (learned)
unhusked rice (paddy)	dhan
wealth	dhon
stream (current)	dhara
dust	dhulo
smoke	dhum (learned)
(an exclamation)	dhik (learned)
debt	dhar

Medial position:

ass; stupid person	gadha
honey (necter)	modhu
(to) entreat	śadha
straight (direct)	śidhe

Final position:

desire (wish)	śadh (śad - f.v.)

unobstructed   ɔbadh (ɔbad – f.v.)

Utterances:

    I have many desires.   amar'ɔnek śadh ache"

4.4.4.1. The following are contrasts between /d/ and /dh/:

Unaspirated		Aspirated	
English	Bengali	English	Bengali
price	dam	abode	dham (learned)
gift	dan	unhusked rice (paddy)	dhan
direction	dik	(an exclamation)	dhik (learned)
afterwards	bade	is obstructed	badhe
heap	gada	ass	gadha
white	śada	(to) entreat	śadha

4.4.4.2. The following are contrasts between dental and retroflexed voiced stops.

4.4.4.2.1. Contrasts between /ḍ/ and /d/ (retroflex and dental voiced unaspirated stops):

Retroflex		Dental	
English	Bengali	English	Bengali
dry land	ḍaŋa	riot	daŋga
egg	ḍim	day	din
bucket	ḍol	swinging	dol

4.4.4.2.2. Contrasts between /ḍh/ and /dh/ (retroflex and dental voiced aspirate stops):

Retroflex		Dental	
English	Bengali	English	Bengali
sound of swallowing a liquid	ḍhɔk ḍhɔk	palpitation	dhɔk dhɔk
you (ord.) doze	ḍhulo	dirt	dhulo
hollow sounding	ḍhɔp ḍhɔpe	dazzlingly white	dhɔp dhɔpe

4.4.5. There is in Bengali a dental (pre-alveolar) flap /r/, which occurs in all positions; try making the flap sound, using the following set:

rɔ
ra
ri
ru
ræ
re
ro

Now pronounce the following Bengali words:

	English	Bengali

Initial position:

	English	Bengali
	(to) keep, (place)	rakha
	color	rɔŋ
	(to) grow angry	raga
	king	raja
	night	rat
	weak, thin, (ill)	roga
	daily	roj

Medial position:

	English	Bengali
	(to) wear	pɔra
	whole, (entire)	śara
	(to) strike, (kill)	mara
	(to) do, make	kɔra

The flap /r/ sound is a little different in final position than in initial or inter-vocalic positions. In final position /r/ becomes somewhat voiceless. Pay special attention to the following examples:

Final position:

	English	Bengali
	necklace; defeat	har
	of the gift	daner
	of me	amar
	of you (ord.)	tomar
	of you (hon.)	apnar
	of him (ord.)	tar

Utterances:

I do work.	ami'kaj kori"
I put it on the table.	amj oʈa'ʈebile rakhi"
I go to the store every day.	ami roj'dokane jai"
Its color is white.	or rɔŋ'śada"
He has work.	tar'kaj ache"

4.4.5.1. The following are contrasts between /ṛ/ and /r/:

	Retroflex		Dental
English	Bengali	English	Bengali
(to) read	pɔṛa	(to) wear	pɔra
(to) step over: thresh	maṛa	(to) strike	mara
reply	śaṛa	whole	śara
bone	haṛ	necklace	har
(to) fly	oṛa	they (yonder)	ora
reprimand; rebuke	taṛa	they (the same)	tara

4.4.6. /bh/ (voiced aspirated bilabial stop).
Before attempting the pronunciation of Bengali words, try the following
series of exercises. Practice the aspirated series until you can
imitate the sound well.

Unaspirated	Aspirated
bɔ	bhɔ
ba	bha
bi	bhi
bu	bhu
bæ	bhæ
be	bhe
bo	bho

Now pronounce the following Bengali words:

English	Bengali
Initial position:	
cooked rice	bhat
steam	bhap

pretence	bhan
(to) think	bhaba
(to) float	bhaśa
wet	bhije
(to) fry	bhaja
(to) forge+	bhola

Medial position:

deep	gobhir
navel	nabhi
splendor	probha (learned)
meeting, assembly	śɔbha

Final position:

gain, result	labh (lab - f.v.)

Note that in lax or rapid speech /bh/ tends to become a sound very like that one represented in English by **v**; some Bengali speakers have a sound which is made by expulsion of breath through a narrow aperture in the lips. Note the usual tendency toward loss of aspiration in final position.

4.4.6.1. The following are contrasts between /b/ and /bh/:

Unaspirated		Aspirated	
English	Bengali	English	Bengali
father	bap	steam	bhap
arrow	ban (learned)	pretence	bhan
thunder	baj	you (fam.) fry	bhaj
nest; rented house	baśa	language	bhaśa
in the seed	bije	wet	bhije
time	bæla	raft	bhæla
sound	bol	you (fam.) forget	bhɔl

4.4.7. /n/ (pre-alveolar nasal).
The American English sound represented by the letter **n** is, like the English stops **t** and **d**, an alveolar sound. The Bengali /n/, however, is pronounced with the tongue farther forward on the alveolar ridge. Put

your tongue in the proper position, and pronounce the following Bengali words:

	English	Bengali

Initial position:

dance	nac
nose	nak
many, various	nana
name	nam
(to) descend	nama
ruin	naś (learned word)

Medial position:

(to) draw, pull	ṭana
police station	thana
oil-mill	ghani

Final position:

gift	dan
ear	kan
betel leaf	pan

4.5. Geminate (doubled) consonants.

There is in Bengali a phenomenon of geminate of doubled consonants, which is unfamiliar to speakers of English. Any consonant which can be held for a period of time can be doubled -- in terms of Bengali, this means any consonant except for the flaps which are by definition sounds made by a single tap of the tongue. Doubling is made by holding the consonant sound for twice the ordinary amount of time it would take to pronounce that consonant. Examples:

4.5.1. /kk/

Single		Doubled	
English	Bengali	English	Bengali
kind of bird (learned)	cɔkor	round	cɔkkor

4.5.2. /gg/

you (ord.) go away	bhago	luck	bhaggo

4.5.3. /cc/

    choose   baca   little boy   bacca (coll.)

4.5.4. /jj/

	Bengali		
straight	śoja	bed	śojja
amusement	mɔja	marrow	mɔjja
worship	pujo	respectable	pujjo

4.5.5. /ṭṭ/

I lick	caṭi	a few, some	caṭṭi (khani) (coll.)
whole wheat flour	aṭa	eight	aṭṭa

4.5.6. /tt/

leaf, page	pata	whereabouts	patta

4.5.7. /ḍc̣/

beginning, initial	adi	kind of cloth	addi (coll.)
pertaining to wine	modo	wine (learned)	moddo

4.5.8. /nn/

weed which grows in water	pana	emerald	panna
blind in one eye	kana	weeping	kanna
(to) agree, obey	mana	surname	manna
(to) weave	bona	flood	bonna

4.5.9. /śś/

I bring up	puśi	adopted	puśśi (coll.)
in the poison	biśe	in the world	biśśe (learned)
guilty	dośi	rascal	dośśi (coll.)

4.5.10. /ll/

garland	mala	boatman	malla
you (ord.) twist	mɔlo	an expert in Kusti, -- a type of wrestling	mɔllo (learned)
cotton	tulo	like	tullo (learned

radish   mulo   price   mullo (learned)

5. Vowels.

5.1. The significant Bengali vowel sounds (arranged according to the Bengali alphabetical order) are:

$$/ɔ, a, i, u, æ, e, o/$$

5.2. A chart of these vowels is as follows:

	Front	Central	Back
High	i		u
Mid	e		o
Lower-mid	æ		ɔ
Low		a	

5.3. All of these sounds will be somewhat familiar to speakers of American English, with the possible exception of /ɔ/. Familiarity with the vowel /ɔ/ will depend upon the speaker's dialect.

5.3.1. Sounds which will be almost identical with some common American English vowel sounds are:

/æ/	as in some dialects of American English	"can"	[khæn]
/a/	as in some dialects of American English	"calm"	[kham]
/ɔ/	as in some dialects of American English	"law"	[lɔ]

Those in whose dialects these sounds do not occur will have to learn them by careful imitation of the Bengali.

5.3.2. Examples of these three vowels in Bengali are:

5.3.2.1. /æ/

46

	English	Bengali

Initial position:

one	æk
now	ækhon
alone	æka
such	æmon

Medial position:

(to) play	khæla
(to) throw	phæla
as if	jæno
how	kæmon
why	kæno
time	bæla
fair (noun)	mæla

/æ/ never occurs in final position in standard Bengali.

5.3.2.2.' /a/

Initial position:

(to) come	aśa
again	abar
light	alo
sky	akaś
you (honorific)	apni
and; also	ar
(to) fetch	ana

Medial position:

food	khabar
red	lal
shawl	śal
time	kal
ear	kan
bad	kharap

Final position:

(to) do	kɔra
(to) read	pɔɽa

(to) play	khæla

5.3.2.3. /ɔ/

Initial position:

silly	ɔga (coll.)
otherwise, (or)	ɔthoba (learned)
eternal	ɔnonto
powerless	ɔśokto

Medial position:

all	śɔb
possible	śɔmbhob
ten	dɔś
juice, (sweetness)	rɔś
fever	jɔr
room, (house)	ghɔr
(to) do	kɔra

Final position: The vowel /ɔ/ rarely occurs finally in standard colloquial Bengali. It is more frequent in some dialects, such as that of Dacca. There are, however, a few examples:

you (fam.) become	hɔ
you (fam.) bear	bɔ

5.4. Sounds which will be recognizable (though not identical to those in American English) are the following: /i, e, o, u/.

5.4.1. In American English, the front vowel sounds /i/ and /e/ are usually pronounced with what is known as an "off-glide". This means that while the vowel sound is being made, the tongue moves upward from its original position, thus varying the quality of the sound. In tne following set of English words, listen for the off-glide.

key	[khiy]	hay	[hiy]
bee	[biy]	lee	[liy]
sea	[siy]	gee	[jiy]
fee	[fiy]		

Now pronounce them yourself, feeling the way in which your tongue moves. Again, in the following set of English words, listen for the off-glides, and then pronounce them yourself:

kay	[khey]	hay	[hey]
bay	[bey]	lay	[ley]
say	[sey]	jay	[jey]
fey	[fey]		

5.4.2. In American English, the so-called "back-rounded" vowels (/o/ and /u/) also have off-glides. These are characterized by upward move- ment of the tongue and by additional lip rounding. In the following sets of English words, listen for the off-glide:

bow	[bow]	hoe	[how]
sow	[sow]	low	[low]
foe	[fow]	joe	[jow]
coo	[khuw]	who	[huw]
foo	[few]	loo	[luw]
sue	[suw]	jew	[juw]
boo	[buw]		

Now pronounce them yourself and feel the way in which your tongue and lips move.

5.4.3. The Bengali vowels /i, e, o, u/ are "pure" vowels -- that is, they are pronounced without an off-glide. The difference between American Eng- lish and Bengali vowels is easy to hear, but less easy to make. You will have to break yourself of the habit of giving an off-glide to the vowels. But proper pronunciation of vowel sounds is a mark of a good speaker of the language. Listen carefully to the following sets of sounds, the first set pronounced by a speaker of English. the second by a speaker of Bengali:

English		Bengali
Orthographic	Phonetic	
bee	[biy]	bi
gee	[jiy]	ji
me	[miy]	mi
bay	[bey]	be
jay	[jey]	je
may	[mey]	me
bow	[bow]	bo
joe	[jow]	jo
mow	[mow]	mo

boo	[buw]	bu
jew	[juw]	ju
moo	[muw]	mu

Now imitate the Bengali pronunciation of the following sounds:

bi ji mi   be je me   bo jo mo   bu ju mu

5.4.4. /i/. Pronounce the following Bengali words:

English	Bengali

Initial position:

this one (hon.)	ini
(proper name)	ila
(interjection)	iś

Medial position:

day	din
he, she (hon.)	tini
in the seed	bije
wet	bhije
sesame seed	til
type of tree	nim
egg	ḍim

Final position:

what	ki
maid-servant	khi
I strike	mari
sari	śaṛi
house	baṛi

5.4.4.1. It should be noted that in certain circumstances the vowel /i/ is pronounced slightly differently than in the above instances. Sometimes the Bengali vowel /i/ is pronounced almost as the American English vowel in the word "sit". Examples of this type of pronunciation of the vowel in Bengali are the following:

but	kintu
sound of laughter	khil khil
station	iśṭeśan

The circumstances in which this variation occurs are too complex to

50

describe here. But listen for it; you will quickly become adjusted to its proper pronunciation.

5.4.5. /e/.

Initial position:

this	e
here	ekhane
of this	er
come!	eśo
this way	edik

Medial position:

(to) buy	kena
I play	kheli
girl	me.e
having eaten	khe.e
district	jela
country	deś

Final position:

who	ke
he, she	śe
there	śekhane
he, she buys	kene

5.4.5.1. It should be noted that in certain circumstances the vowel /e/ is pronounced slightly differently from the above. It is sometimes very like the American English vowel in "set". Examples of this are the following.

a little	ekṭu
boy	chele (note the difference between the two vowels)
thus, such	emni

5.4.6. /o/.

Initial position:

that	o
there	okhane

of that one	or
you (ord.) rise up	oṭho
that way	odik

Medial position:

(to) understand	bojha
sound	bol
(to) forget	bhola
sister	bon
sin; (fault)	doś
above	opor
kind of drum	ḍhol

Final position:

you (ord.) eat	khao
you (ord.) stay	thako
you (ord.) speak	bɔlo
you (ord.) sit	bɔśo

5.4.7. /u/.

Initial position:

means	upae
camel	uṭ
upside down, reversed	ulṭo
proper, right, necessary	ucit
both	ubhɔe
worship (Hindu)	upocar (learned)

Medial position:

very	khub
flower	phul
happy	khuśi
sounds, words	buli
root	mul (learned)
face, mouth	mukh (muk - f.v.)

Final position:

preceptor	guru
cow	goru

sun	bhanu (learned)

5.4.7.1. As with the other vowels, there are circumstances in which the vowel /u/ is pronounced differently -- in this case, almost like the vowel in the English "foot". For example:

son	puttro (learned)

5.4.8. Nasalization.

Nasalization (written as a tilda (˜) over the vowel) is another Bengali language feature, especially in the speech of West Bengal, which is not significant in English. Nasalization of a vowel is made by simultaneous emission of air through both nasal and oral passages during the pronunciation of the vowel. During an ordinary vowel sound, the nasal passage is closed off. During a nasalized sound, it is opened, so that breath escapes through nose and mouth at the same time. Practice the following nasalized vowels with the tape:

Non-nasal	Nasal
ɔ	ɔ̃
a	ã
i	ĩ
u	ũ
e	ẽ
æ	æ̃
o	õ

5.4.8.1. Nasalization of vowels in Bengali will make a difference in what you say. Distinguish carefully between the following:

Non-nasal		Nasal	
English	Bengali	English	Bengali
his (ord.)	tar	his (hon.)	tãr
(to) wash (cloth)	kaca	young	kãca
that one's (ord.)	or	that one's (hon.)	õr
obstacle	badha	(to) bind	bãdha
(to) bloom	phoṭa	mark on forehead	phõṭa
in the market	haṭe	he walks	hãṭe
(to) press	cãpa	kind of flower	cãpa

5.4.9. Vowel sequences. Bengali vowels often occur in sequences of two and sometimes of three. Sequences of two vowels are of two types: either full vowel plus semi-vowel (a single syllable, written in our transcription as two vowels without any mark between), or full vowel plus full vowel (two syllables, written with a period (.) in between). As will be seen below, there are differences both in pronunciation and in meaning between the two types of sequences. Compare the following:

you (ord.) get	pao
leg also	pa.o
I get	pai
leg (emphatic)	pa.i
he (ord.) gets	pae
on the leg	pa.e
brother's or sister's father-in-law	talui
it is a palm, and nothing else	talu.i
this	ei
this is it, and nothing else	e.i
that	oi
that is he, and no one else	o.i
lies down	śoe
having endured	śo.e
he carries	bɔe
in the letter b	bɔ.e
you (ord.) carry	bɔo
you (inf.) also carry	bɔ.o
he takes; legitimate	næe
in the legitimacy	næ.e
expenditure	bæe
in the expenditure	bæ.e
he sings	gae
in the body	ga.e
you (ord.) take	nao
not also	na.o

midwife	dai
responsible	da.i
you (ord.) want	dai
the tea also	da.i
bag	thole
in the bag	thole.e

5.4.10. Syllable structure.

It has been suggested previously that word-stress is not phonemic in
Bengali, that, in fact, all syllables of a multi-syllabic Bengali word
are for all practical purposes stressed equally. The distinction between
Bengali and English in this respect can perhaps best be shown by the pronunciation of loan-words from English current in Bengali. Listen to and
pronounce the following:

railway station	re.lo.eś.ṭe.śan
coke oven	ko.ko.bhen
post office	poś.ṭa.phiś
cabinet minister	mi.niś.ṭar
bath room	baṭ.ṭhrum
pastry	peś.ṭri
ice cream	a.iś.krim
gasoline (petroleum)	pet.ṭrol
control	kɔn.ṭrol
bundle	ban.ḍil
multiplication	mal.ṭi.pli.ke.śan
night-rate, nitrate	na.iṭ.reṭ

Lesson 1, part 1. Conversation.

(To accompany tape).

	Analysis and translation	Bengali
1.	A. Greetings.	A. nomośkar "
2.	B. Greetings.	B. nomośkar "
3.	stem of first person pronoun "me"	ama-
	genitive case ending for stems with vowel final	-r
	"of me, my"	amar
	noun stem, "name"	nam
	proper name	robi
	A. My name is Robi.	A. amar nam ' robi
4.	stem of second person (honorific) pronoun "you"	apna-
	genitive case ending for stems with vowel final	-r
	"of you, your" (honorific)	apnar
	interrogative, "what"	ki
	A. What is your name?	A. apnar nam ' ki "
5.	proper name	ram
	B. My name is Ram.	B. amar nam ' ram "
6.	nominative singular of 2nd person (honorific) pronoun, "you"	apni

interrogative, "where"	kothae
stem of verb "live, remain, stay"	thak-
2nd person (honorific) verbal ending	-en
"you (honorific) do live"	(apni) thaken

A. <u>Where do you live?</u>   A. <u>apni ' kothae thaken</u> "

7.

nominative singular of 1st person pronoun "I"	ami
locative case ending for stems having vowel final	-te
Chicago	śikago
"in Chicago"	śikagote
first person verbal ending	-i
"I live"	(ami) thaki

B. <u>I live in Chicago.</u>   B. <u>ami ' śikagote thaki</u> "

8.

stem of verb "do, make"	kɔr-
2nd person (honorific) verbal ending	-en
"you (hon.) do"	(apni) kɔren

A. <u>What do you do?</u>   A. <u>apni ' ki kɔren</u> "

tumi ki koro

9.

stem of verb "read, study"	pɔr-
1st person present ending	-i
"I study"	(ami) pɔṛi (note vowel change - Lesson 2, grammar, section 1)

B. <u>I study in Chicago.</u>   B. <u>ami' śikagote pɔṛi</u> "

10.

stem of verb "read, study"	pɔr
2nd person (honorific) ending	-en
"you (honorific) study"	(apni) pɔṛen

A. <u>What do you study?</u>   A. <u>apni ' ki pɔren</u> "

tumi ki poro

11.   "Bengali" (language)   baŋla

B. <u>I study Bengali.</u>

B. <u>ami ' baṇla poṛi</u> "

12.　interrogative particle (see grammar, section 8)
"difficult"

ki
śɔkto

A. <u>Is Bengali difficult?</u>

A. <u>baṇla ki ' śɔkto</u> "

13.　"no"
"very"
"easy"

na
khub
śɔhoj

B. <u>No, it is very easy.</u>

B. <u>na ' khub śɔhoj</u> "

sɔhooj

14.　"hot"

gɔrom

A. <u>Is it very hot in Chicago?</u>

A. <u>śikagote ki ' khub gɔrom</u>

15.　stem of verb "be not"
3rd person or impersonal verbal ending
"it is not"

nɔ-

-e

nɔe

B. <u>No, it is not very hot.</u>

B. <u>na ' khub gɔrom nɔe</u> "

nɔy

16.　"cold"

thaṇda

A. <u>Is it very cold in Chicago?</u>

A. <u>śikagote ki ' khub thaṇda</u> "

17.　"yes"

hæ̃

B. <u>Yes, it is very cold.</u>

B. <u>hæ̃ ' khub thaṇda</u> "

18.　interrogative, "how much, how many"
"big, large"

kɔto
bɔṛo

A. <u>How big is Chicago?</u>

A. <u>śikago ' kɔto bɔṛo</u> "

19.　"city"

śɔhor

B. Chicago is a very big city.   B. śikago ' khub bɔɾo śɔhor "

20.   "people"   lok

A. How many people are there in   A. śikagote ' kɔto lok "
Chicago?

21.   negative prefix   ɔn-
      "one"   -ek
      "not one", i.e., "many"   ɔnek
      locative ending with stems   -e
      ending in consonants
      "in the city"   śɔhore

B. There are many people in the   B. śɔhore ' ɔnek lok "
city.

22.   interrogative, "how"   kæmon
      stem of verb "strike"   lag-
      3rd person/impersonal verbal
      ending   -e
      "it strikes"   lage

A. How do you like Chicago?   A. apnar ' śikago ' kæmon lage "
(i.e., "How does Chicago
strike you?")

23.   "good, well"   bhalo

B. Very much.   B. khub bhalo "
I like Chicago very much.   amar śikago ' khub bhalo lage "

Lesson 1, part 2. Drills.

The taped drills based upon the conversation are arranged in the
following manner:

1. Saturation drill #1. The saturation drills are the recorded Bengali
    conversations spoken by two native speakers of Bengali. You are to
    listen carefully to the conversation, following it in the printed
    text. Do not repeat the conversation at this time.

2. Saturation drill #2.

3. Saturation drill #3.

4. Saturation drill #4. In this drill, the English meanings will be
    given first, then the Bengali. The student will listen only.

5. Repetition drill #1. In this drill, the English translation will be
    given first, then the Bengali, then there will be a space left for
    the student to repeat the Bengali sentence. The student's Bengali
    repetition will be recorded, so that the student may check his
    Bengali pronunciation.

6. Response drill #1. Part A of the Bengali conversation will be given
    in Bengali, and the student will supply part B, in Bengali, in the
    space left following part A. The student's response will be recorded.

7. Response drill #2. Part B of the Bengali conversation will be given
    in Bengali, and the student will supply part A, in Bengali (i.e, the
    student will speak part A following the drillmaster's voice saying
    "A"). The student's voice will be recorded.

8. Saturation drill #5.

Lesson 1, part 3. Grammar.

1. /nomośkar/ is the most common form of greeting used between Hindus
(or between a European and a Hindu) in Bengali. You should, however, always be aware that there are other forms of greeting: /śalam/ ("peace")
or in full form /as salam o aleikum/ ("peace be with you") is used when
greeting a Muslim. The return greeting to /as salam o aleikum/ is /o
aleikum as salam/ ("with you be peace").

/nomoskar/ is used for a greeting when meeting and also when parting.

2. The simple present tense is used to denote habitual action. The use of the simple present, for example, in sentences 6-11, implies that the speaker resides habitually or permanently in Chicago, that he habitually studies at the University, etc.

3. -r (sentences 3 ff.) is the genitive (i.e., possessive) case suffix which is used with noun stems which have a vowel final. For stems with consonant final, see Lesson 3, sentence 2, and grammar.

4. -te (sentences 7 ff.) is the locative case (i.e., place in or to which) suffix used with noun stems which have a vowel final. -e is the locative case suffix used with noun stems with either vowel or consonant final, thus:

city	śɔhor	in or to the city	śɔhore
college	kɔlej	in or to the college	kɔleje
Bengali	baŋla	in Bengali	baŋlate
			baŋlae
Calcutta	kolkata	in or to Calcutta	kolkatate
			kolkatae

5. The verb "be" in the present tense affirmative is usually not expressed.

The verb "be not" in the present tense is expressed; i.e., in sentence 15, its stem is /nɔ-/, to which are attached the regular present tense verbal endings.

It is hot in Chicago.	śikagote ' gɔrom "
It is not hot in Chicago.	śikagote ' gɔrom nɔe "
Chicago is a big city.	śikago ' bɔro śɔhor "
Chicago is not a big city.	śikago ' bɔro śɔhor nɔe "
Is it cold in Chicago?	śikagote ki ' ṭhaṇḍa "
It is not cold in Chicago	śikagote ' ṭhaṇḍa nɔe "

5.1. The sequence /hɔe na/ does occur in a limited number of utterances; these occurences will be pointed out as they arise.

5.2. There is usually no verb in the present tense affirmation, and the present tense form of the verb /hɔoa/ can mean only (a) an event as a law or a habit, or (b) a narrated past event.

Chicago is hot	śikago gɔrom"
It gets difficult to drive on Saturdays	śonibare gaṛi calano śɔkto hɔe"
America was discovered four and a half centuries ago	æmerika abiśkar hɔe śaṛe carśo bɔchor age ¹

5.3. Other verbs form their negatives by the addition of the participle /na/.

| I study | ami poṛi | I do not study | ami poṛi na |
| you do | apni kɔren | you do not do | apni kɔren na |

6. The simple present tense is formed by affixing the personal endings to the simple stem of the verb (the verbal noun minus the suffix /-a/; see Lesson 2, part 3, section 1). These endings are:

Person	Stem	Ending
1st (ami)	—	-i
2nd (honorific -- apni)	—	-en
3rd (ordinary -- śe)	-	-e

Examples:

I remain	ami thaki
you (hon.) remain	apni thaken
he (she, it) remains	śe thake

I sit	ami bośi
you (hon.) sit	apni bɔśen
he (she, it) sits	śe bɔśe

The stem-vowel change in the first person will be discussed in Lesson 2.

6.1. Drills. Taped drills on this section of the lesson are arranged in the following manner:

6.1.1. Mutation drill #1. The form of this drill will be as follows:

An English sentence will be given. The student is to translate the sentence into Bengali in the space left for it following the English. The correct Bengali of the sentence will then be given, and the student will repeat the answer, recording. An example:

Master (in English):	I live in the house.
Student (in Bengali):	ami ' baṛite thaki "
Master (in Bengali):	ami ' baṛite thaki "

Student (in Bengali):   ami ' baɽite thaki "

7. Interrogatives begin with the phoneme /k/. Thus:

Bengali	English
ki	what, interrogative particle
kothae	where
kæmon	how
kɔto	how much, how many
kon	which
kæno	why

The distinctions between /kæmon/ and /kɔto/ and between /ki/ and /kon/ should be noted:

7.1. /kɔto/ is an interrogative with reference to quantity or size:

How big (i.e., how much big)   apnar baɽi ' kɔto bɔɽo "
is your house?

How many people are there   ekhane ' kɔto lok "
here?

7.2. /kæmon/ is used in a non-quantitative sense:

How do you like it?   apnar ' kæmon lage "

7.3. Between the interrogatives /ki/ and /kon/, possible confusion results from English equivalents. In English, the word "what" can be used in two ways: to indicate "which of several", and to indicate "what (general) thing". Thus, in English, we can have "in what city do you live" and "what do you do". Bengali distinguishes between these two usages. Thus:

In what (i.e., which) city   apni ' kon ʃohore thaken "
do you live?

In what (i.e., which) chair   apni ' kon ceare bɔʃen "
do you sit?

What do you do?   apni ' ki kɔren "

What do you study?   apni ' ki pɔɽen "

A simple rule is that where in English the word "which" can be used, the Bengali equivalent will be /kon/. A good minimal pair is:

What kind of job do you do?   apni ' ki kaj kɔren "

What particular work do you   apni ' kon kaj kɔren "
do?

Descriptively, it can be said that /kon/ must take a noun following it; /ki/ may or may not.

8. Intonation patterns.

Learning to speak a language well does not consist only of learning the correct reproduction of the individual sounds of that language; the rise and fall of the voice in the utterance of a sentence is also significant This is true in English. For example, pronounce the utterance:

> you're going

first as a statement, then as a question. The difference between the two is the intonation of the utterance. There is no other element which denotes the difference between a statement and a question in this case.

The situation is similar in Bengali. There are three types of intonation patterns so far met, one a statement intonation, and two question intonations.

Listen carefully to the tapes, until you are sure that you can reproduce Bengali intonation patterns exactly.

Pattern 1: Statement.

My name is Robi.	amar nam ' robi "
My name is Ram.	amar nam ' ram "
It is very hot in Chicago.	śikagote ' khub gɔrom "
You (hon.) live in Chicago.	apni ' śikagote thaken "
You (hon.) work (lit. you do work).	apni ' kaj kɔren "
I study Bengali.	ami ' baŋla poɽi "
I study at the college.	ami ' kɔleje poɽi "

Pattern 2: Questions with /ki/ involving a yes-no answer. (/ki/ is not verbally translatable in English).

	apni ki '·kɔren "
Do you do?	apni kɔren ' ki "
	apni ki ' kaj koren "
Do you work?	apni kaj kɔren ' ki "
	śikagote ki ' khub gɔrom "
Is it very hot in Chicago?	śikagote khub gɔrom ' ki "

64

Do you study Bengali?	apni ki ' baŋla pɔṛen "
	apni ' baŋla pɔṛen ki "

Pattern 3: In the following sentences, /ki/ is translatable in English by the interrogative "what".

What do you do?	apni ' ki kɔren "
	apni kɔren ' ki "
What do you study?	apni ' ki pɔṛen "
	apni pɔṛen ' ki "
What is your name?	apnar ' ki nam "
	apnar nam ' ki "
What is your work?	apnar ' ki kaj "
	apnar kaj ' ki "
Where do you live?	apni ' kothae thaken "
	apni thaken ' kothae "
How many people are there in Chicago?	śikagote ' kɔto lok "
How do you like Chicago?	apnar śikago ' kaemon lage "
How (much) different is Bengali?	baŋla ' kɔto śɔkto "

8.1. Drills. Taped drills on this section of the lesson are arranged in the following manner:

8.1.1. Intonation drill #1 (pattern 1, statement intonation)

An English sentence will be given, and the student will translate it into Bengali in the space given. The student will then hear the correct Bengali, and will repeat the correct Bengali in the space given.

8.1.2. Intonation drill #2 (pattern 2, question with /ki/ involving a "yes" or "no" answer)

An English sentence will be given, and the student will translate it into Bengali, recording in the space given. The student will then hear the correct Bengali and will repeat it, recording, in the space given.

8.1.3. Intonation drill #3 (pattern 3, questions with /ki/ meaning "what"). The system will be the same as for the drills above.

9. Word order: In Bengali a modifier precedes that which it modifies:

a <u>hot</u> city	gɔrom śɔhor
<u>Very</u> good (<u>very</u> well)	<u>khub</u> bhalo
<u>easy</u> Bengali	śɔhoj baŋla

10. Bengali sentence formation: Form Bengali sentences (both as questions and statements -- note differences of intonation between the types of formations), from the following outlines and translate them into English. Use forms in parentheses (interrogatives) for question formation.

10.1.

Modifier	Noun	(Interrogative)	Noun	(Interrogative)
amar	nam	(ki)	robi	(ki)
apnar			ram	

10.2.

noun or pronoun	(Interrogative)	verbal modifier or object	verb stem	suffix	(Interrogative)
ami	(ki)	ekhane	thak-		(ki)
apni		śekhane	khæl-		
śe		śɔhore	bɔś-	i/en/e	
ram		baṛite			
robi		śikagote			
		baŋla	pɔṛ-		

10.3.

		kothae			
		ki (what)	kɔr-		

10.4.

Noun	Interro-gative	Modifiers	Noun	(Verb)	Interro-gative
śikago		khub bɔɾo			
	(ki)		śɔhor	(nɔe)	(ki)
bari	_____	choto			
ghɔr	kɔto				
śɔhor	- - - - -	- - - - - -	- - - -		
baŋla	(ki)	śokto			
Noun (locative)					
śikagote		gɔrom			
	kɔto			(nɔe)	
ekhane		thaṇḍa			
baɾite					
śɔhore	(ki)				(ki)

Lesson 1, part 4. Pattern drills.

1. Pattern: sentences 3, 4, 5.

    a. My name is Naresh ([nɔreś]). What is your name?
    b. My name is Shuhash ([śuhaś]). What is your name?
    c. My name is Probash ([probaś]). What is your name?
    d. My name is Shomdeb ([śomdeb]). What is your name?
    e. My name is Shamir ([śomir]). What is your name?

2. Pattern: sentences 3, 5.

    a. My name is Nira ([nira]).
    b. My name is Rita ([rita]).
    c. My name is Shanta ([śanta]).
    d. My name is Shita ([śita]).
    e. My name is Shipra ([śipra]).

3. Pattern: sentences 6, 8, 10.

    a. Where do you live?
    b. Where do you sit?
    c. Where do you play?
    d. Where do you study?

e. What do you do?

4. Pattern: sentences 7, 9.

   a. I live in the city.
   b. I sit in the chair.
   c. I play here.
   d. I study in Chicago.
   e. I study here.

5. Pattern: sentences 6, 8, 10.

   a. What do you do?
   b. What do you study?
   c. What do you play?
   d. What do you study?
   e. What do you read?

6. Pattern: sentence 11.

   a. I study in the college.
   b. I study Bengali.
   c. I play games.
   d. I study language.
   e. I read English.

7. Pattern: sentence 12.

   a. Is the college difficult?
   b. Is Bengali difficult?
   c. Are the games easy?
   d. Is language easy?
   e. Is English very difficult?

8. Pattern: sentence 13.

   a. No, it is not difficult.
   b. No, it is not very difficult.
   c. No, not very easy.
   d. No, language is not easy.
   e. No, it is not difficult.

9. Pattern: sentence 12 and 14.

   a. Is it very hot in the city?

68

b. Is it very cold in the house?
c. Is it very hot there?
d. Is it very cold in Chicago?
e. Is it very cold here?

10. Pattern: 15 and 17.

a. No, it is not very hot.
b. No, it is not very cold.
c. No, it is not very hot there.
d. No, it is not very cold in Chicago.
e. No, it is not very cold here.

11. Pattern: 12 and 14.

a. Is it very cold in the city?
b. Is it very hot in the house?
c. Is it very cold there?
d. Is it very hot in Chicago?
e. Is it very hot here?

12. Pattern: 15 and 17.

a. Yes, it is very cold.
b. Yes, it is very hot.
c. Yes, it is very cold there.
d. Yes, it is very hot in Chicago.
e. Yes, it is very hot here.

13. Pattern: 18.

a. How big is the city?
b. How difficult is Bengali?
c. How cold is Chicago?
d. How hot is your house?
e. How easy is English?

14. Pattern: 19.

a. Chicago is a very big city.
b. Bengali is a very easy language.
c. Chicago is a very cold city.
d. My house is very hot.
e. English is a very difficult language.

15. Pattern: 20.

    a. How many people are there in the city?
    b. How many people are there in the country?
    c. How many people are there in Chicago?
    d. How many people are there in your house?
    e. How many people are there in your college?

16. Pattern: 21.

    a. There are many people in Chicago.
    b. There are many people in the country.
    c. There are many people in the city.
    d. There are many people in my house.
    e. There are many people in my college.

17. Pattern: 22.

    a. How do you like the city?
    b. How do you like Bengali?
    c. How do you like Chicago?
    d. How do you like your house?
    e. How do you like the college?

18. Pattern: 23.

    a. I like the city very much.
    b. I like Bengali very much.
    c. I do not like Chicago very much.
    d. I do not like my house very much.
    e. I like the college very much.

Lesson 1, part 5.   Drills.

Translate into Bengali:

Drill 1

-- What is your name?
-- My name is Naresh.
-- Where do you sit?
-- I sit here.
-- Do you sit in this chair?

Drill 2

-- Where is your house?
-- My house is in the city.
-- How big is your house?
-- My house is very big.
-- In what city is your house?

-- No, I sit in that chair.

-- What do you study?

-- I study Bengali.

-- How do you like Bengali?

-- Very much.

-- Is Bengali very difficult?

-- No, it is not very difficult.

-- It is in Chicago.

-- How do you like Chicago?

-- It is very hot there.

-- Is Chicago a big city?

-- Yes, there are many people in Chicago.

Lesson 1, part 6. Vocabulary

Nouns

Bengali	English
baṛi	house
ghɔr	room
kaj	work
khæla	game
cear	chair
deś	country
iŋriji	English (language)
bhaśa	language
kɔlej	college

Verbs

(Note: verbs are given in stem form; the endings are added directly to the stem; see also Lesson 2, grammar.)

Bengali	English
bɔś-	sit
khael-	play
kɔr-	do, make

Adjectives

Bengali	English
śɔhoj	easy
śɔkto	difficult
choṭo	small

Other

Bengali	English
ei, e	this
oi, o	that
ekhane	here
okhane	there
śekhane	there

Idioms

amar bhalo lage / kharap — me-of good / bad strikes-(it) (I like/dont like it.)

apnar kæmon lage — you-of how strikes-(it) (How do you like it?)

Analysis and translation	Bengali

1.
2nd person ordinary pronoun "you" — tumi

stem of verb "do, make" — kɔr-

2nd person (ordinary) verbal
ending — -o

"you (ordinary) do" — (tumi) kɔro

A. What do you do?   A. tumi ' ki kɔro "

2.
noun stem, "office" — ɔphiś

(note that Bengali /ph/ is
frequently pronounced much like
English f -- see Phonology, 4.2.6.

locative case ending for stems
with consonant final — -e

"in the (an) office" — ɔphiśe

noun stem, "work" — kaj

alternative (high) stem of
verb "do, make" (see grammar,
section 1) — kor-

"I do" — (ami) kori

B. I work in an office.   B. ami ' ɔphiśe kaj kori "

3.
stem of 2nd person (ordinary)
pronoun "you" — toma-

genitive case ending for stems
with vowel final — -r

"of you (ordinary)" — tomar

noun stem, " father" — baba

"your father" — tomar baba

72

demonstrative, "that"   śe
morpheme indicating place   khan-
locative case ending   -e
"in that place, there"   śekhane
2nd/3rd person honorific ending   -en
"he (honorific) does"   kɔren

<u>A.</u> <u>Does your father work there?</u>   <u>A.</u> <u>tomar baba ki ' śekhane</u>
                                                <u>kaj kɔren "</u>

4. 3rd person honorific pronoun
   "he, she"   tini

<u>B.</u> <u>No, he doesn't work there.</u>   <u>B.</u> <u>na ' tini ' śekhane kaj</u>
                                                <u>kɔren na "</u>

5. <u>A.</u> <u>What does your father do?</u>   <u>A.</u> <u>tomar baba ' ki kɔren "</u>

6. "some, any"   kono
   "none at all"   kono ... na

<u>B.</u> <u>He doesn't do any work at all.</u> <u>B.</u> <u>tini ' kono kaj ' kɔren na "</u>

7. noun stem, "brother"   bhai
   present stem of defective verb
   "be"; see grammar, section 3.   ach-
   3rd person (ordinary) verbal
   ending   -e

<u>A.</u> <u>Do you have any brothers?</u>   <u>A.</u> <u>tomar ki ' kono bhai ache "</u>
   (you-of ? any brother there is)

8. form of numeral "two" used in
   compounds   du-
   qualifying suffix, used with
   reference to human beings   -jon

<u>B.</u> <u>Yes, I have two brothers.</u>   <u>B.</u> <u>hæ̃ " amar ' dujon bhai ache "</u>
   (yes, me-of two-(qualifier)
   brother there-is)

9.   3rd person (ordinary) pronoun
stem   ta-

    nominative plural ending, used   -ra
with pronouns and nouns having
reference to living beings

    "they, those people" (ordinary)   **tara**

    3rd person ordinary verbal ending   -e

    (note that the ending is the
same for singular and plural)

    "they (ordinary) live"   tara thake

    A. <u>Where do they live?</u>   A. <u>tara ' kothae thake</u> "

10.   noun stem, "house"   bari
    locative case ending   -te
    "in the house, at home"   barite

    B. <u>They live at home.</u>   B. <u>tara ' barite thake</u> "

11.   "big"   boro

    A. <u>Where does your older brother
work?</u>   A. <u>tomar boro bhai ' kothae
kaj koren</u> "

12.   B. <u>He works in an office.</u>   B. <u>tini ' ophiśe kaj koren</u> "

13.   "little"   choto

    A. <u>What work does your younger
brother do?</u>   A. <u>tomar choto bhai ' ki kaj
kore</u> "

14.   verb stem, "read, study"   por-

    B. <u>My younger brother studies.</u>   B. <u>amar choto bhai ' pore</u> "

15.   3rd person (ordinary) pronoun
stem "he/she/it"   ta-

    genitive case ending for stems
with vowel-final   -r

    "of him/her (ordinary)"   tar

    noun stem, "age"   boeś

	A. How old is he? (how much is his age?)	A. tar bɔeś ' kɔto "
16.	"twenty"	kuṛi
	B. He is twenty. (his age is twenty)	B. tar bɔeś ' kuṛi "
17.	A. Does your younger brother study in college?	A. tomar chɔṭo bhai ki ' kɔleje pɔre "
18.	B. Yes, he studies in college.	B. hæ̃ " śe ' kɔleje pɔre "
19.	stem of verb "go"	ja-
	3rd person (ordinary) ending	-e
	"he goes"	(śe) jae
	"daily, every day"	roj
	A. Does your younger brother go to college every day?	A. tomar chɔṭo bhai ki ' roj kɔleje jae "
20.	noun stem, "week"	śɔptaho
	locative case ending	-e
	"in the week"	śɔptahe (see **grammar**, section 8)
	"four"	car
	noun stem, "day"	din
	B. No, four days a week he does not go to college.	B. na ' śɔptahe ' car din ' śe kɔleje jae na "
21.	"which"	kon
	"which (plural)"	kon kon
	"which day"	kon din
	"which days"	kon kon din
	A. Which days of the week does he not go to college?	A. śe śɔptahe ' kon kon din ' kɔleje jae na "
22.	Sunday	robibar
	Monday	śombar

Tuesday	moŋgolbar
Wednesday	budhbar
"and"	ar

B. He does not go to college Sundays, Mondays, Tuesdays, or Wednesdays.

B. śe robibar ' śombar ' moŋgolbar ' ar budhbar ' koleje jae na "

23.

"only"	kebol
Thursday	brihośpotibar
Friday	śukrobar
Saturday	śonibar

B. He goes to college only Thursdays, Fridays, and Saturdays.

B. śe kebol ' brihośpotibar ' śukrobar ' ar śonibar ' koleje jae "

Lesson 2, part 2.   Drills.

The taped drills will follow the same pattern as in Lesson 1.

Lesson 2, part 3.   Grammar.

1.   Many Bengali nouns, pronouns, and verbs have two alternative stems.
The two alternative verb stems will hereafter be distinguished as "high"
and "low" stems, the terms referring to the height of the stem-vowel
(see chart below). The low-stem form is the basic form, the form which
you will be given throughout this text, since through it the system of
vowel change is more easily understood.

1.1. The basic form -- low stem -- can be considered as the verbal noun
minus the nominal suffix:

Verbal noun		Basic stem
kɔra	"doing"	kɔr-
kena	"buying"	ken-
khæla	"playing"	khæl-
jaoa	"going"	ja-

1.2.   The system of Bengali vowels is charted as follows:

	Front	Middle	Back
High	i		u
Mid	e		o
	æ		ɔ
Low		a	

1.2.1.   The system of vowel alternation is as follows:

When the low-stem vowel is /e/, the high-stem vowel is /i/.
/æ/, /e/.
/o/, /u/.
/ɔ/, /o/.

The stem-vowel /a/ presents a special case, and will be considered in
detail at a later time; for the present, we can consider stems with /a/
as having no vowel change. Stems in /i/ and /u/, these being the
highest vowels, have no higher form.

1.3. In some cases the stem-vowel alternation can be phonologically defined, as for example in sentences 1 and 2 in this exercise. In sentence 1, the verb "do, make" occurs with the stem /kɔr-/. In sentence 2, the same verb occurs with the stem /kor-/. Note that the 1st person (personal ending -i) form of the verb, i.e, /kori/, is the form which occurs in sentence 2. It is a general phonological rule for the language that when a word of this shape: consonant-vowel-(consonant), has for the second vowel either /i/ or /u/, the preceding vowel of the word is high. In sentence 2, the second vowel of /kori/ is /i/, and the /ɔ/ vowel of the low stem becomes the high vowel /o/.

1.3.1. Other examples of this type of vowel-alternation in verb stems are:

Vowel Alternation	Stem	Simple Present Tense Paradigm	
e/i	ken-	ami kini	"I buy"
		tumi keno	"you (ord.) buy"
		apni kenen	"you (hon.) buy"
		śe kene	"he (ord.) buys"
		tini kenen	"he (hon.) buys"
æ/e	khæl-	ami kheli	"I play"
		tumi khælo	"you play"
		apni khælen	"you play"
		śe khæle	"he plays"
		tini khælen	"he plays"
ɔ/o	bɔś-	ami bośi	"I sit"
		tumi bɔśo	"you sit"
		apni bɔśen	"you sit"
		śe bɔśe	"he sits"
		tini bɔśen	"he sits"
o/u	oṭh-	ami uṭhi	"I rise up"
		tumi oṭho	"you rise up"
		apni oṭhen	"you rise up"
		śe oṭhe	"he rises up"
		tini oṭhen	"he rises up"

1.4. Stems with /a/ have no change in the simple present tense.

78

	Stem	Simple Present Tense Paradigm	
	ɟan-	ami ɟani	"I know"
		tumi ɟano	"you know"
		apni ɟanen	"you know"
		śe ɟane	"he knows"
		tini ɟanen	"he knows"
	ɟa-	ami ɟai	"I go"
		tumi ɟao	"you go"
		apni ɟan	"you go"
		śe ɟae	"he goes"
		tini ɟan	"he goes"

Note that stems with vowel final have the ending /-n/ in the honorific forms.

1.5. Drills on these vowel changes will follow the same pattern as in Lesson 1.

1.6. Examples of this type of alternation in pronoun and noun stems are

Vowel Alternation	Genitive	Nominative
o/u	tomar "of you"	tumi "you (ord.)"
	Masculine	**Feminine**
ɔ/o	nɔʈ "actor"	noʈi "actress"

1.7. There are other stem-vowel changes which are not phonologically definable; these will be considered at a later time.

1.8. Write the simple present tense paradigms for the following verb stems:

(to) read	pɔɽ-
(to) drop, throw	phæl-
(to) know, recognize	cen-
(to) hear	śon-
(to) remain	thak-

1.9. The verb /de-/, "give", is irregular in the simple present tense, and has the following paradigm.

ami dii   "I give"

tumi dao	"you (ord.) give"
apni dæn	"you (hon.) give"
śe dæe	"he (ord.) gives"
tini dæn	"he (hon.) gives"

2. The /khan/ morpheme, indicating place, as in sentence 3, is usually used in the locative, i.e., /-khane/. Various kinds of demonstratives and interrogatives can be substituted as the first element of a word, e.g.,

ekhane	"in this place, here"
okhane	"in that place, there" (with specific reference)
śekhane	"in that place, there" (used in a more generalized way than the preceding)
konkhane	"in which place, where"

3. The defective verb /ach-/, sentence 7.

3.1. In statements which imply a permanent condition, some form of the verb /ach-/, which exists only in the simple present and simple past forms, is used. A good rule of thumb is that this verb can be used in statements or questions which may have the expression "there is" in English. In sentence 7, for example, the literal translation is: "Is there any brother of you?"

3.2. The negative form of the verb /ache/, "there is", is /nei/, "there is not":

tomar ki ' kono bhai ache"	Do you have any brothers?
na " amar ' kono bhai nei"	No, I don't have any brothers.

4. There is no simple Bengali equivalent for the transitive English verb "have, possess". As in sentence 7, a possessive construction is formed by the use of the genitive case for the subject and the 3rd person (or impersonal) form of the verb /ach-/, thus:

amar'ækṭa boi ache"	me-of one-(qualifier) book (there)-is	I have a book.
tar'ækṭa bɔṛo kukur ache"	him-of one-(qualifier) big dog (there)-is	He has a big dog.

5. We have now had two types of second person pronoun -- the stems

/apn-/ and apna-/, in Lesson 1, and /tum-/ and /toma-/, in Lesson 2.
The distinction between these two forms is that /apn- apna-/ (used with
verbal ending /-en/) is an honorific form of address, while /tum- toma-/
(used with the verbal ending /-o/) is an ordinary form of address.

5.1.   There is also a distinction between ordinary and honorific forms
of address in the 3rd person. The 3rd person ordinary pronoun forms
are /śe/ (nominative) and /ta-/ (stem to which inflectional endings are
added). The 3rd person honorific pronoun form is /tini/. Note that the
honorific verbal endings are the same for both 2nd and 3rd persons.

apni koren	you do
tini koren	he/she does
apni janen	you know
tini janen	he/she knows
apni jan	you go
tini jan	he/she goes

5.2.   The circumstances which govern the distribution of these forms are
not easily defined, but a basic rule of thumb might be the following:

The polite or honorific form is used by Bengalis when addressing or
referring to a person of superior rank, an elder, or an equal with whom
the speaker is not on intimate terms. The ordinary form is used with
intimate equals and members of one's immediate family; it is also used
by Bengalis when addressing servants. It is to be noted, however, that
a non-native Bengali speaker will not go wrong by using the honorific
form in every circumstance except perhaps when addressing servants. It
is a matter about which it is well to be carful, since the form you use
indicates to the listener your attitude toward him.

5.3.   There is another degree of second person address, of which the
pronoun stem is /to- tu-/. The inflection of this pronoun is:

Nominative:	tui
Genitive:	tor
(Objective:	toke)

The verbal ending is /-iś/, thus: tui janiś "you know"
This form is sometimes used for addressing very intimate friends and

younger family members, sometimes for servants and children, and for animals. It is not a form which a foreigner can often use; therefore there will be little stress laid upon it in these lessons.

6. The nominative stem of the 3rd person pronoun is /śe/ or, in the honorific, /tini/. The inflectional stem, however, is /ta-/ or, in the honorific, /tã-/. Thus:

| He reads his book. | śe'tar boi poṛe" |
| He (hon.) reads his book. | tini'tãr boi poṛen" |

7. The nominative plural ending for pronouns and nouns which have reference to human beings is /-ra/ (for stems with vowel final) and /-era/ for stems with consonant final). Thus:

chele	boy
chelera khae	the boys eat
ta-	3rd person pronoun stem
tara jane	they know
manuś	man
manuśera jae	men go

Note that the rule is not inflexible; the forms /manuśra/ and /lokra/ (people) are possible.

7.1. The personal endings of the verb ? identical for singular and plural:

English	Bengali
I do	ami kori
you (ord.) do	tumi koro
you (inf.) do	tui koriś
you (hon.) do	apni koren
he (she, it) does	śe kore
he (she, it - hon.) does	tini koren
we do	amra kori
you (ord.) do	tomra koro
you (inf.) do	tora koriś

you (hon.) do	apnara kɔren
they (ord.) do	tara kɔre
they (non.) do	tãra kɔren

7.2. Make complete paradigms, singular and plural, for the following verbs:

(to) buy	ken-
(to) go	ja-
(to) play	khæl-
(to) hear	śon-
(to) know	jan-

7.3. Note that, as in sentence 8, when the noun is accompanied by a plural adjective (here /dujon/), it takes no plural suffix.

8. Noun stems ending in /-o/ are inflected by the replacement of final /o/ by the inflectional suffix.

"week"	śɔptaho
"of the week"	śɔptaher
"in the week"	śɔptahe

9. Sentence formation:. construct possible Bengali sentences:

9.1.

Modifier	Noun or Pronoun	Interrogative	Verbal Modifier	Verb Stem	Suffix
	ami tumi apni śe tini tara	(ki)	ekhane śekhane baɽite ghɔre śchore kɔleje (etc.)	ja- kɔr- khæl- pɔɽ- thak-	i/o/en/e
amar apnar tomar tar tãr	baba dada bhai bon ma bondhu	kothae			

9.2.

Modifier	Noun or Pronoun	In-terr.	Modifiers and Nouns		Verb	Suffix	In-terr.
	(Genitive) tomar amar apnar	(ki)	kono baba dada choṭo bhai bɔṛo bondhu		ach-	ə	(ki)
amar tomar apnar bondhur	bɔeś bɔeś	kɔto kuṛi tiriś					

9.3.

Noun or Pronoun	Modifier	Modifier	Noun	Verbal Modifier	Verb	Suffix
ami tumi apni śe ram bhai	śɔptahe	kon kon kon æk du tin robibar śonibar roj	din	kɔleje ekhane bariṭe śɔhore	ja- khæl- pɔṛ aś-	i/o/en/e

Lesson 2, part 4. Pattern drills.

1. Pattern: sentences 1, 5.

   a. What does your younger brother do?
   b. What does your younger brother study?
   c. What does your older brother do?
   d. What does your older brother study?
   e. What work does your father do?

2. Pattern: sentences 2, 12.

   a. He (ord.) goes to college.
   b. He (ord.) studies Bengali.
   c. He (hon.) works at the college.
   d. He (hon.) studies English.

e. He (hon.) works in an office.

3. Pattern: sentence 3.

a. Does your younger brother study there?
b. Does your younger brother speak Bengali?
c. Does your older brother study there?
d. Does your older brother study at the college?
e. Does your older brother work there?

4. Pattern: sentence 4.

a. Yes, he (ord.) studies there.
b. Yes, he (ord.) speaks Bengali.
c. Yes, he (hon.) studies there.
d. No, he (hon.) does not study at the college.
e. No, he (hon.) does not work in the office.

5. Pattern: sentence 5.

a. What work does your younger brother do?
b. What language does your older brother know?
c. What work does your older brother do?
d. What books does your older brother read?
e. What work does your older brother do?

6. Pattern: sentence 6. (Use appropriate pronoun and verb forms.)

a. He doesn't do any work at all.
b. He doesn't know any Bengali at all.
c. He doesn't do any work at all.
d. He doesn't read any books at all.
e. He doesn't study any books at all.

7. Pattern: sentence 7.

a. Do you have any older brothers?
b. Does he have any Bengali books?
c. Do you (hon.) have any younger brothers?
d. Does he have any English books?
e. Does he have any work?

8. Pattern: sentence 8.

a. Yes, I have one older brother.

b. Yes, he has some Bengali books.
c. Yes, I have four younger brothers.
d. Yes, he has some English books.
e. Yes, he has some work.

9. Pattern: sentences 9, 11.

a. Where does he live?
b. Where does he buy books?
c. Where do they study?
d. Where does your older brother live?
e. Where does he work?

10. Pattern: sentences 10, 12.

a. He lives at college.
b. He buys books in the city.
c. They study in the room.
d. He lives at home.
e. He works at the college.

11. Pattern: sentence 15.

a. How old is he?
b. How old is your younger brother?
c. How old is your older brother?
d. How old is your older sister?
e. How old is your father?

12. Pattern: sentence 16.

a. He is thirty.
b. He is twenty.
c. He is twenty-five.
d. He is forty.
e. He is fifty.

13. Pattern: sentence 17.

a. Does he study at the college?
b. Does your younger brother study at the college?
c. Does he live at home?
d. Does he study at home?

e. Does your father live in the city?

14. Pattern: sentence 18.

a. Yes, he studies at the college.
b. Yes, my younger brother studies at the college.
c. Yes, my older brother lives at home.
d. Yes, he studies in the room.
e. Yes, he lives in the city.

15. Pattern: sentence 19.

a. Does he go home every day?
b. Does he study at the college every day?
c. Does he come home every day?
d. Does he study every day?
e. Does your father go home every day?

16. Pattern: sentence 20.

a. No, two days a week he does not go home.
b. No, three days a week he does not go to college
c. No, four days a week he does not come home.
d. No, five days a week he does not study.
e. No, one day a week he stays at the college.

17. Pattern: sentence 21.

a. Which days of the week does he not go home?
b. Which days of the week does he not go to college?
c. Which days of the week does he not come home?
d. Which days of the week does he not study?
e. Which day of the week does he stay at the college?

18. Pattern: sentences 22, 23.

a. He does not go home Sunday and Monday.
b. He does not go to college Sunday, Monday, and Tuesday.
c. He does not come home Monday, Tuesday, Wednesday, and Thursday.
d. He does not study Monday, Tuesday, Wednesday, Thursday, and Friday.
e. He stays at the college Saturday.

a. He goes home only Tuesday, Wednesday, Thursday, Friday, and Saturday.
b. He goes to college only Wednesday, Thursday, Friday, and Saturday.
c. He comes home only Friday, Saturday, and Sunday.
d. He studies only Saturday and Sunday.
e. He comes home Sunday, Monday, Tuesday, Wednesday, Thursday, and Friday.

Lesson 2, part 4. Sentence Drill.

Drill 1

--Where do you (ord.) work?
--I work at the college.
--Do you study there?
--No, I work in the office.
--What work does your father do?
--My father is (a) doctor.
--Where does he live?
--He lives in Calcutta.
--Do you have any brothers?
--Yes, I have three brothers.
--What do they do?
--They study at the college.
--Do you stay at home Mondays?
--Yes, I stay at home two days a week, Monday and Tuesday.

Drill 2

--Have you any sisters?
--Yes, I have two sisters.
--What does the older sister do?
--She studies English.
--Does she speak English?
--No, she speaks only Bengali.
--Where does your younger sister live?
--She lives at my father's house.
--Does your sister have any sons?
--Yes, she has two sons and one daughter.
--How old is the daughter?
--She is ten.

Lesson 2, part 5. Vocabulary.

Nouns

Bengali	English	Bengali	English
rɔkom	kind	bon	sister
ḍaktar	doctor	ma	mother
kolkata, kolikata	Calcutta	dada	older brother
põciś	twenty-five	chele	son, boy
tiriś	thirty	mee	daughter, girl
colliś	forty	bondhu	friend
põcaś	fifty		

Verbs		Adjectives	
Bengali	**English**	**Bengali**	**English**
nac-	dance	Cardinal Numbers:	
bɔl-	say	æk	one
aś	come	dui, du	two
		tin	three
Other		car	four
mattro		pãc	five
kebol	only	chɔe	six
kichu	some, a few	śat	seven
		aʈ	eight
		nɔe	nine
		dɔś	ten
		kaɽi, biś	twenty
		Days of the Week:	
		robibar	Sunday
		śombar	Monday
		moŋgolbaɪ	Tuesday
		budhbar (budbar)	Wednesday
		brihóśpotibar	Thursday
		śukrobar	Friday
		śonibar	Saturday

Lesson 3, part 1. Conversation.

Analysis and translation	Bengali
1. "news"	khɔbor
"what news" -- form of greeting	ki khɔbor
A. **What news?**	A. ki khɔbor "
2. "of you (ordinary)"	tomar
B. **Good. What's the news with you?**	B. bhalo " tomar ' ki khɔbor "
3. demonstrative, "that"	o
qualifying suffix; see grammar, section 2.	-ʈa
"that (particular)"	oʈa
A. **Good. What book is that?**	A. bhalo " oʈa ' ki boi "
4. "one"	æk
qualifying suffix; see grammar, section 2.	-ʈa
"a, an"	ækʈa
noun stem, "poetry, poem"	kobita
genitive case suffix for stems with vowel final	-r
"of poetry"	kobitar
"book of poetry"	kobitar boi
B. (It is) a book of poetry.	B. ækʈa ' kobitar boi "

5.
noun stem, "book"   boi

qualifying suffix; see Grammar, section 2   -ṭa

"that book"   boiṭa

genitive case suffix   -r

"of that book"   boiṭar

A. What is the name of that book?   A. o boiṭar ' nam ki "

6.
name of a book of poems by Tagore   bɔlaka

B. That book's name is Balaka.   B. o boiṭar nam ' bɔlaka "

7.
demonstrative pronoun, "that"   o

qualifying suffix   -ṭa

genitive case suffix   -r

"of that (particular) one"   oṭar

verb stem, "write"   lekh-

noun stem, "writer"   lekhok

interrogative, "who"   ke

A. Who is the writer of it?   A. oṭar ' lekhɔk ke "

8.
name of a famous Bengali poet, Rabindranath (Tagore)   robindronath (ṭhakur)

B. Rabindranath is the writer of it.   B. oṭar lekhɔk ' robindronath "

verb stem, "know, recognize"   jan-

"you (ordinary) know"   (tumi) jano

B. Do you know Rabindranath's name?   B. tumi ki robindronather ' nam jano "

10.
(inflectional) stem of 3rd person (honorific) pronoun   tã-

"of him (honorific)"   tãr

A. No, I don't know his name.   A. na " ami ' tãr nam ' jani na "

11. <u>A</u>. <u>Who is he?</u>   A. <u>tini ke</u> "

12.   "one"   æk

     qualifying suffix, used with
     reference to human beings   -jon

     "one (person)"   ækjon

     noun stem, "poet"   kobi

     <u>B</u>. <u>He is a poet</u>.   B. tini ' ækjon kobi "

13.   noun stem, "song"   gan

     <u>A</u>. <u>Does he write songs?</u>   A. tini ki ' gan lekhen "

14.   for this use of the future tense,
     see grammar, section 3.1.

     basic stem of verb "hear"   śon-

     high stem of verb "hear"   śun-

     sign of the future tense   -b-

     2nd person (ordinary) verbal
     ending used with future tense   -e

     "you (ordinary) will hear"   (tumi) śunbe

     <u>B</u>. <u>Yes. Would you like to hear a</u>
     <u>song by Rabindranath?</u>   B. hæ̃ " tumi ki ' robindronather
                                       gan ' śunbe "

15.   for this use of the genitive case,
     see grammar, section 4.

     verb stem, "hear"   śun-

     sign of the future tense   -b-

     1st person verbal ending,
     future tense   -o

     "I will/shall hear"   (ami) śunbo

     <u>A</u>. <u>Yes, I should like to hear a</u>
     <u>song by him</u>.   A. hæ̃ " ami ' tãr gan ' śunbo "

16.   type of Indian stringed
     instrument   śetar

     verb stem, "play (an instrument)"   baja-

     you (ordinary) will play"   (tumi) bajabe

A. Will you play the sitar?	A. tumi ki ' śetar bajabe "
17. type of instrument, violin	behala
B. No, I shall play the behala.	B. na " ami ' behala bajabo "

18.   2nd person (ord.) pronoun stem — toma-

genitive case suffix with vowel stems — -r

post-position "with" (accompaniment), governing a preceding genitive — śɔŋge

"with you" — tomar śɔŋge

type of Indian drum — tɔbla

A. I shall accompany you on the tabla.   A. ami ' tomar śɔŋge ' tɔbla bajabo "

19. B. Will your brother play the sitar?   B. tomar bhai ki ' śetar bajabe "

20. A. Yes, he will play.   A. hæ̃ " bajabe "

Lesson 3, part 2. Grammar.

1. Genitive case endings. The genitive case ending has two forms:

1.1. The general rule for the formation of the genitive case is that when a word has a vowel final, the suffix is /-r/. When a word has a consonant final, the suffix is /-er/. There is an exception to this rule:

When the word has the shape CV (consonant-vowel) and the final vowel is /i/, /u/, or /a/, the genitive suffix is either /-r/ or /-er/. When the word has the shape CVV (consonant-vowel-vowel), and the final vowel is /i/ or /u/, the genitive suffix is /-er/. Examples:

	English	Nominative	Genitive
CV:	mother	ma	mar, maer
	foot	pa	par, paer
CVV:	book	boi	boier

brother	bhai	bhaier
wife	bou	bouer

But the genitive of /kobi/, "poet", is /kobir/, the word being of CVCV shape.

2. The use of qualifiers.

2.1. There are various qualifiers (sometimes called "particles") in Bengali, which have different usages and meanings. The most commonly used one is the one which we have in sentences 3, 4, 5, 6, 7, and 8 -- i.e., /-ṭa/. It is often difficult to assign a lexical meaning to these qualifiers. They are frequently added to adjectives or, as here, demonstrative pronouns, which are not accompanied by a noun.

Examples:

English	Bengali
What book is that (or, depending on the intonation, "Is that a book?")	oṭa ki boi"
What book is this (or: Is this a book?)	eṭa ki boi"
Is this easy?	eṭa ki'śɔhoj"
Is that bad?	śeṭa ki'kharap"
That is bad.	śeṭa'kharap"
That is easy work.	oṭa'śɔhoj kaj"

When the demonstrative is accompanied by a noun, the qualifier is affixed to the noun. Note also differences in meaning.

What is that book?	o boiṭa'ki"
That work is easy.	o kajṭa'śɔhoj"
This poetry is very beautiful.	o kobitaṭa'khub śundor"

Drill carefully (using the tapes) on these usages and distinctions.

2.1.1. How would you say the following?

That work is difficult.
That is difficult work.

That book is good.
That is a good book.

That poem is beautiful.
That is a beautiful poem.

Is that difficult work?
Is that work difficult?

2.1.2.   The difference might be defined in this way: that when the demonstrative (/e/, /o/, or /śe/) is used adjectivally (i.e., accompanying a noun), the noun takes the qualifier. When it is used pronominally (i.e., standing alone, as the subject or object of the sentence), the demonstrative itself takes the qualifier.

2.2.   Qualifiers are usually added to numerals and other adjectives of quantity even when accompanied by a noun, as in sentence 4. Again, in such cases, there is no transferrable meaning in English. An exception to this rule is when adjectives of quantity accompany nouns referring to money or measure. For example:

"two annas"	du ana
"five rupees"	pãc ṭaka
"two seers"	du śer

The numerals /du/ ("two"), /tin/ ("three") and /car/ ("four") usually take special forms of the qualifier, thus:

I want two books.	ami'duṭo boi cai"
I shall hear three songs.	ami'tinṭe gan śunbo"
I shall eat four mangoes.	ami'carṭe am khabo"

Note that when adjectives of quantity are used, the nouns which they accompany are singular in form.

2.3.   The qualifier /-ṭa/ can be used with reference to any person or object. The qualifier /-jon/, however, as in sentence 2, can be used only in reference to human beings. Although /-ṭa/ can also be used with human reference, the use of /-jon/ is preferable in this situation.

2.4.   Examples of these various usages are as follows:

I shall fetch a book.	ami'ækṭa boi anbo"
I shall fetch that book.	ami'o boiṭa anbo"
I shall fetch that.	ami'oṭa anbo"

He (hon.) will sing a song.	tini'ækṭa gan gaiben"
He (hon.) will sing two songs.	tini'duṭo gan gaiben"
He (hon.) will sing that song.	tini'o ganṭa gaiben"
He (hon.) will sing that (one).	tini'oṭa gaiben"
I have a book.	amar'ækṭa boi ache"
I have a brother.	amar'ækjon bhai ache"

3. The simple future tense.

'3.1. The two uses of the future tense which are illustrated in this lesson are the following:

   a. The indication of action that will take place in the future time.

   b. An expression equivalent to the English "would you ..." (i.e., do you want to) as in sentence 15.

3.2. The future tense is formed by the addition of the future sign /-b-/ to the high stem of the verb, unless the vowel of the verb stem is /a/, and with the exception of the stem /hɔ-/. If the vowel of the stem is /a/ or the stem is /hɔ-/, the low vowel is preserved in the future tense. The personal endings of the future tense are then added to the stem + h complex. The future tense personal endings are:

1st person (ami)	-o
2nd person (ordinary -- tumi)	-e
2nd person (inferior -- tui)	-i
3rd person (honorific -- apni)	-en
3rd person (ordinary -- śe)	-e
3rd person (honorific -- tini)	-en

3.3. Sample simple future paradigms are:

śon-   "hear"

ami śunbo	I shall hear
tumi śunbe	you (ord.) will hear
tui śunbi	you (inf.) will hear
apni śunben	you (hon.) will hear
śe śunbe	ɹe (ord.) will hear
tini śunben	he (hon.) will hear

ken- "buy"

ami kinbo	I shall buy
tumi kinbe	you (ord.) will buy
tui kinbi	you (inf.) will buy
apni kinben	you (hon.) will buy
śe kinbe	he (ord.) will buy
tini kinben	he (hon.) will buy

khæl- "play"

ami khelbo	I shall play
tumi khelbe	you (ord.) will play
tui khelbi	you (inf.) will play
apni khelben	you (hon.) will play
śe khelbe	he (ord.) will play
tini khelben	he (hon.) will play

kɔr- "do, make"

ami korbo	I shall do
tumi korbe	you (ord.) will do
tui korbi	you (inf.) will do
apni korben	you (hon.) will do
śe korbe	he (ord.) will do
tini korben	he (hon.) will do

jan- "know"

ami janbo	I shall know
tumi janbe	you (ord.) will know
tui janbi	you (inf.) will know
apni janben	you (hon.) will know
śe janbe	he (ord.) will know
tini janɓen	he (hon.) will know

ja- "ɡo"

ami jabo	I shall gɔ
tumi jabe	you (ord.) will go

tui jabi	you (inf.) will go
apni jaben	you (hon.) will go
śe jabe	he (ord.) will go
tini jaben	he (hon.) will go

3.4. There are two types of verbs which are irregular in the future. The first is the stem /hɔ-/ "be, become". This preserves its low stem in the future, except where it is changed by a final high vowel:

hɔ-   "be, become"

ami hɔbo	I shall become
tumi hɔbe	you (ord.) will become
tui hobi	you (inf.) will become
apni hɔben	you (hon.) will become
śe hɔbe	he (ord.) will become
tini hɔben	he (hon.) will become

Note however that there are other stems of shape Cɔ-, which take the high stem in the future.

3.5. The second class of verbs which is irregular in the future tense is the one which includes the stems /ca-/ "want", /ga-/ "sing", /śɔ-/ "bear, endure", and /bɔ-/ "carry". They are conjugated thus:

ca-   "want"

ami caibo	I shall want
tumi caibe	you (ord.) will want
tui caibi	you (inf.) will want
apni caiben	you (hon.) will want
śe caibe	he (ord.) will want
tini caiben	he (hon.) will want

śɔ-   "endure"

ami śoibo	I shall endure
tumi śoibe	you (ord.) will endure
tui śoibi	you (inf.) will endure
apni śoiben	you (hon.) will endure

śe śoibe	he (ord.) will endure
tini śoiben	he (hon.) will endure

4. The genitive case can be used to denote authorship, as in sentences 15 and 16. Another example:

noun stem "story"	gɔlpo
"Is that a story by Mitra?"	oʈa ki'mittrer gɔlpo"

5. **Syntax.**

Form possible Bengali sentences:

	Modifiers	Noun	Interro-gative	Complement	Noun	Interro-gative
5.1.		eʈa	(ki)	bhalo		
		oʈa		śɔkto		
		śeʈa		śɔhoj		
		boiʈa				
5.2.		oʈa	(ki)	gɔlper	boi	(ki)
		eʈa		bhalo		
		śeʈa		śɔkto		
		boiʈa		śɔhoj		

	Modifiers	Noun	Interro-gative	Noun	Verb	Interro-gative
5.3.	boiʈar robindronather ramer	nam	(ki)		jan-	(ki)
	or oʈar er	lekhɔk	(ke)			(ki)
	eʈar boiʈar	lekhɔk	(ki)	robindronath ram		

5.4.

Modi-fiers	Noun (Subject)	Interro-gative	Modi-fiers	Noun (Object)	Verb	Interro-gative
	ami	(ki)	amar	gan	baja-	(ki)
	tumi		tomar	śetar	śon-	
	tomra		apnar	tɔbla		
			tar	gɔlpo		
amar	bhai		tãr			
tomar	ma		bhalo			
ramer	baba		kharap			
			śohoj			
			śɔkto			
			ækʈa			

Lesson 3, part 3. Pattern Drills.

1. Pattern: grammar, section 2.1.

    a. Is that a book?
    b. Is that a poem?
    c. Is that a novel?
    d. Is that a play?
    e. Is that a story?

2. Pattern: grammar, section 2.1.

    a. Yes, this is a book.
    b. Yes, this is a poem.
    c. Yes, this is a novel.
    d. Yes, this is a play
    e. Yes, this is   story.

3. Pattern: sentence 3.

    a. What book is that?
    b. What poem is that?
    c. What novel is that?
    d. What play is that?
    e. What story is that?

4. Pattern: sentence 4.

   a. It is a book of songs (use singular form).
   b. It is a poem by (i.e., of) Rabindranath.
   c. It is a novel by Rabindranath.
   d. It is a play by Rabindranath.
   e. It is a story by Somdev.

5. Pattern: sentence 5.

   a. What is the name of that book?
   b. What is the name of that poem?
   c. What is the name of that novel?
   d. What is the name of that play?
   e. What is the name of that story?

6. Pattern: sentence 6, grammar section 2.

   a. That book's name is Bicitra [bicittra]. That is the name of the book.
   b. That poem's name is Balaka [bɔlaka]. And that is the name of the book.
   c. That novel's name is Gora [gora]. That is the name of the novel.
   d. That play's name is Raja [raja]. That is the name of the play.
   e. That story's name is Trene [ṭrene]. That is the name of the story.

7. Pattern: grammar, section 2.

   a. Is that a very good book?
   b. Is that a book of poetry?
   c. Is that a good novel?
   d. Is that a difficult play?
   e. Is that a Bengali story?

8. Pattern: grammar, section 2.

   a. Yes, it is a good book.
   b. Yes, it is a book of poetry.
   c. Yes, it is a very good novel.
   d. No, it is an easy play.
   e. Yes, it is a Bengali story.

9. Pattern: sentence 7.

   a. Who is the author of it?
   b. Is Rabindranath the author of the book?
   c. Is Rabindranath the author of it?
   d. Is Rabindranath the author of the play?
   e. Is Somdev the author of the story?

10. Pattern: sentences 8, 9.

   a. Rabindranath is the writer of the book. Do you know his name?
   b. Yes, he is the writer of it. Do you know his name?
   c. Yes, he is the writer of the novel. Do you know his name?
   d. Yes, he is the writer of the play. Do you know his name?
   e. Yes, he is the writer of the story. Do you know his name?

11. Pattern: sentences 10, 11.

   a. No, I don't know his name. Who is he?
   b. Yes, I know his name.
   c. Yes, I know his poetry.
   d. Yes, I know his stories.
   e. No, I don't know his name. Who is he?

12. Pattern: sentence 12, 13.

   a. He is a writer. You will hear his name.
   b. He is a good writer. You will read his poetry.
   c. He is a very good writer. You will read his novels.
   d. He is a poet. You will hear his songs.
   e. He is a friend. And he is a writer.

13. Pattern: sentence 14.

   a. Is he a poet of Bengal? *
   b. Is he a writer of poems?
   c. Is he a writer of many novels?
   d. Is he a writer of stories?
   e. Is he a friend of yours (i.e., of you)?

14. Pattern: sentence 15.

   a. Yes. Would you like to hear his Bengali?

---

* /baŋladeśer ækjon kobi/ -- "one of Bengal's poets."

b.   Yes.   Would you like to hear a song by him? (i.e., a song of his?)

c.   Yes.   Would you like to read his novels?

d.   Yes.   Would you like to read his stories?

e.   Yes.   Would you like to hear a song by him?

15.   Pattern: sentence 16.

a.   Yes, I should like to hear his Bengali.

b.   Yes, I should like to hear a song by him.

c.   Yes, I should like to read his novels.

d.   Yes, I should like to read his stories.

e.   Yes, I should like to hear a song by him.

Pattern: sentence 17.

a.   Will you read his poetry?

b.   Will you play the sitar?

c.   Will you read a novel?

d.   Will you read a story?

e.   Will you sing a song?

16.   Pattern: sentence 18.

a.   Yes, I shall read a poem.

b.   No, I shall play the tabla.

c.   No, I shall read a story.

d.   No, I shall read a poem.

e.   Yes, I shall sing a song.

17.   Pattern: sentence 19.

a.   I shall read with you.

b.   I shall play the sitar with you.

c.   I shall read a story with you.

d.   I shall read a poem with you.

e.   I shall sing a song with you.

Lesson 3, part 4.   Sentence Drill.

Drill 1

--What book is that?

--This book?   Its name is Gitanjali [gitanjoli].

--I do not know that name. Who is its author?

--It is a book by Rabindranath.

--Is it a novel?

--No, it is a book of poetry.

--Is it a good book?

--Yes, it is a very good book.

--Is it in Bengali?

--No, it is in English. Shall I read a poem?

--Yes, I should like to hear a poem (i.e., I shall hear ...).

--I shall read the first poem.

--That is a good poem. Now will you sing a song by Rabindranath?

--No, I shall not sing. My brother will sing.

--Will you play the tabla?

--Yes, I shall play the tabla. Will you dance?

--Yes, I shall dance.

Drill 2

--This is a good story.

--What story?

--A story by Bonaphul [bonaphul].

--Is that his real name?

--No, his real name is Balai Chand Mukhopadhyay [balai cand mukhopaddhae]. He is a good writer.

--In which country does he live?

--He lives in Bengal. Will you read this story?

--I cannot. I do not know Bengali.

--Will you learn Bengali?

--My brother speaks Bengali well. He will read it.

--Is Bengali difficult?

--No, it is easy. You will learn Bengali quickly.

--That will be good.

--Yes, that will be good.

Lesson 3, part 5. Vocabulary.

naṭok	play
nɔbhel	novel
kobita	poetry, poem

iŋriji	English (language)	gan ga-	sing (a song)
baŋla	Bengali (language)	(Fut.: gan gai-)	
gan	song	par-	be able
deś	country	śekh-	learn
baŋladeś	Bengal		
gɔlpo	story		
lekha	writing		
prothom	first	ba	or
ditio	second	ar	and
tritio	third	pɔre	after, afterwards
aśol	true, original	age	before
taɽataɽi	quick, quickly	ækhon	now
kon	which		
ke	who		

Idiom: ta hole   that becomes-(if)   then, if that is so

1. The following items and formations should now be at your command and you should know their particular place of occurence in a sentence.

Noun stems:

nam	name	baɾi	house
baŋla	Bengali (language)	ghɔr	room
śikago	Chicago	kolkata	Calcutta
śɔhor	city	bɔeś	age
kaj	work	śɔptaho	week
baba	father	din	day
ma	mother	boi	book
bhai	brother	gɔlpo	story
bon	sister	kobita	poem, poetry
chele	son, boy	nɔbhel	novel
mee	daughter, girl	lekhɔk	writer
rɔkom	kind	kobi	poet
ɖaktar	doctor	gan	song
iŋriji	English (language)		

Personal Pronouns:

ami	I	ɑmra	weˈ
tumi	you (ordinary)	ꞁtomra	you (ordinary)ˈ
tui	you (inferior)	ꞁtora	you (inferior)ˈ
apni	you (honorific)	ꞁapnara	you (honorific)ˈ
śe	he, she (ordinary)	ꞁtara	they (ordinary)ˈ
tini	he, she (honorific)	ꞁtãra	they (honorific)ˈ

Adjectives:

bhalo	good	thanɖa	cold
gɔrom	hot	bɔro	big

choṭo	small	śohoj	easy
onek	many	śokto	difficult
kichu	a few, some		

Other modifiers:

ei, e	this
oi, o	that
śei, śe	that (non-specific reference)
ekhane	here
śekhane	there
prae	about
khub	very

Interrogatives:

ki	what
ki	? (i.e., involving yes-no answer)
ke	who
koto	how many, how much
koṭa	how many (an easily countable number)
kæmon	how
kothae	where
kon	which

Verb stems:

kɔr-/kor-	do, make
thak-	be, remain, live
pɔṛ-/poṛ-	read, study
lag-	strike, touch
bɔś-/boś-	sit
khæl-/khel-	play (a game)
ach-, (ache)	be, (have)
ja-	go
jan-	know, recognize
śon-/śun-	hear
baja-	play (an instrument)
nac-	dance
bɔl-/bol-	say, speak
gan ga-/ gan gai-	sing
par-	be able

śekh-	learn	

Other:

ar	and	
ba	or	

Numbers, 1-10 (See Lesson 2, part 5.)
Days of the week (See Lesson 2, part 5.)

2. Genitive case suffix.

Thus far we have seen that the genitive suffix in Bengali appears in two variant forms, /-er/ and /-r/. Their selection depends upon the structure of the word taking the ending.

2.1. The suffix is /-er/:

2.1.1. If the word ends in a consonant; examples are:

robindronath	robindronather	"of (or by) Rabindra-nath"
śohor	śohorer	"of city"
ghɔr	ghɔrer	"of room"
gan	ganer	"of song"
kaj	kajer	"of work"

2.1.2. If the word is monosyllabic and ends in a sequence of two vowels; examples are:

boi	boier	"of book"
bhai	bhaier	"of brother"
bou	bouer	"of wife"

2.2. The suffix is /-r/:

2.2.1. If the word is not monosyllabic and ends in a vowel; examples are:

baṛi	baṛir	"of house"
śikago	śikagor	"of Chicago"
kobita	kobitar	"of poetry"

2.3. The suffix is either /-er/ or /-r/ if the word is monosyllabic and ends in /-a/ or /-i/; examples are:

ma	maer, mar	"of mother"
pa	paer, par	"of foot"
ghi	ghier, ghir	"of ghi" (i.e., butter)

3. Locative case suffix (place in or to which).

The locative suffix in Bengali has two variants, /-e/ and /-te/. The choice of a particular suffix is determined phonologically.

3.1. The suffix is /-e/:

3.1.1. If the word ends in a consonant; examples are:

śɔhor	śɔhore	"in city"
kɔlej	kɔleje	"in college"
gan	gane	"in song"

3.1.2. If the word is monosyllabic and ends in a vowel or a sequence of vowels:

pa	pa.e	"on foot"
boi	boi.e	"in book"

3.2. The suffix is /-te/ if the word is multisyllabic and ends in a vowel:

baṛi	baṛite	"in house"
goru	gorute	"on cow"

3.3. The suffix /-te/ is freely variant with /-e/ if the word is multisyllabic and ends in either /-a/ or /-ɔ/:

śikago	śikagote, śikagoe	"in Chicago"
kolkata	kolkatate, kolkatae	"in Calcutta"

4. The following inflections should now be at your command:

Person	Nominative	Genitive
1st	ami	ama-r
2nd (ord.)	tumi	toma-r
2nd (hon.)	apni	apna-r
2nd (inf.)	tui	tor

3rd (ord.)	śe	ta-r
3rd (hon.)	tini	tã-r

5. The following inflectional endings of finite verbal forms should now be at your command:

5.1. Simple present tense:

Person	Stem		Tense sign	Ending	
	V-stem	C-stem		V-stem	C-stem
1st (ami)	ja-	jan-		-i	-i
2nd (ord. - tumi)				-o	-o
2nd (inf. - tui)				-ś	-iś
2nd (hon. - apni)				-n	-en
3rd (ord. - śe)				-e	-e
3rd (hon. - tini)				-n	-en

5.2. Simple future tense:

Person	Stem		Tense sign	Ending	
	V-stem	C-stem		V-stem	C-stem
ami	ja-	jan-	-b-	-o	-o
tumi				-e	-e
tui				-i	-i
apni				-en	-en
śe				-e	-e
tini				-en	-en

6. The formation of negatives:

We have had so far three types of negatives, the negative verb "be not" (/nɔ-/), the negative particle /na/, which serves to negate other verbs, and the particle /nei/, "there is not".

6.1. Negative verb "be not":

It is hot in the city.	śɔhore'gɔrom"
It is not hot in the city.	śɔhore'gɔrom nɔe"

6.2. Negatives of other verbs:

I know.	ami jani"
I do not know.	ami jani na"
I like it.	amar'bhalo lage"
I do not like it.	amar'bhalo lage na"

6.3. The particle /nei/:

There are trees in the garden.	bagane'gach ache"
There is no tree in the garden.	bagane'gach nei"
I have a pen.	amar'kɔlom ache"
I have no pen	amar'kɔlom nei"

Lesson 4, part 1. Conversation.

Analysis and Translation	Bengali
1. 2nd person (ord.) pronoun stem	toma-
genitive plural ending (for pronouns and nouns with reference to human beings)	-der
"of you, your" (ordinary plural)	tomader
"so many"	æto
"people"	lok
"why"	kæno
"why so many people"	æto lok kæno

A. Why are there so many people at your house?

A. tomader barite ' æto lok kæno "

2. "today"	aj
noun stem, "sister"	bon
"of sister"	boner
noun stem, "wedding"	bie

B. Today is my sister's wedding.

B. aj ' amar boner ' bie "

3. "that is why"	tai
noun stem, "people"	lok
"of people"	loker
noun stem, "crowd"	bhiɽ
"a crowd of people"	loker bhiɽ

B. That is why there is a crowd of people.

B. tai ' loker bhiɽ "

4. noun stem, "sister"   bon

    genitive plural ending (for nouns   -eder
    with reference to human beings)

    "of sisters"   boneder

    "among" (post-p ition with   moddhe
    preceding geni e)

    "among sister   boneder moddhe

    inflectional stem of interrogative
    pronoun "who"   кa-

    genitive case ending   -r

    "of whom"   kar

    A. Who among your sisters is getting   A. tomar boneder moddhe '
        married?   kar bie "

        (your sisters among whose wedding)

5. B. It is my little sister's wedding.   B. amar ' choto boner bie "

6.   "of whom"   kar

        post-position "with", with
        preceding genitive   śɔŋge

        "with whom"   kar śɔŋge

        verb stem, "be"   hɔ-

        "(he/she/it) will be"   hɔbe

    A. Whom is she marrying?   A. kar śɔŋge ' tar bie hɔbe

        (with whom her wedding will-be)

7.   surname, "Sen"   śen

    B. She will marry the Sens' son.   B. śeneder cheler śɔŋge '
                                                 tar bie hɔbe "

8.   noun stem, "boy"   chele

        qualifying suffix, see grammar,
        section 4.   -ţi

        "the boy"   cheleţi

    A. What does the boy do?   A. cheleţe ' ki kɔre "

9.	noun stem, "student"	chattro
	"college student"	kɔlejer chattro

B. He is a college student.	B. śæ ' kɔlejer chattro "

10.	nominative plural suffix for nouns
	with reference to human beings	-era

A. Where do the Sens live?	A. śenera ' kothae thaken "

11.	3rd person (honorific) pronoun stem	tã-
	nominative plural case ending for
	pronouns and noun stems with re-
	ference to human beings	-ra
	"they (honorific)"	tãra
	name of a town	rajpur
	noun stem, "market"	bajár
	post-position, "near", with
	preceding genitive	kache
	"near the market"	bajarer kache

B. They live in Rajpur, near the
market.	B. tãra 'rajpure ' bajarer
kache ' ' thaken "

12.	noun stem, "brother"	bhai
	nominative case plural ending
	for noun stems	-ra
	"brothers"	bhaira
	"to the wedding"	biete
	verb stem, "come"	aś-
	3rd person future "(he/she/it/they)
	will come"	aśbe

A. Will your brothers come to the
wedding?	A. tomar bhaira ' biete
aśbe ki "

13.	"all, every one" (reference to
	human beings)	śɔkole

B. Yes, they will all come.	B. hæ " tara śokole ' aśbe

14. 2nd person (ord.) pronoun stem   tom-
     nominative case plural ending   -ra
     "you (ord. plural)"   tomra
     noun stem, "night"   rattri
     "in/on the night"   rattre
     "on the night of the **wedding**"   bier rattre
     noun stem, "song"   gan
     verb stem, "sing"   ga-
     "will (you) sing songs"   gan gaibe
     Note irregular future; see **Lesson**
     3, part 2. Section 3.5.

     A. <u>Will you sing songs on the night</u>   A. <u>tomra ' bier rattre ' gan</u>
        <u>of the wedding?</u>   <u>gaibe ki "</u>

15. first person pronoun stem   am-
     nominative plural ending   -ra
     "we"   amra

     B. <u>Yes, we shall sing songs.</u>   B. <u>h̃æ " amra ' gan gaibo "</u>

16. noun stem, "girl"   mee
     genitive plural suffix   -der
     "of the girls"   meeder

     "among", post-position with
     preceding genititive   moddhe
     "among the girls"   meeder moddhe
     inflectional stem of
     interrogative, "who"   ka-
     nominative plural suffix   -ra
     "who" (nominative plural)   kara

     A. <u>Who among the girls will sing</u>   A. <u>meeder moddhe ' kara</u>
        <u>songs?</u>   <u>gan gaibe "</u>

17. noun stem, "friend"   bondhu
     "friends" (nominative plural)   bondhura
     "friends of my sister"   amar boner bondhura

     B. <u>Friends of my sister will sing.</u>   B. <u>amar boner bondhura</u>
                                                     <u>gan gaibe "</u>

18. **A.** <u>What songs will they sing</u>?   **A.** <u>tara ' ki gan gaibe</u>

19.   name of a 14th or 15th century   conḍidaś
        Vaisnava religious poet "servant
        of Çandi"
        name of goddess   conḍi
        "servant, slave"   daś
        type of religious (Vaisnava) song   kirtton

    B. <u>They will sing kirtan (songs) of   **B.** <u>tara conḍidaśer kirtton
    Candidas.</u>   gaibe</u> "

20.   conjunction, "and, also"   o
        "you also"   tum·o

    A. <u>Will you also sing songs?</u>   **A.** <u>tumi·o ki ' gan gaibe</u> "

21. **B.** <u>Yes, I also will sing songs.</u>   **B.** <u>hã̀ ' ami·o 'gan gaibo</u> "

22.   1st person pronoun stem   ama-
        genitive plural suffix   -der
        "of us, our"   amader

    B. <u>Will you listen to our songs?</u>   **B.** <u>tumi ki 'amader gan '
                                                                     śunbe</u> "

23. **A.** <u>Yes, I should like to listen.</u>   **A.** <u>hã̀ " śunbo</u> "

24.   "all right"   beś
        "in that case"   ta hole
        2nd person ordinary pronoun stem   toma-
        objective case suffix (see Grammar,
        Section 1.)   -ke
        verb stem, "call"   ḍak-
        "I shall call"   ḍakbo
        "I shall call you"   tomake ḍakbo
        "I shall call on you tonight"   rattre tomake ḍakbo

    B. <u>All right. In that case, I shall   **B.** <u>beś " ta hole ' rattre
    call on you tonight.</u>   tomake ḍakbo</u> "

25. "seven"   śat

     qualifying suffix, see grammar,
     section 4.2.   -ṭa

     "seven o'clock"   śatṭa

     post-position, "before", with
     preceding gentiive   age

     "before seven o'clock"   śatṭar age

A. Will you call before seven o'clock?   A. tumi ki ' śatṭar age '
                                             ḍakbe "

26. "eight"   aṭ

     qualifying suffix, see grammar,
     section 4.2.   -ṭa

     "eight o'clock"   aṭṭa

     post-position, "after", with
     preceding genitive   pɔre

     "after eight o'clock"   aṭṭar pɔre

B. No, I shall call after eight.   B. na " ami 'aṭṭar pore
                                             ḍakbo " /

Lesson 4, part 2. Grammar.

1. The objective case, sentence 24.

1.1. For the time being, we can consider that the objective case in
Bengali takes the singular case ending /-ke/ and the plural case ending
/-der/ or /-derke/ for pronouns and nouns which have human reference. A
more elaborate statement describing this case inflection will be given
in Lesson 7.

1.2. The objective case suffix indicates that a personal noun or pronoun
is the óbject of the verb. The object of the verb has no case suffix
when it has an inanimate or abstract reference. For example.

     Uninflected:

          He speaks Bengali.   śe'banla bɔle"
          I will hear the song.   ami'ganta śunbo"

<u>Inflected</u>:

I shall call your <u>brother</u>.   ami'tomar <u>bhaike</u> dakbo".

I know <u>him</u>.   ami'<u>take</u> jani"

2. Plurals.

2.1. A plural of a noun or pronoun indicates that the referrent is more than one in number. Note that when a noun is accompanied by an adjective of number, the noun <u>does</u> <u>not</u> <u>take</u> <u>a</u> <u>plural</u> <u>suffix</u>. For example:

boy	chele	boys	chelera	two boys	dujon chele
sister	bon	sisters	bonera	many sisters	ɔnek bon
book	boi	books	boigulo	some books	kichu boi

2.2. The plurals of nouns referring to animate beings and of pronouns are formed by the addition of one of a set of plural suffixes to the noun or pronoun stem. These case suffixes are:

Nominative	-ra / -era
Genitive	-der / -eder
Objective	-der / -eder, -derke / -ederke

Except in pronominal stems and noun stems with /e/ final, where the suffix is always /-ra/, /-der/ (or /-derke/), there is free variation between /-ra ~ -era/, etc., irrespective of whether the stem has a consonant or vowel final.

2.3. A sample plural paradigm of /chele/, "boy" is:

"boys" (nominative)   chelera

"of boys (genitive)   cheleder

"(to) boys" (objective) cheleder, chelederke

2.4. A sample plural paradigm of the personal pronouns is:

Person	Nominative	Genitive	Objective
1st	amra	amader	amader, amaderke
2nd (ordinary)	tomra	tomader	tomader, tomaderke
2nd (inferior)	tora	toder	toder, toderke
2nd (honorific)	apnara	apnader	apnader, apnaderke
3rd (ordinary)	tara	tader	tader, taderke

3rd (honorific)	tãra	tãder	tãder, tãderke

Note: Pronouns and nouns referring to human beings are very rarely used in the locative. For such an expression as "among the boys", Bengali usually employs a so-called post-position or similar device -- /cheleder moddhe/ (see below, section 6.).

2.5. Although only nouns denoting animate objects and personal pronouns can form their plurals by means of the suffixes /-ra/, etc., all nouns (but not personal pronouns) can form plurals by means of the suffix /-gulo/.   A sample plural paradigm of /boi/, "book", is:

"books" (nominative)	boigulo
"of books" (genitive)	boigulor
"books" (objective)	boiguloke (very rare -- inanimate nouns are usually uninflected in the objective case)
"on/in books" (locative)	boigulote

2.6. The suffix /-gulo/, when used with nouns referring to animate beings, indicates particularization:

what do boys (in general) do?	chele'ki kɔre"
what do (those particular) boys do?	chelegulo'ki kɔre"

2.7. Nouns denoting both animate and inanimate objects are uninflected in the plural when the reference is general (i.e., there is no contrast between singular and plural formations):

"mango falls", or "mangos fall"	am pɔre
"flower blooms", or "flowers bloom"	phul phoṭe
"boy plays", or "boys play"	chele khæle

When the reference is particular, nouns denoting both animate and inanimate objects take /-gulo/ in the plural:

"mangos (in general) fall"	am pɔre
"(those particular) mangos fall"	amgulo pɔre
"flowers (in general) bloom"	phul phoṭe
"(those particular) flowers bloom"	phulgulo phoṭe
"boys (in general) play"	chele khæle
"(those particular) boys play"	chelegulo khæle

2.8. In sum:

2.8.1. With animate nouns and pronouns:

      -ra/-era   nominative plural suffix, group reference.
      -der/-eder   genitive plural suffix, group reference.
      (-der/-eder,   objective plural suffix, group reference.
      -derke/-ederke)

2.8.2. With all nouns:

      -gulo   nominative plural suffix, particular reference.
      -gulor   genitive plural suffix, particular reference.
      -guloke   objective plural suffix, particular reference.
      -gulote   locative plural suffix, particular reference.

2.8.3. To put it another way: plurals of animate nouns can be formed in three ways:

2.8.3.1. The noun is uninflected, when the reference is to a general class of beings:

      one girl   ekti mee
      two girls   duṭi mee
      He has one or more daughters.   tãr mee ache "

2.8.3.2. The noun takes the suffix /-ra/-era, -der/-eder, -derke/-ederke/ when the reference is to a class or species or clan.

      On the night of the wedding,   bier rattre ' meera gan gaibe "
      the girls (all or some) will
      sing.

2.8.3.3. The noun takes the suffix /-gulo, -gulor, -guloke/ when the reference is to a particular or specific surveyed concrete group.

      On the night of the wedding,   bier rattre ' meegulo gan
      those particular girls will   gaibe "
      sing.

2.8.4. Plurals of inanimate nouns can be formed in two ways:

2.8.4.1. The noun is uninflected, when the reference is to the general class of objects:

      Flowers are red.   phul lal

2.8.4.2. The noun takes the suffix /-gulo, -gulor, -guloke, -gulote/ when the reference is to a particular group within the class:

>   Those flowers are red.   phulgulo lal

2.9. Mutation drills.

2.10. In a sequence of plural nouns, only the last noun in the sequence takes the plural suffix. For example,

>   "the mangos and bananas and berries"   am kɔla ar jamgulo

3. Interrogative pronoun (ordinary) stem /ka-/, as in sentence 4.

The interrogative pronoun "who" is declined in this way:

	Singular	Plural
Nominative	ke (hon. ke)	kara (hon. kāra)
Genitive	kar (hon. kār)	kader (hon. kāder)
Objective	kake (hon. kāke)	kader (hon. kāder)

The equivalent non-personal **pronoun**, "which", is /konʈa/:

>   which of your dogs   tomar kukurgulor'konʈa"
>   which of your books   tomar boigulor'konʈa"

4. Qualifier -ʈi, as in sentence 8.

4.1. In addition to the uses of the qualifier already mentioned (see Lesson 3, part 2. Section 2.) the qualifier can be added to a noun stem to give the force of the English definite article "the" or of the demonstrative "that". So here, /cheleʈi/, "the boy, that particular boy".

4.2. The use of the qualifiers /-ʈi/ and /-ʈa/.

The two qualifiers are used under the same circumstances with both animate and inanimate nouns. There is a slight qualitative distinction between the two. The qualifier /-ʈi/ is frequently used to suggest that the speaker has a personal, positive feeling with reference to the person or object about whom or which he is speaking, and /-ʈa/ in more ordinary circumstances. It is to be noted, however, that the /-ʈi/ suffix is often considered a polite form; as such, it can be used exclusively and in all types of circumstances with complete correctness.

5. Formation of the feminine.

5.1. Many, though by no means all, nouns in Bengali form a feminine by the addition of the suffixes /-i/, /-ini/, or /-ni/.

5.2. Some nouns which have /-o/ final replace the final /-o/ with /-i/, as:

> chattru   "student" (masc.)   chattri   "student" (fem.)

5.3. Nouns which have other vowels final frequently add the /-ni/ suffix to the noun stem, as:

> dhópa   "washerman"   dhopani (l.t.) "washerwoman"

5.4. Nouns which have consonants final frequently add the suffix /-ini/ to the stem, as:

> bagh   "tiger"   baghini   "tigeress"

5.5. It should be carefully noted that the feminines in Bengali are a "closed class", that is, that one cannot always predict what the feminine of a given noun will be, or even if it has a feminine form. The student, therefore, will have to learn by experience and by rote which feminines exist and what their forms are.

6. Bengali phrases of place or time, in which, accompaniment, agency, etc., are expressed by means of post-positions. Most of these post-positions govern a preceding genitive. Some of the most common ones are:

śoŋge	"with"	amar śoŋge	"with me"
moddhe	"among"	meeder moddhe	"among the girls"
pore	"after (time)"	etar pore	"after this"
age	"before (time)"	etar age	"before this"
jonne	"for (the sake of)"	tar jonne	"for him/it, for his/ its sake"
opore	"on top of"	tebiler opore	"on top of the table"

7. Form possible Bengali sentences.

7.1.

Modifiers		Post-positional phrase		Subject	Verb
kader		kar	śɔnge	bie	hɔbe
amar	boner, -eder	tar			
tomar	bhaier -der	tomar			
apnar	bondhur, -der	apnar			
tar	cheler, -der	meer			
amader		bondhur			

7.2.

Post-positional phrase			Subject	Object	Verb	
amar	boner, -eder	śɔnge	ami	gan	gai-b-	o/
tomar	bhaier, -der	moddhe	tumi	kaj	kor-b-	e/
tar	bondhur, -der	jonne	apni	ki		en
		pɔre	ke			
			kara			

Lesson 4, part 3. Pattern Drills.

Pattern: sentence 1.

a. Why are there so many people in your room?
b. Why are there so many friends at your house?
c. Why are there so many people here?

___

d. Why are there so many books on your table?
e. Why are there so many books in your room?

2. Pattern: sentences 2, 3.

a. Today is my brother's wedding; that is why there is a crowd.
b. Today is my sister's wedding; that is why there is a crowd there.
c. Today is my son's wedding; that is why there is a crowd at my house.

    d. Today is my exam; that is why there are so many books.

    e. Today is my exam; that is why there are so many books here.

3. Pattern: sentence 4.

    a. Which of your brothers is getting married?

    b. Which of your sisters is getting married?

    c. Which of your sons is getting married?

    ———

    d. To which of your friends do the books belong * (i.e., of your friends, whose book?)

    e. To which of your brothers do the books belong?

4. Pattern: sentence 5.

    a. It is my elder brother's wedding.

    b. It is my younger sister's wedding.

    c. It is my younger son's wedding.

    ———

    d. They are Ram's books.

    e. They are my younger brother's books.

5. Pattern: sentence 6.

    a. Whom is he marrying? (use /bie hɔ-/)

    b. Whom is your sister marrying? (use /bie hɔ-/)

    c. Whom is your son marrying? (use /bie hɔ-/)

    ———

    d. With whom does your friend live?

    e. With whom does your brother study?

6. Pattern: sentence 7.

    a. He is marrying Ram's daughter.

    b. She is marrying Ram's son.

    c. He is marrying my friend's daughter.

    ———

* There is an idiomatic peculiarity here. Any of the following is acceptable:

--tomar bondhuder moddhe'kar boi"

--tomar bondhuder moddhe' eigulo kar boi"

--tomar bondhuder moddhe'ei boigulo kar"

    d. He lives with his friends.

    e. He studies with me every day.

7. Pattern: sentence 8.

    a. What does your elder brother do?

    b. What work does the boy do?

    c. What work does your friend do?

    _____

    d. What does he study?

    e. What do you (plural) study?

8. Pattern: sentence 9.

    a. He is a student.

    b. He is a college student.

    c. He is an artist.

    _____

    d. He studies Bengali.

    e. We learn songs.

9. Pattern: sentence 10.

    a. Where do they live?

    b. Where does the boy live?

    c. Where does he live?

    _____

    d. Where does he study?

    e. Where will you (plural) study?

10. Pattern: sentence 11.

    a. They live near the city.

    b. He lives in Calcutta, near my house.

    c. He lives in Calcutta, near your house.

    _____

    d. He studies at the college near the market.

    e. We will study here, near the window.

11. Pattern: sentence 12.

    a. Will your sisters come to your brother's wedding?

    b. Will your friends come to your sister's wedding?

    c. Will your friends come to your son's wedding?

d. Will you go to his college?

e. Will he come daily to your room?

12. Pattern: sentence 13.

a. Yes, they will come.

b. Yes, they will all come.

c. Yes, they will all come to the wedding.

d. Yes, I will go to his college.

e. Yes, he will come to my room every day.

13. Pattern: sentence 14.

a. Will you (plural) hear songs on the night of the wedding?

b. Will they sing good songs on the night of the wedding?

c. Will they sing kirtan [kirtton] (songs) on the night of the wedding?

d. Will you study Bengali at the college?

e. Will you study music with him?

14. Pattern: sentence 15.

a. Yes, we will listen to many songs.

b. Yes, they will sing many good songs.

c. Yes, they will sing many kirtan (songs).

d. Yes, I will study Bengali there.

e. Yes, we will learn music.

15. Pattern: sentence 16.

a. Who among the boys will sing songs?

b. Who among the girls will sing songs?

c. Who among you (plural) will sing songs?

d. Who among your friends will study Bengali?

e. Who among your friends will learn music?

16. Pattern: sentence 17.

a. Friends of my son will sing songs.

126

    b. Friends of my daughter will sing songs.

    c. Friends of mine will sing songs.

---

    d. They all will study Bengali.

    e. My friends all will learn music.

17. Pattern: sentence 18.

    a. What songs will they sing?

    b. What songs will her friends sing?

    c. What songs will your friends sing?

---

    d. What writing will they read?

    e. What songs will they learn?

18. Pattern: sentence 19. (Use /-gulo/ throughout, where plural is required.)

    a. They will sing many songs.

    b. They will sing kirtan songs.

    c. We will sing Rabindranath's songs.

---

    d. They will read poetry.

    e. They will learn bhajan [bhɔjon] (songs).

19. Pattern: sentence 20.

    a. Will you also sing many songs?

    b. Will you also sing kirtan (songs)?

    c. Will you also sing Candidas's [condidaśer] songs?

---

    d. Will you also read poetry?

    e. Will you also learn bhajan (songs)?

20. Pattern: sentence 21, 22.

    a. Yes I also shall sing songs. Will you listen?

    b. Yes, I also shall sing kirtan (songs). Will you listen to the songs?

    c. Yes, I also shall sing his songs. Will you listen?

---

    d. Yes, I also shall read poetry. Will you listen to poetry?

    e. Yes, I also shall learn bhajan (songs). Will you listen to a bhajan (song)?

21. Pattern: sentence 23.

   a. Yes, I should like to listen.
   b. No, I should not like to listen.
   c. Yes, we all should like to listen.

   ———
   d. Yes, I should like to listen to a poem.
   e. Yes, I should like to hear a song.

22. Pattern: sentence 24.

   a. All right. In that case, you will hear the songs tonight.
   b. All right. In that case I shall not call you tonight.
   c. All right. In that case, you will come here tonight.

   ———
   d. All right. In that case, I shall read a poem tonight.
   e. All right. In that case, I shall call you tonight.

23. Pattern: sentence 25.

   a. Will I come before eight o'clock?
   b. Will you sing before nine o'clock?
   c. Will you call me before ten o'clock?

   ———
   d. Will you read before seven o'clock?
   e. Will you call me before six o'clock?

24. Pattern: sentence 26.

   a. No, I shall call you after nine.
   b. No, I shall sing after ten.
   c. No, I shall call you after ten.

   ———
   d. No, I shall read after eight.
   e. No, I shall call you after seven.

Lesson 4, part 4. Sentence Drill.

Note: Use ordinary plural forms throughout.

Drill 1

--There will be a celebration at our house today. Will you come?
--What time will it be?

128

--It will be at eight o'clock tonight.

--Will there be a crowd of people?

--Yes, many people will come.

--Then I shall not come. I do not like a crowd.

--But they are all your friends. Ram and Naresh will come there.

--All right, then, we shall come. What is the celebration?

--Today is Sarasvati-puja [sɔrossoti-pujo]. Do you know who Sarasvati is?

--Yes, she is the goddess of learning and of art.

--Yes. We shall sing songs on the day of Sarasvati-puja.

--What kind of songs will you sing?

--Kirtan [kirtton] songs. The tune of these songs is very beautiful.

--Who are the writers of kirtan-songs?

--Vaisnava-bhaktas. Their names are Candidas [condidaś], Jnanadas, [gændaś], and Vidyapati [biddapoti].

--Are they modern writers?

--No, they are very ancient.

--Who (plural) will sing their songs?

--Some [baijis] will come. My friends will also sing.

--I shall not sing. My voice is bad.

Drill 2

--Somdev will come to my house tonight. Will you come with him?

--What time will he go?

--He will come at seven o'clock sharp. Probhas will come too.

--Will Ila sing? She has a beautiful voice.

--Yes, she will sing kirtan songs.

--Then I shall come. Those songs are very sweet.

--Many people will be coming. They will all bring their instruments.

--What is the celebration?

--Today is Sarasvati [sɔrossoti] puja in Bengal.

--Will the people of Bengal sing songs for her?

--Yes, she is the goddess of music.

--Then I shall come at seven.

Lesson 4, part 5. Vocabulary.

porikkha   examination
utśɔb   celebration

bidda	learning	śekh-	learn
kɔla	art	aś-	come
śoŋgit	music	an-	bring, fetch
śur	melody	pɔchondo kɔr-	like
śomɔe	time		
boiṣɳɔb	Vaiṣṇava	roj; protidin	everyday, daily
bhɔkto	devotee	aj	today
pɔchondo	liking	kal (agami kal--)	tomorrow
dada	elder brother		
gula	throat, voice	kal (gɔto kal --)	yesterday
rattri	night	śɔkole	all
śɔrośśoti	Sarasvati		
debi	goddess	tai	therefore, that is why
jɔntro	instrument	kintu	but
śilpi	artist		
baiji	professional female singer and dancer		
bandhobi	friend (feminine)		

adhunik	modern
purono	old
miṣṭi	sweet
pracin	ancient

Idioms:

kɔṭar śomɔe aśbe	What time will you come?
aṭṭar śomɔe aśbo	I shall come at eight.
aj rattre (rate)	tonight

<u>Lesson 5, part 1. Conversation.</u>

<u>Analysis and translation</u>	<u>Bengali</u>

1.   honorific suffix attached to the   -babu
given name of a male person
addressed.

    noun compound, "mother and father"   ma-baba
(see grammar, section 1.)

    <u>A</u>. <u>Ram, where do your mother and</u>   <u>A</u>. <u>rambabu ' apnar ma-baba '</u>
    <u>father live?</u>   <u>kothae thaken "</u>

2.   "before, formerly"   age

    name of a city, capital of
East Pakistan   ḍhaka

    "in Dacca"   ḍhakae

    simple past tense stem of verb
/ach-/, "be"   chi-

    sign of the simple past tense   -l-

    honorific verbal ending   -en

    "(they - honorific) were"   (tãra) chilen

    <u>B</u>. <u>My mother and father were in</u>   <u>B</u>. <u>amar ma-baba age ' ḍhakae</u>
    <u>Dacca before.</u>   <u>chilen "</u>

3.   "this"   e/æ

    morpheme indicating time   -kon

    "this time, now"   ækhon

    name of a city, capital of West
Bengal   kolkata

    <u>B</u>. <u>Now they live in Calcutta.</u>   <u>B</u>. <u>ækhon ' kolkatae thaken "</u>

4. 2nd person (hon.) pronoun stem   apna-
    genitive case plural suffix   -der
    "of you (hon. plural)"   apnader

<u>B</u>. <u>Where is your home?</u>   B. <u>apnader baɽi ' **kothae** "</u>

5. 1st person pronoun stem   **ama-**
    genitive case plural suffix   **-der**
    "of us"   **amader**
    name of a city and a district
    in western West Bengal   **birbhum**
    3rd person simple past tense
    verbal ending   **-o**
    "it (she/ he) was"   **chilo**

<u>A</u>. **Our house was in Birbhum before.**   A. <u>amader baɽi age ' birbhume chilo "</u>

6. 1st person nominative pronoun
    stem   am-
    nominative plural case suffix   -ra
    "we"   amra
    conjunctive, "too, also"   o
    "we also"   amra.o

<u>A</u>. **Now we also live in Calcutta.**   A. <u>ækhon amra.o ' kolkatae thaki "</u>

7. "which"   kon
    noun stem, "place"   jaega
    "in which place"   kon jaegae
    "in which part of Calcutta"   kolkatae kon jaegae

<u>B</u>. <u>In which part of Calcutta do you live?</u>   B. <u>kolkatae ' kon jaegae thaken "</u>
    (Calcutta-in which place-in
     you live)

8. noun stem, "tank" -- small man-
    made pond for water storage   dighi
    noun stem, "bank, edge, side"   dhar

	"on the side of the tank"	dighir dhare

A. Now we live by the side of the tank.

A. amra ækhon ' dighir dhare ' thaki "

9. name of a section of north Calcutta

śambajar

1st person simple past verbal ending

-um

"(we) were"

(amra) chilum

A. Formerly we were in Syambazar.

A. age ' śambajare chilum "

10. post-position, "with" with preceding genitive

śɔŋge

"with you (honorific)"

apnar śɔŋge

"more, and, in addition"

ar

"who in addition, who else"

ar ke

B. Who else lives with you in Calcutta?

B. apnar śɔŋge ' kolkatae ' ar ke thaken "

11. noun stem, "family"

śɔŋśar

A. Our family is very large.

A. amader śɔŋśar ' khub bɔro "

12. noun stem, "elder brother"

dada

noun stem, "elder brother's wife"

boudi

A. My mother, father, elder brother, and sister-in-law live with me.

A. amar śɔŋge ' ma-baba ' dada ' ar boudi thaken "

13. "how many"

kɔ-

qualifier

-ṭi

"how many"

kɔṭi

noun stem, "boy"

chele

noun stem, "girl"

mee

compound noun, "boys and girls, children"

chele-mee

B. How many children does your elder brother have?

B. apnar dadar ' kɔṭi chele-mee "

14. alternative stem of numeral "one" — ek-
    qualifier — -ṭi
    "one" — ekṭi
    stem of numeral "two", used in compounds — du-
    qualifier — -ṭi
    "two" — duṭi

A. My elder brother has a son and two daughters.
A. amar dadar 'ekṭi chele ' ar duṭi mee "

15. noun stem, "father's younger brother" — kaka
    noun stem, "father's younger brother's wife" — kakima
    compound noun, "father's younger brother and his wife" — kaka-kakima
    nominative plural case suffix — -ra
    "father's younger brothers and their wives" — kaka-kakimara

B. Do your aunts and uncles live with you?
B. apnar kaka-kakimara ki ' apnar śɔnge thaken "

16. "now" — ækhon
    emphatic suffix, here translatable as "even" — -o
    "even now, still" — ækhono

A. No, my aunts and uncles still live in Syamabazar.
A. na " kaka-kakimara ' ækhono śambajare thaken "

17. B. What does your eldest uncle do?
B. apnar bɔro kaka ' ki kɔren "

18. loan word, "professor" — prophasar

A. Before, he was a professor.
A. tini age ' prophesar chilen "

19. "some, something" — kichu
    emphatic suffix, see Grammar, section 7. — -i

134

"something (emphatic)"   kichui

"nothing at all" see Grammar,   kichu na
section 7.

A. Now he does nothing at all.   A. ækhon ' kichui kɔren na "

20.   "that"   śe

       "what"   ki

       "what is that?" or "how can
       that be?"   śe ki

       3rd person (honorific) pronoun
       stem   tã

       objective case ending   -ke

       "him (objective)"   tãke

       high stem of verb "see"   dekh-

       simple past tense sign   -l-

       1st person past tense suffix   -um

       "I saw"   dekhlum

B. How can that be? I saw him in   B. śe ki " ami ækhon ' tãke
the office (just) now.   ɔphiśe dekhlum "

21. A. In what office did you see him?   A. kon ɔphiśe ' tãke ækhon
                                         dekhlen "

22. B. I saw him in his office.   B. ami tãke ' tãr ɔphiśe '
                                         dekhlum "

23.   perhaps   hɔeto

A. Perhaps he has some business   A. tãr hɔeto 'ɔphiśe kono
in the office.   kaj ' ache "

24.   but   kintu

A. But he doesn't work there.   A. kintu tini śekhane ' kaj
                                     kɔren na "

Lesson 5, part 2. Grammar

1.   Compound nouns.

Compound nouns are common in Bengali; they are made up or two or more noun stems. The case or number inflection, where there is one, is added to the last member of the compound only. Therefore such compounds are treated inflectionally as simple nouns. Examples:

ma-baba	"mother-father, mother and father"
bhai-bon	"brother-sister, brother and sister"

In some cases, meanings of compound nouns are extended beyond the meaning of their elements:

gach-pala	"trees and things like that"
bone'gach-palagulo' taṛataṛi gɔjae"	"In the forest trees and other things (i.e., vines, bushes, etc.) grow very quickly."

2. Simple past tense.

2.1. The primary uses of the simple past tense are:

a. Connected narrative to describe a series of actions in past time.

b. To express action which has taken place in the immediate past.

2.2. The sign of the simple past tense is -l-, which is added to the high stem of all verbs except those of CVC- shape with /a/-vowel stems.

2.3. The personal endings for the simple past tense are:

1st	-um (Note alternatives: -am, -em.)
2nd (ordinary)	-e
2nd (inferior)	-i
2nd (honorific)	-en
3rd (ordinary)	-o
3rd (honorific)	-en

2.4. Examples:

ken-	"buy"	ami	kin-l-um
		tumi	kin-l-e
		tui	kin-l-i
		apni	kin-l-en

		śe	kin-l-o
		tini	kin-l-en
kɔr-	"do"	ami	korlùm
		tumi	korle, etc.
khæl-	"play"	ami	khellum
		tumi	khelle
ot̯h-	"rise up"	ami	ut̯hlum
		tumi	ut̯hle, etc.

<u>But</u> CaC- stems have no vowel change:

jan-	"know"	ami	janlum, etc.

Stems of shape CV-, even where the stem-vowel is /a/, take the high stem. For example:

pa-	"get"	ami	pe-l-um
		tumi	pe-l-e
		tui	pe-l-i
		apni	pe-l-en
		śe	pe-l-o
		tini	pe-l-en

2.5.   The verb /ja-/, "go", has an irregular stem in the simple past. The stem /ja-/, is inflected in this way:

ami	ge-l-um
tumi	ge-l-e
tui	ge-l-i
apni	ge-l-en
śe	gæ-l-o
tini	ge-l-en

2.6.   Give full paradigms for the following verb stems.

pɔɽ-	"read"	phæl-	"drop"
śon-	"hear"	de-	"give"
par-	"be able	kha-	"eat"

2.7.   In lesson 7, more intensive work on the simple past is given.

3.   The stem of the simple past tense of the verb "be" (/ach-/) is /chi-/. The sign of the simple past and the simple past personal endings are added to this stem. The simple past is the only past tense in which this verb occurs.

4.   Plural verbal endings. Note that there is no variation in verbal personal endings between the singular and plural numbers. Thus:

ami jani   "I know"   amra jani   "we know" etc.

5.   The qualifier /-ți/, as in sentence 13.

The form /kɔ-/ is an adjective of quantity. The use of the qualifier in sentences 13 and 14 is the use which we have noticed before -- namely, that the qualifier is added to numerals and other adjectives denoting quantity when followed by a noun.

6.   The bound morpheme /-khon/ indicates time:

æxkhon   "this time, now"
kɔkhon   "which time, when"
ɔnekkhon   "much time"

7.   There are two particles, /-i/ and /-o/, which give emphasis to the word to which they are attached. Often an emphatic negative is expressed in Bengali by the use of the construction

(positive)-(emphatic) ... (verb) + na

as in sentence 19:

something-(emphatic) does-do not   kichui kɔren na
He does nothing at all.

Other examples, using the /-o/ emphatic suffix as in sentence 16, might be:

they sometimes-(emphatic) there   tara kɔkhono'śekhane
do-go not   jae na"
They never go there (at all).

they somewhere-(emphatic) do-go not   tara kothao'jae na"
They do not go anywhere (at all).

He reads no books (at all).   śe kono boi'pɔṛe na"

8. When the subject of a sentence is plural the complement takes no plural suffix; e.g.,

| They are writers. | tãra'lekhɔk" |
| They were students. | tãra'chattro chilen" |

9. Construct possible Bengali sentences:

Modifier	Subject	Verbal Modifiers		Verb		
amar amader tor toder tomar tomader	ma-baba/ra bhai-bon/era chele-mee/ra	pɔre ækhon age	kothae kolkatae śɔhore ekhane e jaegae	chi - thak -	-l- -b-	um/e/en/o o/e/en/e
	ami/amra tui/tora tumi/tomra apni/apnara	pɔre ækono	dighir dhare tader śɔnge tar kache			

Lesson 5, part 3. Patterns.

1. Pattern: sentence 1.

    a. Where do your brother and sister live?
    b. Where do your children live?
    c. Where do your brothers and sisters live?
    d. Where do your aunts and uncles live?
    e. Where do their children live?

2. Pattern: sentence 2.

    a. They were in Calcutta before.
    b. They were in Dacca before.
    c. Their house was in Faridpur [phoridpur].
    d. They were with Ram before.
    e. They were in Ram's house before.

Pattern: sentence 3, 4.

a. Now they live in Dacca. Where is your home?

b. Now they live in Calcutta. Where is your home?

c. Now they live in Burdwan [bɔrdhoman]. Where is your brother's home?

d. Now they live with me. Wnere is your uncle's home?

e. Now they live with their father. Where is your children's home?

3. Pattern: sentence 5, 6.

a. Now we also live in Dacca.

b. Now we also live in Calcutta.

c. Now he also lives in Burdwan.

d. Now he also lives with his children.

e. Now they also live with us.

4. Pattern: sentence 7.

a. In which part of Dacca do you live?

b. In which part of the city do you live?

c. In which part of Burdwan does he live?

d. In which part of the house does he live?

e. In which room of the house do they live?

5. Pattern: sentence 8.

a. Now we live by the side of the river.

b. Now we live by the side (use /paśe/) of the Kali temple.

c. Now he lives by the side (use /paśe/) of the temple.

d. Now he lives beside (use /paśe/) me.

e. Now they live in the big room.

6. Pattern: sentence 10.

a. Who else lives with you?

b. Who else lives by the side of the temple?

c. Who else lives with him?

d. Who else lives beside you?

e. Who else lives in that room?

7. Pattern: sentence 11.

a. Our family is very large.

    b. Many large families.

    c. His family is very large.

    d. My brother lives with his large family.

    e. Our family is very small.

Pattern: sentence 12.

    a. My aunts and uncles live with us.

    b. My brothers and sisters live near (/kache/) us.

    c. His children live with him.

    d. My uncle also lives with him.

    e. Only the children live in that room.

8. Pattern: sentence 13.

    a. How many children do they have?

    b. How many children does your sister have?

    c. How many children does he have?

    d. How many children does your brother have?

    e. How many children do you have?

9. Pattern: sentence 14.

    a. They have two sons and two daughters.

    b. She has one son and two daughters.

    c. He has three sons and four daughters.

    d. My brother has one son and one daughter.

    e. We have one son and one daughter.

10. Pattern: sentence 15.

    a. Do your mother and father live with you?

    b. Do your aunts and uncles live near you?

    c. Dc his brothers live with him?

    d. Does your sister live with him?

    e. Do your brothers live with you?

11. Pattern: sentence 16.

    a. No, they still live in Calcutta.

    b. No, they still live in Dacca.

    c. No, they still live in the city.

    d. No, she still lives with my brother.

    e. No, they still live with my father.

12. Pattern: sentence 17.

    a. What does your father do?
    b. What does your uncle do?
    c. What do your brothers do?
    d. What does your brother do?
    e. What do they do?

13. Pattern: sentence 18.

    a. Formerly, he was a writer.
    b. Formerly, he was a poet.
    c. Formerly, they were writers.
    d. Formerly, he was an artist.
    e. Formerly, they were students.

Pattern: sentence 19.

    a. Now he writes nothing at all.
    b. Now he reads nothing at all.
    c. Now they write nothing at all.
    d. Now he does nothing at all.
    e. Now they study nothing at all.

14. Pattern: sentence 20.

    a. How can that be? I saw his writing just now.
    b. How can that be? I saw his book of poetry just now.
    c. How can that be? I saw their writing just now.
    d. How can that be? I saw him in the studio just now.
    e. How can that be? I saw them in class just now.

15. Pattern: sentence 21.

    a. Which book of his* did you see?
    b. Which poetry book did you see?
    c. Which writing did you see?
    d. In which studio did you see him?
    e. In which class did you see them?

16. Pattern: sentence 22.

    a. I saw his poetry book.

------

* tār kon boita

    b.   I saw his big book.

    c.   I saw their new book.

    d.   I saw him in his friend's studio.

    e.   I saw them in Bengali class.

17. Pattern: sentence 23, 24.

    a.   He wrote poetry, but he doesn't write now.

    b.   He wrote books, but he doesn't write now.

    c.   They wrote books, but they don't write now.

    d.   He went there, but he doesn't work there now.

    e.   They went to class, but they don't study there now.

Lesson 5, part 4. Sentence Drill.

Drill 1

--Shall I sit with you a while?

--Yes, we shall gossip a while. I have (just) finished my work.

--How many children do you have?

--I have two sons and two daughters.

--How old are your daughters?

--My older girl is twenty. The younger is only four.

--Where does the older one live?

--She lives with us at home.

--What does she do?

--She used to be a student before. Now she is a teacher in Calcutta.

--In what part of Calcutta is her shcool?

--It is in north Calcutta, by the side of Citpur Road.

--How many children are there in her class?

--About ten, I think. There were twenty, but ten have just gone home.

Drill 2.

--Where do your brother and sister-in-law live now?

--They used to live in Birbhum. Now they live in Calcutta, near you.

--Where in Calcutta do they live?

--In south Calcutta, near the Kali temple.

--What does your brother do?

--He used to be a teacher. Now he is an artist.

--Yes, I know now.* Their children go to school with our children.
--Do they do often to the temple?
--Yes, but I never go to the temple. He often comes into my shop.
--Is he well?
--Yes, I saw him a little while ago. He is well.

Lesson 5, part 5. Vocabulary.

śikkhɔk	teacher (m.)	dækh-	see, look
śer		ja-	go
maśṭar mosae		śeś kɔr-	finish
sikkhoitri	teacher (f.)		
didimoni		paśe	beside
chattro	student (m.)	bhirore	within (post-position)
chattri	student (f.)	bhitore	
dhopa	washerman	kache	near (post-position)
dhopani	washerwoman		
dokan	shop	kichukkhon	a while
mondir	temple	ækhon	now
iśkul	school	ekhuni	now (emphatic); just now
śɔŋśar	family		
poribar		prae	often
roḍ	road	kɔkhono na	never
rasta			
bharot	India	uttor	north
bharotbɔrśo		dokkhin	south
		purbo	east
		pościm	west

Idioms:	amar mone hɔe	I think, it seems to me
	gɔlpo kɔr-	talk, gossip
	eimattro	just now
	śe ki'bhalo ache"	Is he well?
	apni ki'bhalo achen"	Are you (hon.) well?
	tumi ki'bhalo acho"	Are you (ord.) well?

---

* Use simple past -- the recognition has taken place in the immediate past.

Lesson 6, part 1. Conversation.*

Analysis and translation	Bengali
1. Note: no subject is expressed; /apni/ is understood from the context and verbal suffix.	
verb stem, "want"	ca-
honorific verbal ending	-n
"(you honorific) want"	can
A. What do you want?	**A.** ki can "
2. **B.** I want a book.	**B.** ækṭa boi cai "
3. 1st person pronoun stem	ama-
objective case ending (see grammar, section 1.1)	-ke
"(to) me" (objective)	amake
"that, (those)"	oi
"new"	notun
"history"	itihaś
noun stem, "book"	boi
plural suffix	-gulo
"books"	boigulo
verb stem, "show"	dækha-
honorific ending for verb stems with vowel final	-n

---

* With apologies to the booksellers of Bengal, who do not act this way
at all, and suffer from our attempt to combine the bargaining situation
with vocabulary and grammar useful to the student.

"please show"   dækhan
(for this imperative usage,
see grammar, section 2.2.)

B. <u>Please show me those new</u>   B. amake ' oi notun itihaś
<u>history books.</u>   boigulo ' dækhan "

4.   **high stem** of verb "buy"   kin-

         sign of future tense   -b-

         honorific verbal ending   -en

         "(you hon.) will buy"   (apni) kinben

A. <u>Will you buy the books now?</u>   A. <u>apni ki ækhon ' boigulo kinben</u>

5.   **high stem** of verb "look,
         look at"   dekh-

         sign of future tense   -b-

         1st person future verbal ending   -o

         "(I) shall look at"   dekhbo

         Note: the change in word order, with /ækhon/ coming first in the
         sentence, emphasizes the concept <u>now</u>, <u>at</u> <u>this</u> <u>time</u>.

B. <u>No, I shall look at the books</u>   B. na " ækhon ami ' boigulo
<u>now.</u>   dekhbo "

6.   "afterwards"   pɔre

         "this"   e

         "plural suffix   -gulo

         "these"   egulo

         high stem of verb "take"   ni-

         ending for past active
         participle   -e

         PAP, "taking, having taken",   nie
         see Grammar, section 4.

         stem of verb "go"   ja-

         "take away (i.e., take and go)"   nie ja.

B. <u>Afterwards I shall take them.</u>   B. <u>pɔre ami ' egulo nie jabo</u> "
    (Afterwards I them having-
    taken shall-go)

7.   "the books"   boigulo

          "of the books"   boigulor

          noun stem, "price"   dam

          verb stem, "give"   de-

          sign of future tense   -b-

          honorific verbal ending   -en

          "you (hon.) will give"   (apni) deben

     A. <u>Will you pay for the books now?</u>   A. <u>apni ki ækhon ' boigulor dam deben "</u>

8.   noun stem, "brother"   bhai

          objective case ending   -ke

          "(to) brother"   bhaike

          verb stem, "send"   paṭha-

          "you (hon.) will send" --   pathaben
          indicative or imperative;
          for the imperative usage,
          see grammar, section 3.

     B. <u>No, send (them) to my brother.</u>   B. <u>na " amar bhaike ' pathaben "</u>

9. B. <u>He will pay.</u>   B. <u>śe ' dam debe "</u>

10.   "the price"   damṭa

          high stem of irregular verb
          "give"   di-

          honorific ending   -n

          "please give"   din
          (imperative -- see grammar,
          section 5.1.)

     A. <u>No, please pay now.</u>   A. <u>na " apni ækhon ' damṭa din "</u>

11.   "all right"   accha

          "how much"   kɔto

          "how much (price)"   kɔto dam

     B. <u>All right. How much are the books?</u>   B. <u>accha " boigulor ' kɔto dam "</u>

12. numeral, "three"   tin-

     form of qualifier used with
     /tin/   -ṭe

     Note: no plural suffix is used with the noun when the noun is
     accompanied by an adjective of quantity.

     "these three books"   ei tinṭe boi

     "the price of these three books" ei tinṭe boier dam

   A. The price of these three books   A. ei tinṭe boier dam ' pãc
     is five rupees.   ṭaka "

13. "very great, excessive"   beśi

     "very greatly excessive"   bɔṛo beśi

   B. That's too much.   B. bɔṛo beśi dam "

14. numeral, "four"   car

     "rupee"   ṭaka

     locative case ending   -te

     in (within) four rupees"   car ṭakate

   B. Give me the books for (i.e.,   B. car ṭakate ' ei boigulo din "
     within) four rupees.

15. noun stem, "book"   boi

     plural suffix   -gulo

     locative case ending   -te

     "in books"   boigulote

     "five"   pãc

     "hundred"   śo

     "page"   pata

   A. No. There are five hundred   A. na " ei boigulote ' pãc śo
     pages in these books.   pata "

16. "so much"   æto

     "small"   kɔm

     "so small"   æto kɔm

     noun stem, "price"   dam

     locative case ending   -e

locative case ending	-e
"in (within) price"	dame
"within (for) so small a price"	æto kɔm dame

A. <u>I shall not give (them to you) for such a small price.</u>   A. <u>æto kɔm dame ' debo na</u> "

17.
"book"	boi
"the (particular) book"	boiṭa
"this (particular) book"	ei boiṭa

B. <u>How much will you sell this book for.</u>   B. <u>kɔto dame ' ei boiṭa deben</u> "

18. A. <u>I'll give (you) this one for two rupees.</u>   A. <u>du ṭakate ' eṭa debo</u> "

19.
"but"	kintu
"in this (particular) book"	ei boiṭate

Note that the locative suffix comes after the qualifier.

"only"	mattro
"hundred"	śo
"one hundred"	æk śo
"one hundred pages"	æk śo pata

B. <u>But there are only one hundred pages in this book.</u>   B. <u>kintu ' ei boiṭate ' mattro æk śo pata</u>

20. B. <u>Why is it so expensive?</u>   B. <u>æto dam kæno</u> "

21.
"this"	e
"this (particular) one"	eṭa
"in this (particular) one"	eṭate
"picture"	chobi
"there is. there are"	ache

A. <u>There are many pictures in this one.</u>   A. <u>eṭate ' ɔnek chobi ache</u> "

22. **B.** <u>Will you give me the book for</u>   **B.** æk ṭakate ' boiṭa deben ki "
   <u>one rupee?</u>

23.   "another"   onno
       "shop"   dokan
       "in another shop"   onno dokane
       high stem of verb "look"   dekh-
       honorific imperative ending   -un
       "please look"   dekhun

   A. <u>No, please go and look in</u>   **A.** <u>na " apni onno dokane '</u>
   <u>another shop.</u>   <u>dekhun "</u>

Lesson 6, part 2. Grammar.

1. The objective case inflectional ending, as in sentences 3 ff.

1.1. The objective case ending is used with <u>pronouns</u> <u>and</u> <u>nouns</u> <u>denoting</u>
<u>persons</u>. Except in certain circumstances, inanimate nouns are left un-
inflected in the objective case (see below, 1.3.)

1.2. When a verb has both a "direct" and an "indirect" object, the case
ending is used with the indirect object, and the direct object is left
uninflected. Thus, in sentence 3, the indirect object /amake/ takes the
case inflection, while the direct object /boigulo/ is left uninflected.

Another example of this situation is:

> amake'tomar cheleṭa dao"
> Give your son to me / give me your son

1.3. A rare exception to the rule that inanimate nouns do not take
objective case inflection, is when a particular object or group of
objects is designated. In sentence 14, for example, where particular
books are under discussion, the objective case ending <u>may</u> be used, thus:

> Give me the (particular)   car ṭakate'ei boiguloke din"
> books for four rupees.

This option is, however, not usually taken in normal speech.

1.4. Some Bengali verbs do not take indirect objects. Among these
verbs are "read" and "sing"; in such cases, a post-positional construction
is used. This will be treated in its proper place.

2.   The formation of the present imperative, as in sentence 3.

Do not let our use of the term "imperative" confuse you. There are
reasons for our using it to designate both a command, ("Go!", "Read!",
"Please go!", "Please read!") and what is sometimes called an "optative",
("Let me/him go", "Let me/him read"). The grammatical analysis of the
construction "let me go" in English and Bengali is too complex to allow
explication here. Assume, then, that we arbitrarily assign the term
"first person imperative" to such constructions as "let me read", and the
term "third person imperative" to such constructions as "let him read".

2.1.   The present imperative of regular verb stems is formed by the use
of the present indicative, usually without the personal pronoun in the
first and second person ordinary. Thus:

kini	'let me/us buy"	jai	'let me/us go"
keno	"buy!"	jao	"go!"

2.2.   In the 3rd person ordinary and in the 2nd and 3rd person honorific
forms, the imperative is formed by the addition of the suffixes /-uk, -k/
and /-un, -n/, respectively; the use of the alternative suffixes depends
upon whether the verb stem has a consonant or vowel final.

kinun	"please buy"	jan (colun)	"please go"
kinuk	"let him/her/it (ord.) buy	jak (coluk)	"let him/her/it (ord.) go"
kinun	"let him (hon.) buy"	jan (colun)	"let him (hon.) go"

2.3.   Give imperative forms for the following:

poɽ-
kɔr-
śon-
oʈh-
phæl-
pa-

3.   Future imperative, as in sentence 8.

The future imperative (i.e., the indicated action is to be performed at
some time in the future) of all persons except for the 2nd person ordinary

is the simple future without the personal pronoun. The formation of the future imperative of the 2nd person ordinary will be discussed in a later lesson.

4. Formation and use of the past active participle, as in sentence 6.

The past active participle is formed by the high stem of a verb with the ending /-e/. There are many "compound verbs" in Bengali, as here in sentence 6, some of which consist of the non-finite past active participle plus an inflected or finite form of another verb. The past active participle is often translatable either as "-ing" or "having ...-en"; here, for example, either "taking" or "having taken". There will be a more full discussion of the past active participle and of compound verbs in Lesson 8.

5. The verbs /de-/, "give" (as in sentence 9) and /ne-/, "take" form an irregular verb class. A paradigm of the simple present, past, and future tenses will be:

Person	Present	Past	Future
1st	dii	dilum	debo/dobo
2nd (ord.)	dao	dile	debe
2nd (hon.)	dæn	dilen	deben
2nd (inf.)	diś	dili	dibi
3rd (ord.)	dæe	dilo	debe
3rd (hon.)	dæn	dilen	deben

5.1. The 3rd person ordinary and the honorific imperative forms are also irregular, being formed by means of the high-stem /di-/:

3rd (ord.)	dik
2nd and 3rd (ord.)	din

6. The use of the locative in various contexts, including the buying and selling context, is a peculiar one. The best translation for such a use might be "within what price ..." "within five rupees ...", etc. Thus:

kɔto dame deben   how-much price-within give-will
                                      How much will you sell it for?

7. Form possible Bengali sentences:

7.1.

Subject	(Int.)	Indirect Object	Direct Object		Verbal Modifier	Verb	(Neg.)
ami	(ki)	amake		ki			(na)
tumi		tomake		eṭa	ækhɔn		
apni		apnake		oṭa	pɔre	dækha-	
śe		take	ækṭa	boi		de-	
tini		tãke	duṭo		aj	paṭha-	
amra		amader (ke)			kal		
tomra		tomader (ke)	baŋla	boi	śekhane	ken-	
apnara		apnaker (ke)	notun	boigulo	onno	nie ja-	
tara		tader (ke)	itihaś		dokane		
tãra		tãder (ke)	bɔro	dam		de-	
ram			boier				
lekhɔk		ramke	boigulor				
		bhaike					
		lekhɔkke					

7.2.

Subject	Modifier	Object	(Int.)	Verb
ami	boier	dam		an-
tumi	boigulor			de-
	eṭar		kɔto	
	oṭar		ki	
	egulor			

7.3.

Subject	Indirect Object	Modifier	(Int.)	Direct Object	Verb	(Neg.)
ami	amake	æk ṭakate	(ki)	eṭa	de-	(na)
tumi	tomake	du		oṭa	paṭha-	
		tin		boiṭa	ken-	
	bhaike					
		kɔto dame				
		bɔro				
		choṭo				

7.4.

Modifier	Subject		
boiţate boigulote	mattro	æk śo	pata
		du śo	
		ɔnek	

Lesson 6, part 3. Patterns.

Note: from this point for the **next** several lessons, only the **first** three of the patterns will be heard on the tape. The last two you will be expected to produce in class.

1. Pattern: sentence 1. (use honorific)

     a. What do you hear?
     b. What do you see?
     c. What do you buy?
     ____
     d. What do you read?
     e. What do you want?

2. Pattern: sentence 2.

     a. I hear a song.
     b. I see a book.
     c. I buy books.
     ____
     d. I read books.
     e. I want many books.

Pattern: sentence 3, grammar section 1.4.

     a. Please sing that song.
     b. Please show me that book.
     c. Please show me those new books.
     ____
     d. Please send me those new books
     e. Please send me those new Bengali books.

3. Pattern: sentence 4.

    a. Will you hear the song now?

    b. Will you listen to the poetry now?

    c. Will you buy the books in this shop?

    _____

    d. Will you buy the books now?

    e. Will you read the books afterwards?

4. Pattern: sentence 5.

    a. No, I shall read this book now.

    b. No, I shall read the poetry now.

    c. No, I shall read the books here.

    _____

    d. No, I shall read the books now.

    e. Yes, I shall not read the books now.

Pattern: sentence 6.

    a. Afterwards I shall listen to the song.

    b. Afterwards I shall listen to the poetry.

    c. Afterwards I shall take them.

    _____

    d. Afterwards I shall buy them.

    e. Afterwards I shall read them.

5. Pattern: sentence 7.

    a. Will you pay for that book now?

    b. Will you pay for that poetry book now?

    c. Will you pay for those books now?

    _____

    d. Will you pay for them now?

    e. Will you pay for the Bengali books now?

6. Pattern: sentence 8.

    a. No. Send it to my brother.

    b. No. Send the book to my sister.

    c. No. Send them to my father.

    _____

    d. No. Send the books to my brother.

    e. No. Send the books to me.

Pattern: sentence 9.

a. He will pay you.

b. She will pay you.

c. He will pay for the books (i.e., "he will give the price of the books").

------

d. He will pay for them.

e. I shall pay you afterwards.

7. Pattern: sentence 10.

    a. No, please pay (me) now.

    b. No, please pay us now.

    c. No, let him pay now.

------

    d. No, let him pay for them now.

    e. No, please pay for them now.

8. Pattern: sentence 11.

    a. All right. How much is it?

    b. All right. How much is the book?

    c. All right. How much are the books?

------

    d. All right. How much are they?

    e. All right. How much are the Bengali books?

9. Pattern: sentence 12.

    a. The price of that book is three rupees.

    b. Its price is five rupees

    c. The price of these five books is ten rupees.

------

    d. The price of those two books is four rupees.

    e. Their price is thirty rupees.

10. Pattern: sentence 13.

    a. That is too little. (khub kɔm dam)

    b. That is too much.

    c. That price is too much.

156

d. That price is too little.

e. That is too much.

Pattern: sentence 14.

a. Give (me) the book for four rupees.

b. Give it to me for three rupees.

c. Give (me) the five books for five rupees.

----

d. Give them to me for six rupees.

e. Give them to me for ten rupees.

11. Pattern: sentence 15.

a. No. There are only two hundred pages in this book.

b. No. There are many pages in this book.

c. No. There are six hundred pages in these five books.

----

d. No, there are only two pictures in these books.

e. No, there are many pictures in these books.

Pattern: sentence 16.

a. I shall not sell it (i.e., give it) for such a large price.

b. I shall not sell it to you for such a small price.

c. I shall not sell them for five rupees.

----

d. I shall not sell them for six rupees.

e. I shall not sell them to you for such a small price.

12. Pattern: sentence 17.

a. All right   How much will you sell these for?

b. All right. How much will you sell those for?

c. .All right. How much will you sell these books for?

----

d. All right. How much will you sell these pictures for?

e. All right. How much will you sell me these books for?

13. Pattern: sentence 18.

a. I'll give those for ten rupees.

b. I'll give you those for seven rupees.

c. I'll give you these books for five rupees.

----

d. I'll give you those pictures for one rupee.

e. I'll give you these books for nine rupees.

14. Pattern: sentence 19, 20.

a. But there are only one hundred pages in those books. Why are they so expensive?

b. But there are only two pictures in them. Why are they so expensive?

c. But there are only two hundred pages in them. Why are they so expensive?

_____

d. But there are two pictures here. Why are they so cheap?

e. But there are only three books here. Why are they so expensive?

15. Pattern: sentence 21.

a. There are many pictures in those books.

b. There are five hundred pages in them.

c. There are twenty pictures in them.

_____

d. There are many pictures in this shop.

e. There are many pictures in those three books.

16. Pattern: sentence 22.

a. Will you give me the books for five rupees?

b. Will you give me them for four rupees?

c. Will you give me those books for three rupees?

_____

d. Will you give me this one for two rupees?

e. Will you give me those three books for six rupees?

17. Pattern: sentence 23.

a. No, please look in another shop.

b. No, please look in another place.

c. No, please look in that shop.

_____

d. Yes. Please look at these other pictures.

e. No. Please go to another shop.

Lesson 6, part 4.   Sentence Drill.

Drill 1

--What do you want?
--I want a sari.
--For your wife?
--No, for my sister. Please show me those two red silk saris.
--These are very fine Murshidabad silk saris. Your sister will like them.
--This is not very good material. How much will you sell them for?
--Fifty rupees. But for you, I shall give them for thirty.
--That is too much. Give me the saris for twenty-five.
--All right. For you they are twenty-five. Please pay now.
--No, send the saris to my sister. I shall pay you later.
--No, sir, please pay me now, or I shall not give them to you.
--Then I shall not buy them. I am an honest man.
--But I am a poor man. I shall sell you these saris for such a small
  price and make no profit.
--Then I shall go to another shop.
--Yes, please go.

Drill 2

--How much will you sell these sandals for?
--I shall sell you the sandals for ten rupees, sir.
--That is too much.
--They are very fine sandals, sir.
--They are very bad sandals. Please show me those Kashmiri shawls.
--I shall sell you this shawl for thirty rupees.
--The color is very dark. Have you any light-colored shawls?
--This one is exactly the color of ivory. Its price is fifty rupees.
--All right. I shall give you twenty-five.
--For forty I shall sell it, sir.
--All right. Send it to my brother. He will pay you.
--I shall send it to him. Please give me twenty rupees now.
--All right. You will become very rich.
--There will be no profit, sir. I am a poor man.

Lesson 6, part 5. Vocabulary.

śaṛi	sari	bæc-	sell
silk	silk	ken-	buy
kapoṛ	cloth, material		
mɔśae, mośae	sir, gentleman	śundor	fine, beautiful
labh	profit	śɔt	honest
cɔppol, coṭi	sandals	gorib	poor
śal	shawl	phike,	
hatirdāt	ivory	halka	light
rɔŋ	color	ghɔno	dark; thick
		dhoni	rich
accha	all right, OK	lal	red
		pɔ̃ciś	twenty-five
		tiriś	thirty
		colliś	forty
		pɔ̃ncaś	fifty

Review II

1. Bring up to date your file of word cards, to include all the new vocabulary of Lessons 4-6

1.1.
bhiɽ	crowd
bie	wedding
bajar	market
gan	song
bondhu	friend
kirtton	type of religious song
boisŋɔb	Vaiṣṇava
mababa	mother and father
jaega	place
dighi	tank
śɔŋśar	family
boudi	sister-in-law
kaka	paternal uncle (father's younger brother)
kakima	father's younger brother's wife
chelemee	children
śilþi	artist
śikkhɔk	teacher (m.)
śikkhoittri	teacher (f.)
chattro	student (m.)
chattri	student (f.)
dhopa	washerman
dhopani	washerwoman
dokan	shop
mondir	temple
iśkul	school
itihas	history

dam	price
ṭaka	rupee
pata	page, leaf
chobi	picture
rasta	street
śaṛi	sari
silk	silk
kapoṛ	cloth, material
mośae; mɔśae	sir, gentleman
labh	profit
cɔppol, coṭi	sandals
śal	shawl
hatirdāt	ivory
rɔŋ	color

1.2.	æto	so many
	kɔṭa, kɔṭi	how many
	ka –	who (inflectional stem)

1.3.	kæno	why

1.4.	aś-	come
	śɔn-	hear, listen to
	ḍak-	call, shout
	pɔchondo kɔr-	like
	chil-	simple past stem of ach-, "be"
	oṭh	rise up
	pa-	get, receive
		go
	gɔ-/ge-	past stem, "go"
	dækh-	see, look
	śeś kɔr-	finish
	ca-	want
	dækha-	show
	nie ja-	take (away)
	paṭha-	send
	bæc-	sell
	ken-	buy

1.5. śɔkole   all
      uttor   north
      dokkhin   south
      purbo   east
      pościm   west

1.6. conḍidaś   proper name of medieval poet
      biddapoti   proper name of medieval poet
      gænḍaś   proper name of medieval poet

1.7. purono   old
      miśṭi   sweet
      pracin   ancient
      beśi   a lot, very much
      śundor   fine, beautiful
      śɔt   honest
      gorib   poor
      phike, halka   light
      ghɔno   dark; thick
      dhoni   rich

1.8. aj   today
      kal   yesterday, tomorrow
      gɔtokal   yesterday
      agamikal   tomorrow
      ækhon   now
      prothome   at first
      kichukkon   a while
      kichu   some, a little
      prae   often

1.9. tai   conjunction - "that is why"
      ɔ   "also"
      kintu   but

1.10. śɔŋge   with
      kache   near
      moddhe   within, among
      age   before (time or place)

pɔre	after (time or place)
dhare	beside, on the edge of
paśe	beside
bhitore; bhetore	within, inside

1.11.
beś	all right
accha	OK, all right

1.12.
põncaś	fifty
tiriś	thirty
põciś	twenty-five
colliś	forty
śo	hundred

2. The plural.

2.1. Nouns can be divided into two broad classes. Class I is a class of nouns which denote animate objects. This class may be subdivided into nouns which denote human beings and nouns which denote other types of animate beings. These subdivisions will be referred to as Class I.a. and Class I.b. respectively. Class II nouns include all other types of nouns.

2.2. The plural suffixes:

Nominative	-ra, era	chelera	lokera
Genitive	-der, -eder	cheleder	lokeder
Objective	-der (ke), -eder (ke)	chelederke, cheleder	lokederke, lokeder

These suffixes are used by Class I nouns, and within that class only rarely by Class I.b. nouns.

2.3. The plural suffix /-gulo/, to which are added the case endings of the singular, can be used with both classes of nouns:

Nominative	chelegulo	kukurgulo	gachgulo
Genitive	chelegulor	kukurgulor	gachgulor
Objective	cheleguloke	kukurguloke	gachguloke
Locative	---	---	gachgulote

2.4. These two sets of suffixes are often used interchangeably. The use
of one or the other of the suffixes, however, may have significance.
Frequently, the /-ra, -era/ suffix is used to indicate particulars within
the class.

Examples:

/lok'ʃɔhore thake"/	"(all) people live in the city"
/lokera'ʃchore thake"/	"the people live in the city"
/lokgulo'ʃɔhore thake"/	"those (particular) people live in the city"

2.5. There are, then, three levels of plural usage, though the distinctions are not always kept perfectly clear by Bengali speakers.

2.5.1. No plural suffix (see below, section 2.6.):

/dhopa'kapoɽ kace"/	"(all) washermen (i.e., washermen as a class) wash clothes"

2.5.2. /-era, -ra/ plural suffix:

/dhopara'kapoɽ kace"/	"the washermen (as opposed to others) wash clothes"

2.5.3. /-gulo/ plural suffix:

/dhopagulo'kapoɽ kace"/	"(those particular) washermen (within the caste) wash clothes"

2.6. The plural number is not always expressed by means of suffixes.

2.6.1. When an adjective implying plural number is present, the plural
suffix is not used.

Example:

/ʃekhane'ɔnek lok"/	"many people are there"

2.6.2. Reduplication frequently has a plural or a distributive meaning
(see below, Lesson 8).

Examples:

/ke ke'aʃbe"/	"who all will come, what (various) people will come"
/kothae kothae'jabe"/	"to what (various) places will you go"

2.6.3. If the subject or the sentence is plural, its complement does not have to agree in number.

Example:

/tara'duṣṭu chele"/   "they are naughty boys"

2.6.4. When the reference is to a class of objects, the plural suffix may be omitted:

Example:

/boier dam'beśi"/   "books are expensive"

2.6.4.1. When the reference is to a particular group within a class, however, the plural suffix can be used:

Example:

/boigulor dam'beśi"/   "(those) books are expensive"

2.7. The suffix /-gulo/ may be used with certain adjectives of quantity, e.g., /kɔto/ and /ɔnek/, and with demonstrative pronouns and adjectives.

2.7.1. The plural suffix /-gulo/ may be used with the demonstratives /e, o/, "this, that", when they are used as pronouns.

Example:

/egulo ki'boi"/   "are these books?"

2.7.2. When the demonstrative is used as an adjective, the plural suffix is attached to the noun which it modifies.

Example:

/e boigulo ki'bhalo"/   "are those books good?"

3. Qualifiers.

3.1. There are two sets of qualifiers which are commonly used in Bengali. These sets are /-ṭa, -ṭi/ and /-khana, -khani/.

3.1.1. The qualifier /-ṭa, -ṭi/ may oe used with all nouns.

3.1.2. The qualifier /-khana, -khani/ (increasingly rare in spoken Bengali, thus not stressed in the lessons) is used with inanimate objects which are square, flat, or cubical in shape, e.g., /boi/, "book", /baṛi/, "house", etc.

Example:

/amake'boikhana din"/   "Please give me the book."

3.2.   The qualifiers/-ṭa, -khana/, of which the final vowel is /a/, are
used with reference to ordinary objects, toward which the speaker feels
no special emotion.

The qualifiers /-ṭi, -khani/, of which the final vowel is /i/, are used
with reference to objects toward which the speaker feels a particular
attraction.

3.3.   Qualifiers are used with numerals and other adjectives of quantity
when followed by a noun.

Example:

/ækṭa boi cai"/   "I want a book."

3.4.   Qualifiers may be added to a singular noun to give the force of the
English definite article.

Example:

/kɔto dame'boiṭa deben"/   "How much will you sell the book
                                  for?" (lit. give the book for)

3.4.1.   The case endings are added after the qualifier, in cases of this
kind.

Example:

/chèleṭake'boiṭa dao"/   "Give the book to the boy."

3.5.   Qualifiers may be added to demonstratives without a following noun --
i.e., when the demonstrative is the subject or object of the sentence.
When the demonstrative functions as an adjective, the qualifier is used
with the following noun.

Examples:

/oṭa'ki boi"/   "What book is that?"
/o boiṭa'ki"/   "What is that book?"

4.   Verbal inflection.

You should now have three verb tenses at your command: the simple present the simple future, and the simple past.

4.1. Future

Verbs except for /a/-stem verbs form their future tense by the addition
of the future morpheme /-b-/ and the future personal endings to the <u>high</u>
stem of the verb. The following are exceptions to this rule.

4.1.1. The verb /hɔ-/, "be, become" forms its future with the low stem.

> ami hɔbo
> tumi hɔbe
> tui hobi -- (Note: the stem changes here for
> apni hɔben   phonological reasons)
> śe hɔbe
> tini hɔben

4.1.2. Other vowel-stem verbs, of which the vowel is /ɔ/, take the alternate stem /Coi-/ in the future. Thus the verb /śɔ-/, "bear",

> ami śoibo
> tumi śoibe
> tui śoibi
> apni śoiben
> śe śoibe
> tini śoiben

4.1.3. Certain vowel stem verbs in /a/ also take an alternate stem for
the future: /Cai-/; thus the verbs /ca-/ "want" and /ga-/ "sing":

> ami   caibo   gaibo
> tumi   caibe   gaibe
>
> etc.

4.1.4. Vowel-stem verbs in /e/, i.e., /de/, "give" and /nę-/, "take",
preserve their low stems in the future.

4.2. Simple past

The simple past is formed by the addition of the /-l-/ (past) morpheme
and the past tense personal endings to the high stem of the verb,
except for CaC- verbs, which preserve their low stems.

5. We have had the various uses and meanings of /o/.

Demonstrative, "that"	amake o boiṭa dao	"Give me that book'
Conjunctive, "and"	amra·o jabo	"We too will go"
Emphatic	ækhono baṛite thake	"Even now they live in the house"
2nd person ord. personal ending	tumi śekhane jao	"You go there"

Analysis and Translation	Bengali
1.	
noun stem, "river"	nodi নদী
noun stem, "bank"	dhar ধার
"bank of the river"	nodir dhar নদীর ধার
post-position, "from", preceding genitive optional	theke থেকে
"from the river-bank"	nodir dharer theke, nodir dhar theke
	নদীর ধারের থেকে, নদীর ধার থেকে
alternative stem of verb "come"; see Grammar, section 3.	e- এ
sign of simple past tense	-l- ল–
honorific verbal ending	-en এন
"you came" (simple past)	apni elen আপনি এলেন
"you came now" (i.e., "you just came")	apni ækhon elen আপনি এখন এলেন

A. <u>Rambabu, have you just come from the river bank?</u>

A. <u>rambabu " apni ki ækhon ' nodir dhar theke ' elen "</u>

রাম্বাবু, আপনি কি এখন নদীর ধার থেকে এলেন ।

2.	
"daily"	roj রোজ
noun stem, "bank"	dhar ধার
locative case ending	-e –ে
"to/on the bank"	dhare ধারে
"to the river bank"	nodir dhare নদীর ধারে

B. Yes, I go to the river bank every day.

B. hæ̃ " ami roj ' nodir dhare ' jai "

হাঁ, আমি রোজ নদীর ধারে যাই ।

3. A. Why do you go?

A. kæno jan "

কেন যান ?

4.   verb stem, "walk"   hãṭ- হাঁট-
      verbal noun suffix   -a -া
      verbal noun, "walking"   hãṭa হাঁটা

B. Walking on the river bank is good.

B. nodir dhare hãṭa ' bhalo "

নদীর ধারে হাঁটা ভাল ।

5.   noun stem, "fish"   mach মাছ
      high stem of verb "buy"   kin- কিন-

B. And I buy fish every day.

B. ar ami roj ' mach kini "

আর আমি রোজ মাছ কিনি ।

6.   high stem of verb "buy"   kin- কিন-
      sign of simple past tense   -l- -ল-
      honorific verbal ending   -en
      "you bought (simple past)"   apni kinlen আপনি কিনলেন

A. Did you buy fish there today?

A. apni ki aj ' śekhane ' mach kinlen "

আপনি কি আজ সেখানে মাছ কিনলেন ?

7.   name of a type of fish   rui mach রুই মাছ
      name of a type of fish   katla mach কাতলা মাছ
      high stem of verb "buy"   kin- কিন-
      sign of simple past tense   -l- -ল-
      1st person verbal ending   -um -ুম
      for simple past tense
      "I bought (simple past)"   ami kinlum আমি কিনলুম

B. Yes, I bought <u>rui and katla</u>   B. hæ̃ " ami ' rui <u>a̧r katla maoh '</u>
<u>fish.</u>   <u>kinlum</u> "

                                           হাঁ , আমি র‍ুই আর কাত্লা মাছ কিনল‍ুম ।

8.   noun stem, "fisherman"   jele জেলে

      objective case ending   -ke -কে

      "(to) the fisherman"   jeleke জেলেকে

      high stem of verb "give"   di- দি-

      sign of simple past tense   -l- -ল-

      honorific verbal ending   -en -েন

      "you gave (simple past)"   apni dilen আপনি দিলেন

      Note: /jeleke/ is the indirect object of the verb /dilen/; /dam/ is the direct object of the verb.

  A. <u>How much did you pay the</u>   A. <u>jeleke ' kɔto dam ' dilen</u> "
     <u>fisherman?</u>

                                           জেলেকে কত দাম দিলেন ?

9.   B. <u>I gave the fisherman one</u>   B. <u>ami jeleke ' æk ṭaka dilum</u> "
     <u>rupee.</u>

                                           আমি জেলেকে এক টাকা দিল‍ুম ।

10. "very, quite"   beś বেশ

      adjective, "cheap"   śɔsta সস্তা

      adverb, "cheaply"   śɔstae সস্তায়

      high stem of verb "get, acquire"   pe- পে-

      "you got (simple past)"   apni pelen আপনি পেলেন

  A. <u>You got the fish very</u>   A. <u>apni machgulo ' beś śɔstae ' pelen</u> "
     <u>cheaply.</u>

                                           আপনি মাছগ‍ুলো বেশ সস্তায় পেলেন ।

11. verb stem, "come"   aś আস-

      2nd person honorific imperative ending   -un -‍ুন

      Why don't you come, please come   asun na আস‍ুন না

      Note: /na/ here does not have the force of a negative, see Grammar, section 7.

	"together, in one group"	ækɔɔŋge	একসঙ্গে

B. Yes. Why don't you come to our house; then we will eat together.

B. hæ̃ " amader barite asun na " ta hole ' ækɔɔŋge khabo "

হাঁ, আমাদের বাড়ীতে আসুন না ৷ তা হলে একসঙ্গে খাবো ৷

12. A. All right, I shall come tonight.

A. accha " ami aj rattre ' aśbo "

আজ্ঞা, আমি আজ রাত্রে আসবো ৷

13.
alternative stem, "how much"	kɔ-	ক-
qualifier (see Grammar, section 6, for this usage)	-ʈa	-টা
noun stem, "time"	śomɔe	সময়
idiomatic usage: "at what time"	kɔʈar śomɔe	কটার সময়

B. At what time will you come?

B. apni ' kɔʈar śomɔe ' aśben "

আপনি কটার সময় আসবেন ?

14.
numeral "eight"	aʈ	আট
qualifier	-ʈa	-টা
"at eight o'clock"	aʈʈar śomɔe	আটটার সময়

A. I shall come at eight o'clock.

A. aʈʈar śomɔe ' aśbo "

আটটার সময় আসবো ৷

15.
verb stem "come"	aś	আস-
alternate verbal noun suffix	-ba-	-বা-
genitive case ending	-r	-র
"of coming"	aśbar	আসবার
post-position, "before", with preceding genitive	age	আগে
"before coming"	aśbar age	আসবার আগে
loan word, "telephone"	phon	ফোন
compound verb, "(to) telephone"	phon kɔr-	ফোন কর-

"(please) phone (future)"   phon korben   ফোন করবেন

For this use of the future imperative, which is identical in form with the simple future honorific, see Grammar, section 4.2.)

B. **All right. (Please) phone me before you come.**

B. accha " asbar age ' amake phon korben "

আচ্ছা , আসবার আগে আমাকে ফোন করবেন ।

16. verb stem, "telephone"   phon kɔr-   ফোন কর–
    verbal noun suffix   -ba-   –বা–
    genitive case ending   -r   –র
    "of telephoning"   phon korbar ফোন করবার
    post-position, "after",   pɔre   পরে
    with preceding **genitive**
    "after calling"   phon korbar pɔre   ফোন করবার পরে

A. **All right. I shall come after calling you.**

A. accha " apnake phon korbar pɔre ' ami asbo "

আচ্ছা , আপনাকে ফোন করবার পরে আমি আসবো ।

17. post-position, "with" with   śɔŋge   সঙ্গে
    preceding genitive
    "with you (honorific)"   apnar śɔŋge   আপনার সঙ্গে
    Note that below, /apnar/ is not stated.
    noun stem, "wife"   stri   স্ত্রী
    verb stem, "bring, fetch"   an-   আন–

B. **Will you bring your wife with you?**

B. śɔŋge ' apnar strike ' anben ki "

সঙ্গে আপনার স্ত্রীকে আনবেন কি ?

18. Note: for this usage of the future tense, see Grammar, section 4.1.

A. **She is going to her sister's house.**

A. śe ' tar boner barite ' jabe "

সে তার বোনের বাড়ীতে যাবে ।

19. "so, therefore"   tai   তাই

verb stem, "bring"	an- আন-
verbal noun suffix	-a -া
verbal noun, "bringing	ana আনা

Note that the verbal noun, like other verbal forms, can take an object. /take/ in this sentence is the object of the verbal noun /ana/.

"possible"	ŝɔmbhɔb সম্ভব
"it will not be possible"	ŝɔmbhɔb hɔbe na সম্ভব হবে না

A. <u>So it won't be possible</u>
<u>to bring her.</u>

(i.e., Bringing her will
not be possible)

A. <u>tai ' take ana ' ŝɔmbhɔb hɔbe na "</u>

তাই তাকে আনা সম্ভব হবে না।

20.
"then, in that case"	ta hole তা হলে
"sons" (objective case plural)	chelederke, cheleder
	ছেলেদেরকে , ছেলেদের

B. <u>Then will you bring your</u>
<u>sons?</u>

B. <u>ta hole ' apnar chelederke '</u>
<u>anben ki "</u>

তা হলে আপনার ছেলেদেরকে
আনবেন কি ?

21.
"them" (objective case plural)	taderke, tader তাদেরকে , তাদের
PAP of verb /ne-/, "take"	nie নিয়ে
verb stem, "go"	ja- যা
compound verb stem "take" (from this place to that)	nie ja- নিয়ে যা-
"taking them"	taderke nie jaoa তাদেরকে নিয়ে যাওয়া
verb stem, "go"	ja- যা-
alternative verbal noun suffix,(see Grammar, section 2.2.)	-oa -ওয়া
verbal noun, "going"	jaoa যাওয়া
"difficult"	ŝɔkto শক্ত
"going will be difficult"	jaoa ŝɔkto hɔbe যাওয়া শক্ত হবে

A.	It will be difficult to take them.	A.	taderke nie jaoa ' śɔkto hɔbe "

A. It will be difficult to take them.
(i.e., Taking them will be difficult.)

A. taderke nie jaoa ' śɔkto hɔbe "

তাদেরকে নিয়ে যাওয়া ·ক্ত হবে ৷

22. alternative verb stems, "sleep"

ghuma-, ghumo- ঘুমা– , ঘুমো–

A. They will be sleeping tonight.

A. tara ' rattre ghumobe "

তারা রাত্রে ঘুমোবে ৷

Lesson 7, part 2.   Grammar.

1. Review the formation of the simple past tense: Lesson 5, Grammar, 2.

2. The formation and usage of verb nouns (sentences 4, 15, 16, 19, 21).

2.1. Verbal nouns are formed by the addition of one of the suffixes /a/, /oa/, (or /ano/, which will be dealt with in a later lesson) to the simple stem of the verb, or the suffix /ba/ to the high stem of all verbs except /a/-stems. To the verbal noun suffix is added the inflectional case ending, if any. A verbal noun can be inflected for all four cases, as any other noun.

Stem	Verbal noun suffix	Inflected forms
bɔl- ("speak")	-a	bɔla bɔlar (bɔlake -- rare) bɔlate
bɔl- ("speak")	-ba	bolba bolbar
pa- ("get")	-oa	paoa paoar (paoake -- rare) paoate
	-ba	paba pabar

2.2. The use of the suffixes /a/ and /oa/ depends upon the shape of the verb stem. When the stem shape is Ca-, the suffix is /oa/:

jaoa	"going"
paoa	"getting"
deoa	"giving"

When the stem has the shape CVC-, the suffix is /a/:

kena	"buying"
pɔṛa	"reading"

2.3. The verbal noun suffix /-ba/ is frequently used, with stems of all shapes, when the case of the verbal noun is genitive. The genitive case suffix is added to the verbal noun suffix:

jabar age ' ami ḍakbo "   I shall call (i.e., call aloud) before going.

eṭa kenbar pɔre ' ami aśbo "   I shall come after buying it.

2.4. The verbal noun suffix is usually translatable by the English verbal noun suffix "-ing":

baŋla bɔla ' śɔkto "   Speaking Bengali is difficult.

śekhane jaoa '·ɔśɔmbhɔb "   Going there is impossible.

eṭa paoa ' śɔhoj hɔbe "   Getting it will be easy.

2.5. The verbal noun can take an object, as can any other verbal form; in the second example in 2.3., the object of the verbal noun is /eṭa/.

2.6. A verbal noun is used in Bengali in some cases in which an "infinitive" can be used in English.

śekhane jaoa ' ɔśɔmbhɔb "   To go there is impossible.
                                  Going there is impossible.

2.6.1. Note that in English, the "infinitive" has two separate functions; though in both functions its form is the same, there is a difference in functional characteristics. Take these two examples:

To study is a good thing.
I ought to study now.

In the first of these two examples, "to study" is the subject of the sentence; it functions as a noun. In the second example, "to study" is a function of "ought". In the first example, "to study" can be replaced by "studying", with no change of meaning; it is, then, a verbal noun, and must be translated by one in Bengali. Thus:

pɔṛa'bhalo jiniś"   To study is a good thing. or:
Studying is a good thing.

3. The verb /aś-/, "come" (sentence 1).

3.1. The verb /aś-/ is an irregular verb, having the two stems /aś-/ and /e-/. The stem /e-/ occurs in the present ordinary imperative /eśo/, and in free variation with /aś-/ in the simple past. Thus:

aślum	elum
aśle	ele
aśli	eli
aślen	elen
aślo	elo
aślen	elen

Like other verbs with /a/-vowel stems, **/aś-/** retains its low stem in the simple future.

4. Uses of the future (sentences 15, 18).

4.1. In Bengali the simple future tense may be used for any action which will take place, regardless of what tense occurs in the English.

śe śekhane jabe"   He **will go** there.
He **is going** there (in the future).

4.2. The **future honorific imperative** is identical in form with the simple future honorific. When the imperative is signified, the personal pronoun is usually omitted:

apni jaben"   You (hon.) will go.
jaben"   (Please) go (in the future).

5. As in sentences 3 and 17, a personal pronoun can frequently be omitted, when the reference is clear from context. When such a pronoun is the subject of a verb and is omitted, the person of the subject will of course be indicated by the personal ending of the verb. The number of

178

the subject, however, will not be clear. Therefore take care, in the
omission of a pronoun subject, that there is no confusion between, say,
2nd and 3rd person honorific, or as to the number of the subject.

6. Use of the qualifier /-ṭa/ as in sentences 13 and 14. Refer to
Lesson 3, Grammar, 2.2.: Qualifiers are added to numerals and other
adjectives of quantity when accompanied by a noun.

7. Use of /na/ as in sentence 11.

When used with a present imperative form, /na/ does not have the force
of a negative, but as a polite request, "why don't you ...". Examples:

     (apni) aśun na"   Why don't you come; please come.
     (apni) khan na"   Why don't you eat; please eat.

8. Form possible Bengali sentences:

Subject	Indirect Object	Interr.	Verbal Modifiers	Direct Object	Verb
ram	jeleke	ki	roj	mach (gulo)	aś-
ami	amake		aj	eṭa	ja-
apni	tāke		ækhon	śeṭa	ken-
tumi	amaderke		rattre		ne-
śe	taderke		kɔṭar śɔmoe	æto ṭake	an-
tini	tomaderke		nodir dhar(er) theke		de-
tara	meeke		śɔhorer kache		
			śekhane		

Lesson 7, part 3. Patterns.

1. Pattern: sentence 1.

   a. Ram, have you just come from the city?
   b. Ram, has he (ord.) just come from the city?
   c. Ram, has he (hon.) just gone to the city?
   d. Ram, has he (hon.) just gone to the river bank?
   e. Ram, has he (ord.) just come from the store?

2. Pattern: sentence 2.

    a. Yes, I go to the city every day.
    b. Yes, he comes from the city every day.
    c. Yes, he goes to the city every day.
    d. Yes, he walks on the river bank every day.
    e. Yes, he goes to the store every day.

3. Pattern: sentence 3.

    a. Why do you go?
    b. Why does he (ord.) come?
    c. Why does he (hon.) go?
    d. Why does he (hon.) walk?
    e. Why does he (ord.) go?

4. Pattern: sentence 4.

    a. Going to the city is fun.
    b. Coming here is easy.
    c. Buying there is easy.
    d. Walking there is good.
    e. Going to the store is fun.

5. Pattern: sentence 6.

    a. Did you buy things there today?
    b. Did he buy food here today?
    c. Did he buy books there today?
    d. Did he eat there today?
    e. Did he walk there today?

6. Pattern: sentence 7.

    a. Yes, I bought cloth and sandals.
    b. Yes, he bought rice and sweets.
    c. Yes, he bought poetry and history books.
    d. Yes he ate fish and rice today.
    e. Yes, he took his clothes there today.

7. Pattern: sentence 8.

    a. How much did you pay the weaver?
    b. How much did he pay the sweet-maker?

180

    c. How much did he pay the grocer?

    d. How much did he pay the fisherman?

    e. How much did he pay the washerman?

8. Pattern: sentence 9.

    a. I gave the weaver ten rupees.

    b. He paid him three rupees.

    c. He paid him twenty rupees.

    d. He paid the fisherman two rupees.

    e. He paid the washerman five rupees.

9. Pattern: sentence 10.

    a. You got the cloth very cheaply.

    b. You got the sweets very cheaply

    c. You got the books very cheaply

    d. He did not get the fish very cheaply.

    e. He did not give the washerman very much.

10. Pattern: sentence 11.

    a. Yes. Why don't you come to my house and see the cloth.

    b. Yes. Why don't you come to his house and eat the sweets.

    c. Yes. Why don't you come to his house and read the books.

    d. Yes. Why don't you come to his house and eat the fish.

    e. No. Why don't you go to the washerman's house and give him ten rupees.

11. Pattern: sentence 12.

    a. All right. I shall come tomorrow.

    b. All right. We shall go this evening.

    c. All right. We shall go tomorrow evening.

    d. All right. We shall go tonight.

    e. All right. I shall go afterwards.

12. Pattern: sentence 13.

    a. At what time will you come?

    b. At what time shall we go?

    c. At what time tomorrow shall we go?

    d. At what time tonight shall we go?

    e. At what time will you go?

13. Pattern: sentence 14.

    a. I shall come at five o'clock.

    b.   We shall go at six o'clock.

    c.   We shall go at seven o'clock.

    d.   We shall go at nine o'clock.

    e.   I shall go at ten o'clock.

14. Pattern: sentence 15.

    a.   All right. Will you phone me before you come?

    b.   All right. Will you phone me before we go?

    c.   All right. Will you phone him before we go?

    d.   All right. Will you tell me before we go?

    e.   All right. Will you phone me before you see him?

15. Pattern: sentence 16.

    a.   All right. I shall come after calling you.

    b.   All right. We shall go after my calling you.

    c.   All right. We shall go after my calling him.

    d.   All right. We shall go after my telling you.

    e.   All right. I shall see him after calling you.

16. Pattern: sentence 17.

    a.   Will you bring your sister with you?

    b.   Shall we bring our wives with us?

    c.   Shall I bring my brother with me?

    d.   Shall we bring our friends with us?

    e.   Will you bring your son with you?

17. Pattern: sentence 18.

    a.   No, I won't bring her. She is going to her friend's house.

    b.   No, we won't bring them. They are going to a friend's house.

    c.   No, you won't bring him. He is going to his friend's house.

    d.   No, we won't bring them. They are going to Ram's house.

    e.   No, I won't bring him. He is going to Lila's house.

Pattern: sentence 19.

    a.   So, it won't be possible to bring her.

    b.   So, it won't be possible to bring them.

    c.   So, it won't be possible to bring him.

    d.   So, it won't be possible to bring Ram.

    e.   So, it won't be possible to bring Lila.

18. Pattern: sentence 20.

    a. Then will you bring your brother?

    b. Then will they bring their friend?

    c. Then will we bring his friend?

    d. Then will we bring our children?

    e. Then will you bring your daughter?

19. Pattern: sentence 21.

    a. No, it will be difficult to bring him.

    b. No, it will be difficult to bring their friend.

    c. No, it will not be possible to bring him.

    d. No, it will not be possible to bring them.

    e. No, it will be difficult to bring her.

Pattern: sentence 22.

    a. He will be studying in the evening.

    b. Their friend will be sleeping in the evening.

    c. He will be going home in the evening.

    d. They will be sleeping in the evening.

    e. She will be working in the evening.

Lesson 7, part 4. Sentence Drill.

Drill 1

--Hello, Ram. Is Naresh-babu at home?

--Yes, sir. He came in a little while ago. (Please) come in the house.

--Will you tell him that I am here?

--Yes sir. I shall call him.

--Hello, Naresh.

--Hello Probhas. Why are you in Calcutta?

--I arrived this morning. I have some work outside the city. I have brought some <u>śɔndeś</u> for your children.

--Fine. Will you come and eat with us this evening?

--All right. What time?

--At eight sharp. Is your wife with you?

--No, but my three sons are at the station.

--Good. Will you bring them with you?

----No, they are going (i.e., "will go") to their friends' house tonight.

--How long will you be here?

--I leave tomorrow. Will you come with me to Ashim's [ośimer] house?

--When are you going?

--Right now.

--No, I just came from the university, and I'm very tired. I'll **see** you tonight.

--All right. See you later.

Drill 2

--Where have you just come from?

--I have just come from the tank. It is beautiful there in the **evening**.

--Do you have business (i.e., "work") there?

--No. It is beautiful; that is why I go there every evening.

--What is that in your hand?

--It is a garland. I just bought it from a man on the side of the **road**.

--To whom will you give it?

--I shall give it to my sister. She is coming to my house tomorrow morning.

--Will she stay with you long?

--She will leave before tomorrow night. She lives outside the **city**.

--I shall come and see her. Will her children be with her?

--No, her children are at home. Come at six tomorrow evening.

--Good. I'll see you then.

Lesson 7, part 5. Vocabulary.

śɔkal	morning	ṭhik	exactly
bikel	afternoon	klanto	tired
śondhe, śondhebæla	evening	śɔŋge	with
śɔndeś	type of Bengali sweet	jonne	for, for the sake of
mala	garland	theke	from (place)
hat	hand	kachtheke	from (person)
mɔja	fun	bhetore, bhitore	within
tãti	weaver	baire	outside
mɔera	sweet-maker		
mudi	grocer		

184

Expressions of time:

kichukkhon	a little time, a little while
kɔtokkhon	how much time, how long (when the answer is expected to be in terms of a short while --i.e., minutes or hours).
ɔnekkhon	much time, a long time (in terms of minutes or hours)
kichu din	a few days
kɔto din	how long (when the answer is expected to be in terms of days or weeks)
ɔnek din	a long time (not necessarily literally "many days").
kɔkhon	when, at what time (on the same dav)
kɔbe	when, on what day
kɔtar śɔmoe	at what time, at what hour
ekʈu age	a little while ago

Idioms:

dækha kɔbe	See you later (lit. "seeing will be").
dækha korbo	See you later (lit. "seeing (I) shall make").

The full forms of these idiomatic expressions are:

apnar sɔnge'dækha hɔbe"
apnar sɔnge'dækha korbo"

In the first of them, the subject of the sentence is the verbal noun /dækha/ -- therefore the verb is in the third person and is the inactive verb /hɔ-/. The subject of the second is the pronoun /ami/, and the verb is the active /kɔr-/ -- the subject of the sentence is actively bringing the "seeing" about.

Analysis and Translation	Bengali

1.
"when, on what day,
after how long"

kɔbe   কবে

noun stem, "Bengal"

baṇladeś বাংলাদেশ

A. Ram, when are you going
to Bengal?

A. ram ' tumi kɔbe ' baṇladeśe jabe "
রাম , তুমি কবে বাংলাদেশে যাবে ?

2.
name of a Bengali
month -- April-May

boiśakh, bośek বৈশাখ , বোশেখ

noun stem, "end"

śeś শেষ

"at the end of Boiśakh"

boiśakher śeśe বৈশাখের শেষে

B. I shall go at the end of
Boiśakh.

B. ami ' boiśakher śeśe ' jabo "
আমি বৈশাখের শেষে যাবো ।

3.
inflectional stem of in-
terrogative pronoun "who"

ka- কা–

objective case suffix

-ke –কে

"whom" (objective)

kake কাকে

high stem of verb /ne-/,
"take"

ṅi- নি–

past active participial
ending,(see Grammar, 1.)

-e –য়ে

"taking, having taken"

nie নিয়ে

compound verb, "take away"

nie ja- নিয়ে যাওয়া

A. <u>Whom will you take with you?</u>

A. <u>tomar ś**ɔ**nge ' kake nie jabe "</u>

তোমার সঙ্গে কাকে নিয়ে যাবে ?

4.   noun stem, "wife"   stri স্ত্রী

Note that the objective case suffix is attached to the last member of the series /stri ... cheleke/.

B. <u>I shall take my wife and little boy.</u>

B. <u>ami ' amar stri ' ar choṭo cheleke ' nie jabo "</u>

আমি আমার স্ত্রী আর ছোট ছেলেকে নিয়ে যাবো ।

5.   noun stem, "road, way, path"

"on the road, on the way"

"where"

"what various places"

(For this **type** of reduplica- see Grammar, 2.)

high stem of verb /ghur-/ "turn around, spin around"

last active participial ending

"having turned around"

compound verb, "visit"

pɔth (pɔt) পথ

pɔthe পথে

kothae কোথায়

kothae kothae কোথায় কোথায়

ghur- ঘুর–

-e –ে

ghure ঘুরে

ghure ja- ঘুরে যা–

A. <u>What various places will you visit on the way?</u>

A. <u>tumi pɔthe ' kothae kothae ' ghure jabe "</u>

তুমি পথে কোথায় কোথায় ঘুরে যাবে ।

6.   name of the city, London   lɔnḍon লণ্ডন

B. <u>Having visited London, I shall go to Calcutta.</u>

B. <u>ami lɔnḍon ghure ' kolkatae jabo "</u>

আমি লণ্ডন ঘুরে কলকাতায় যাবো ।

7.   alternative stem of verb /ja-/, "go" -- See Grammar, 3.   gi- গি–

past active participle ending   -e –য়ে

"going, having gone"   gie গিয়ে

"having gone to Calcutta"   kolkatae gie   কলকাতায় গিয়ে

A. What will you study when you get to Calcutta?   **A.** tumi kolkatae gie ' ki porbe "

তুমি কলকাতায় গিয়ে কি করবে ?

8. **B.** When I go to Calcutta I shall study Bengali.   **B.** kolkatae gie ' ami banla porbo "

কলকাতায় গিয়ে আমি বাংলা পড়বো ।

9. "again"   abar আবার

high stem of verb, /pher-/ "turn, return"   phir- ফির-

past active participial ending   -e -ে

"returning, having returned"   phire ফিরে

compound verb, "return" (from there to here)   phire aś- ফিরে আস-

A. When will you come back again to this country?   **A.** abar kɔbe ' e deśe phire aśbe "

আবার কবে এ দেশে ফিরে আসবে ?

10. noun stem, "year"   bɔchor বছর

post-position, "after" (preceding genitive optional)   pɔre পরে

compound verb, "return (from here to there)"   phire ja- ফিরে যা-

B. After two years. When will you go back to Bengal?   **B.** du bɔchor pɔre " tumi kɔbe 'banla deśe phire jabe "

দু বছর পরে । তুমি কবে বাংলা দেশে ফিরে যাবে ?

11. loan word, "degree"   digri ডিগ্রী

(Note: for this usage of the term /deś/, see Grammar, 5.)

188

A. I shall return to the
   country after taking my
   degree.

A. ami digrita nie ' dese phire jabo "

আমি ডিগ্রীটা নিয়ে দেশে ফিরে যাবো ।

12.   "which"
       "which (various)"
       "seeing, having seen"

kon কোন

kon kon কোন কোন

dekhe দেখে

B. What various places will
   you see on the way home?

B. tumi pɔthe ' kon kon jaega dekhe '
   dese phirbe "

তুমি পথে কোন কোন জায়গা দেখে দেশে
ফিরবে ?

13.   noun stem, "Europe"

       high stem of verb /bæɽa-/,
       "wander about"

       "wandering about, having
       wandered about"

iurop ইউরোপ

beɽi- বেড়ি-

beɽie বেড়িয়ে

A. I also shall wander about
   Europe and then return
   home.
   (I also Europe-in having-
   wandered-about home returning shall-go)

A. ami.o ' iurop beɽie ' bari phire
   jabo "

আমিও ইউরোপ বেড়িয়ে বাড়ী ফিরে
যাবো ।

14.   "from" post-position,
       preceding genitive
       optional
       loan word, "camera"
       "for me"
       PAP, "taking, having taken"
       compound verb, "bring" (lit.
       "having taken come")

theke থেকে

kæmera ক্যামেরা

amar jonne আমার জন্যে

nie নিয়ে

nie aś- নিয়ে আস-

B. Will you bring me a
   camera from Europe?

B. tumi ki amar jonne ' iurop theke '
   ækta kæmera nie aśbe "

তুমি কি আমার জন্যে ইউরোপ থেকে
একটা ক্যামেরা নিয়ে আসবে ?

15. high stem of verb /an-/, "bring, fetch"

"bringing, having brought"

"I shall give", alternative forms

en-   এন-
ene   এনে

debo, dobo   দেবো , দোবো

A. Yes, 1 shall bring one (for you.) What priced camera do you want?

A. hæ̃ " ene dobo " kɔto damer ' kæmera cao "

হাঁ , এনে দোবো । কত দামের ক্যামেরা চাও ?

16. negative verb stem, "be not"

"twenty"

high stem of verb "buy"

"buying, having bought"

nɔ -   ন-

kuṛi   কুড়ি

kin-   কিন-

kine   কিনে

B. Not very expensive. Buy one for twenty rupees and bring it.

B. beśi damer nɔe " kuṛi ṭaka die ' ækṭa kæmera kine ' nie eśo "

বেশী দামের নয় । কুড়ি টাকা দিয়ে একটা ক্যামেরা কিনে নিয়ে এসো ।

17. quickly, immediately

taṛataṛi   তাড়াতাড়ি

A. Do you want the camera right away?

A. tumi ki ' kæmeraṭa ' taṛataṛi cao "

তুমি কি ক্যামেরাটা তাড়াতাড়ি চাও ?

18. genitive verbal noun, "of coming"

noun stem, "time" or "at the time"

"at the time of coming, when (you) come"

aśbar   আসবার

śɔmoe   সময়

aśbar śɔmoe   আসবার সময়

B. No, bring it with you when you come.

B. na " aśbar śɔmoe ' tomar śɔŋge ' nie eśo "

না । আসবার সময় তোমার সঙ্গে নিয়ে এসো ।

Lesson 8, part 2. Grammar.

1. Formation and usage of the past active participle.

1.1. The past active participle is formed by the addition of the suffix /-e/ to the <u>high</u> <u>stem</u> of the verb.

Stem	Past Active Participle	Translation
ken-	kin-e	buying, having bought
khæl-	khele	playing, having played
śon-	śun-e	hearing, having heard
kɔr-	kor-e	doing, having done
ɟan-	jen-e	knowing, having known
de-	di-e	giving, having given
pa-	pe-e	received, having received

1.2. There are large numbers of what are called "compound verbs" in Bengali; these compound verbs are made up, in some cases, of a non-finite verbal form (here a past active participle) plus an inflected or finite verbal form. The semantic signalling of these compounds is often clear. We have, for example, in sentence 3, the compound /nie ja-/, "taking (or 'having taken'), go" i.e., "take away". In other cases, as will be seen later, the meaning is not so easily derived from the elements. It is therefore wise to consider these compound verbs for the present as verbal units, rather than as a cluster of two or more separate verbal elements. The verb "take" will thus be considered as /nie ja-/, rather than as /nie/ plus /ja-/; the verb "wander about", as in sentence 5, will be considered as /ghure ja-/, rather than as /ghure/ plus /ja-/.

1.3. The past active participle is frequently used to express sequences of thought, and avoids a series of clauses connected by "and". An example is in sentence 6, which could be translated, "I shall visit London, and (then) I shall go to Calcutta". When used in this way, and not as an element of a compound verb, the past active participle marks the end of a clause and of a breath-group.

1.4. Note carefully that this sequential type of construction can be used <u>only</u> when the subjects of all clauses are the same. Thus, you can say:

kolkatae gie ' ækʈa boi likhbe "   When he goes to Calcutta, he
                                     will write a book.

This type of construction could <u>not</u> be used to express:

When <u>I</u> go to Calcutta, <u>he</u> will write a book.

There must be one <u>inflected</u> verb for each subject in the sentence.

2. Repetition, as in sentence 5, gives either a distributive or intensive
meaning. In sentence 5, the meaning is distributive, i.e., "what different or various places". Other examples might be: /din din/, "daily,
day after day, every day"; /bone bone/, "throughout the forest, in all
the parts of the forest".

3. The irregular verb /ja/, "go", as in sentence 7.

The verb /ja-/ is regular, within its class of vowel-stem verbs in /a/,
for the simple present and simple future, i.e., /ami jai/ "I go", and
/ami jabo/ "I shall go", etc. In the simple past and in the past active
participle forms, there are alternative stems. A paradigm of the simple
past is:

> ami   gelum
>
> tumi gele
> tui   geli
> apni gelen
>
> śe   gælo
> tini gelen

The stem for the past active participle is /gi-/. Therefore, PAP /gie/,
"going, having gone".

4. There is sometimes some confusion as to which of the several
equivalents of the verb "be" should be used in which circumstances. At
this point, the following rules of usage might be noted:

4.1. The stem /thak-/ is used when permanence or habitual condition is
implied:

chelemee'baṛite thake"   The children are (i.e., reside) in the
                          house

4.2. The stem /ach-/ is used when continuity is implied:

chelemee'baṛite ache"   The children are (still, even now) in the house.

4.3. No verb is used when the condition is temporary:

chelemee'baṛite"   The children are in the house (but they may not be there much longer).

4.4. The stem /hɔ-/ is used in the sense of "to become, to be born, to be posted at some place".

chelemee'baṛite hɔe"   The children get born in the house.

5. The term /deś/ has several meanings in Bengali. A Bengal villager may mean by it his village and the countryside he knows well. A sophisticated Bengali may mean by it all India. The meaning of the term varies according to the sophistication of the speaker, and the place where he is when he is speaking. A Bengali in the United States might mean by /deś/, India; a Bengali in Delhi might use the term to refer to Bengal; a Bengali villager might use it to refer to his village. In this sense, it is used much like the English "home".

6. Form possible Bengali sentences:

Subject	Verbal Modifier	Verb$_1$	Verbal Modifier	Verb$_2$
ami	lɔnḍon	ghure	kolkatae	aś
amra	pæris	gie	śɔhore	ja-
tumi	kothae	dekhe	baṛite	
tomra	kothae kothae			
apni	śekhane			
apnara				
	Direct Object		Direct Object	
	eṭa	nie	eṭa	nie aś
	oṭa	kine	oṭa	nie ja-
	cɔppol	dekhe	boigulo	phire ja-
	śaṛiṭa	gie		dekhe
				pher-
				kine an-

Lesson 8, part 3. Patterns.

1. Pattern: sentence 1.

   a. When will you go back to India?
   b. When will you go back to Bengal?
   c. When will you come back to Bengal?
   d. When will you come back here?
   e. When will he come back here?

2. Pattern: sentence 2.

   a. I shall go at the end of Caitro [coittromaś].
   b. I shall go at the beginning of Asarh [aśaṛmaś].
   c. I shall come back at the end of Phalgun [phalgunmaś].
   d. I shall come back at the end of the month.
   e. He will come back here at the end of the week.

3. Pattern: sentence 3.

   a. Whom will you take with you?
   b. What will you take with you?
   c. Whom will you bring with you?
   d. What will you bring with you?
   e. Whom will he bring with him?

4. Pattern: sentence 4.

   a. I shall take my wife with me.
   b. I shall take my clothes with me.
   c. I shall bring my children with me.
   d. I shall bring my books with me.
   e. He will bring his brother with him.

5. Pattern: sentence 5.

   a. What (various) countries will you visit on the way?
   b. What (various) cities will you visit on the way?
   c. What (various) places will you visit on the way?
   d. What (various) shops will you visit on the way?
   e. What (various) places will he visit on the way?

6. Pattern: sentence 6 (use PAP).

194

    a. Having visited Europe, I shall go to India.
    b. Having visited London, I shall go back to Bengal.
    c. Having visited Paris, we shall go back to Bengal.
    d. Having visited the book shops, I shall come back here.
    e. Having visited Calcutta, they will come back here.

7. Pattern: sentence 7 (use PAP, though other constructions are possible).

    a. What will you do when you go to India?
    b. What will you do when you go back to Bengal?
    c. What will you do when you come back to Bengal?
    d. What will you do when you come back here?
    e. What will they do when they come back here?

8. Pattern: sentence 8 (use PAP).

    a. When I go back to India, I shall write a book.
    b. When I go back to Bengal, I shall buy a sari.
    c. When I come back to Bengal, I shall study Bengali.
    d. When I come back here, I shall call you.
    e. When they come back here, they will call us.

    Pattern: sentence 9.

    a. When will you come back?
    b. When will you come back to Bengal?
    c. When will you go back?
    d. When will you come back home?
    e. When will we come back here?

9. Pattern: sentence 11 (use PAP).

    a. I shall return after taking my degree.
    b. I shall return to Bengal after taking my degree.
    c. I shall go back after finishing my work.
    d. I shall come back after buying the books.
    e. We shall come back after buying the cloth.

10. Pattern: sentence 12 (use PAP).

    a. What (various) countries will you see on the way home?
    b. What (various) places will you see on the way home?
    c. What (various) cities will you see on the way home?
    d. What (various) shops will you see on the way home?

e.   What (various) places will we see on the way home?

11.   Pattern: sentence 13.

   a.   I also shall wander in many countries and them return home.
   b.   I also shall wander in many places and then return home.
   c.   I also shall wander in various cities and then return home.
   d.   I also shall wander in many shops and then return home.
   e.   We also shall wander in many places and then return home.

12.   Pattern: sentence 14.

   a.   Will you bring me books from Europe?
   b.   Will you being me cloth from London?
   c.   Will you bring me sandals from Poona [puna]?
   d.   Will you bring me sweets from the shop?
   e.   Will we bring them a sari from the shop?

13.   Pattern: sentence 15.

   a.   Yes, I shall bring (one). What priced books do you want?
   b.   Yes, I shall bring (some). What priced cloth do you want?
   c.   Yes, I shall bring (some). What priced sandals do you want?
   d.   Yes, I shall bring (some). What priced sweets do you want?
   e.   Yes, we shall bring (one). What priced sari does she want?

14.   Pattern: sentence 16.

   a.   Buy some for fifty rupees and bring them.
   b.   Buy the cloth for twenty rupees and bring it.
   c.   Buy the sandals for ten rupees and bring them.
   d.   Buy the sweets for five rupees and bring them.
   e.   Buy one for thirty rupees and bring it.

   Pattern: sentences 17, 18.

   a.   I do not want them right away. Bring them with you when you
        come. (/tomar/ optional)
   b.   I do not want it right away. Bring it with you when you come.
        (/tomar/ optional)
   c.   I do not want them right away. Take them with you when you go.
        (/tomar/ optional)
   d.   I do not want them right away. I shall eat them when I come.
   e.   She does not want it right away. She will wear it when she goes.

Lesson 8, part 4. Drills.

Note: Use compound verb forms wherever possible.

Drill 1

--Rahim [rohim], are you going back to Calcutta soon?

--Yes, I shall be going there at the end of next month.

--Will you stop at many places on the way?

--Yes, I shall visit Delhi [dilli] and Benares [banaros] on my way.

--Will you take your family with you?

--No, not this time. I shall go alone.

--Do you know how long you will be staying in Calcutta?

--About two months.

--Will you study when you have reached Calcutta?

--Yes, I shall write a book.

--Will you do me a favor? (i.e., will you do a favor of me?)

--What favor shall I do for you?

--Will you bring me a sari and sandals form Calcutta?

--Yes, I shall bring them. What price sari do you want?

--Not very expensive. Buy a sari for thirty rupees and sandals for ten.

--Do you want the sari right away?

--No, bring it with you when you come.

Drill 2

--I'll go home now. But I'll come back tonight.

--Will you stop on the way home and give this to Somdev?

--Yes, I'll stop there on the way. Where does he live?

--Get down from the tram at the corner of Hajra Road and go (use simple future) to the third house on the left.

--All right. I won't get lost. Where shall I catch the tram (or: "get up on the tram")?

--In front of the house.

--All right. What shall I take for him?

--Take this watch for him. I brought (use simple past) it for him from America.

--How much did it cost?

--I got it for thirty dollars.

--It is a nice watch. What did you bring for me?
--Nothing. Why do you keep sitting there? Go along.
--All right. I'll come back and see you tonight.

Lesson 8, part 5. Vocabulary.

śuru	beginning	tham-	stop
śɔŋśar	family	harie ja-	get lost (/haṛa-/ "lose")
upokar	favor, help		
jama, kapoṛ	clothes	neme aś-	get down (/nam-/ "descent")
ghoṛi	watch, clock		
moṛ	corner, junction	bośe thak-	remain sitting (/bɔś-/ "sit")
mas	month		
beṛal	cat	bośe ach-	remain sitting
		nie aś-	bring (/ne-/ "take")
		lekh	write
ɔnek, nana	various	dhɔr-	catch
ekhuni	right away	pɔr-	wear
æka	alone		
ebar	this time	śamne	in front of -- post position with genitive
bã dik	left (side)		
dan dik	right (side)		
agami	next, approaching		

Bengali months:

bośek, boiśakh	April-May
joṣṭi, joiṣṭho	May-June
aśaṛ	June-July
srabon	July-August
bhaddro	August-September
aśśin	September-October
kartik	October- November
ɔgghran, ɔgrohaon	November-December
poś, pouś	December-January
magh (mag)	January-February
phalgun	February-March
cot, coittro	March-April

Lesson 9, part 1. Conversation.

Analysis and Translation	Bengali
1. proper name (Muslim)	mustapha মুসতাফা
noun stem, "necessity"	dɔrkar দরকার
"there is"	ache আছে
"it is necessary"	dɔrkar ache দরকার আছে
"it is necessary to go, there is a necessity of going"	jabar dɔrkar ache যাবার দরকার আছে

<u>A.</u> <u>Mustafa, is it necessary for you to go home now?</u>

<u>A.</u> <u>mustapha ' tomar ækhon ' barite jabar ' dɔrkar ache ki "</u>

মুসতাফা , তোমার এখন বাড়াতে যাবার দরকার আছে কি ?

2. emphatic suffix	-i -ই
"right now, right away"	ekhuni এখুনি

Note: the locative suffix on /bari/ is optional in this context.

<u>B.</u> <u>Yes, I have to go home right away.</u>

<u>B.</u> <u>hæ̃ " amar ekhuni ' bari jabar ' dɔrkar ache "</u>

হাঁ , আমার এখুনি বাড়ী যাবার দরকার আছে ।

3. alternative stem of verb "go"	gi- গি-
past active participial ending	-e -য়ে
"going, having gone"	gie গিয়ে

A. When you go home, what will you do?

A. tumi baɽi gie 'ki korbe "

তুমি বাড়ী গিয়ে কি করবে ?

4.   "much, many"

noun stem, "work" (singular)

"much work, many jobs"

ɔnek   অনেক

kaj   কাজ

ɔnek kaj   অনেক কাজ

B. I have a lot of work.

B. amar ' ɔnek kaj ache "

আমার অনেক কাজ আছে ।

5.   "that"

plural suffix

"those"

Note that /ɔnek kaj/ in sentence 4 is a plural formation, though singular in English.

noun stem, "end, finish"

compound verb, "finish"

śe   সে

-gulo   -গুলো

śegulo   সেগুলো

śeś   শেষ

śeś kɔr-   শেষ কর—

B. When I go home, I shall finish that.

B. baɽi gie ' śegulo śeś korbo "

বাড়ী গিয়ে সেগুলো শেষ করবো ।

6.   "again"

verb stem, "return"

PAP, "returning, having returned"

compound verb, "returning come, return here"

abar   আবার

pher-   ফের—

phire   ফিরে

phire aś´   ফিরে আস—

A. Will you come back here again?

A. tumi ekhane ' abar phire aśbe ki "

তুমি এখানে আবার ফিরে আসবে কি ?

7. B. No, I won't come back here today.

B. na " ekhane aj ' phire aśbo na "

না , এখানে আজ ফিরে আসবো না ।

8.   "once more, again"

ækbar   একবার

A. When you finish your work, will you meet me again?

A. tumi ' kaj śeś kore ' amar śɔnge ' ækbar dækha korbe ki "

তুমি কাজ শেষ করে আমার সঙ্গে একবার দেখা করবে কি ?

9. B. No, I won't be able to see you again today.

B. na " tomar śɔnge ' aj abar ' dækha kɔra ' śɔmbhɔb hɔbe na "

না , তোমার সঙ্গে আজ আবার দেখা করা সম্ভব হবে না ।

10. noun stem, "time"
"get time, find time"

śɔmoe   সময়
śɔmoe kɔr-   সময় করা–

A. Can't you find a little time today?

A. aj tomar ' ektu śɔmoe kɔra ' śɔmbhɔb hɔbe na "

আজ তোমার একটু সময় করা সম্ভব হবে না ?

11. B. Why? Is there some need?

B. kæno " kichu dɔrkar ache ki "

কেন ? কিছু দরকার আছে কি ?

12. A. Yes, there is some need.

A. hæ̃ " ektu dɔrkar ache "

হাঁ , একটু দরকার আছে ।

13. B. OK, in that case I'll come back tonight.

B. accha " ta hole ' ami rattre ' phire aśbo "

আচ্ছা , তা হলে আমি রাত্রে ফিরে আসবো ।

14. 2nd person ordinary imperative stem of /as-/ "come"

"come!" (2nd ordinary imperative)

eś-   এস–

eśo   এসো

A. No, come back when you
have finished your work.

A. na " tumi ' tomar kaj śeś
kore ' phire eśo "

না , তুমি তোমার কাজ শেষ করে ফিরে
এসো ।

15.   proper name (f.)   roti   রতি

B. Look, I have to meet
Roti today.

B. dækho " aj rotir śɔŋge ' amar
dækha kɔrar ' dɔrkar ache "

দেখ , আজ রতির সঙ্গে আমার দেখা
করার দরকার আছে ।

16.   verb stem, "learn"   śekh-   শেখ-
        verb stem, "teach"   śekha-   শেখা-
        "today"   aj   আজ
        "today also"   ajo   আজও

A. Why? Is she going to teach
you English again today?

A. kæno " śe ki ajo tomake ' iŋriji
śekhabe "

কেন? সে কি আজও তোমাকে ইংরিজী
শেখাবে ?

17.   "some" - a bound form   kɔtok-   কতক-
        "some (plural)"   kɔtokgulo   কতকগুলো
        3rd person ordinary
        genitive pronoun   tar   তার
        post-position, "from (a
        person)" with preceding   kach theke   কাছ থেকে
        genitive
        "from him, from her"   tar kach theke   তার কাছ থেকে

B. No, I have to get some
poetry books from her
today.

B. na " aj tar kach theke ' amar
kɔtokgulo kobitar boi ' nebar
dɔrkar ache "

না, আজ তার কাছ তেকে আমার
কতকগুলো কবিতার বই নেবার
দরকার আছে ।

18.   adjective (bound), "coming"   agami-   আগামী-
        "tomorrow"   agamikal   আগামীকাল

A. Go and get the books of poetry tomorrow.

A. tumi ' agamikal gie   kobitar boigulo ' nie eśo "

তুমি আগামীকাল গিয়ে কাঁবতার বইগুলো নিয়ে এসো ।

19. B. No, I won't be able to go tomorrow.

B. na " agamikal ' amar jaoa ' śɔmbhɔb hɔbe na "

না , আগামীকাল আমার যাওয়া সম্ভব হবে না ।

20. PAP of /an-/, "bring, fetch"
compound verb, "bring and give"

ene   এনে

ene de-   এনে দে–

A. Then I shall get you the books tomorrow.

A. ta hole ' ami tomake ' agamikal ' boigulo ene dobo "

তা হলে , আমি তোমাকে আগামীকাল বইগুলো এনে দোবো ।

21. A. I can go.

A. amar jaoa ' śɔmbhɔb hɔbe "

আমার যাওয়া সম্ভব হবে ।

22. B. Good. In that case, I shall come back right away.

B. beś " ta hole ' ami taṛataṛi ' phire aśbo "

বেশ । তা হলে , আমি তাড়াতাড়ি ফিরে আসবো ।

23. "much, a lot"
"much time"
verbal noun, "remaining"

beśi   বেশী
beśikkhon   বেশীক্ষণ
thaka   থাকা

B. But I won't be able to spend much time with you.

B. tɔbe ' tomar śɔnge ' amar beśikkhon thaka ' śɔmbhɔb hɔbe na

তবে তোমার সঙ্গে আমার বেশীক্ষণ থাকা সম্ভব হবে না ।

24. adjective, "right, exact"
idiom: "that's all right"
noun stem, "word, story, subject matter"

ṭhik   ঠিক
ṭhik ache   ঠিক আছে
kɔtha   কথা

"speak, say"	bɔl- বল—
"converse"	kɔtha bɔl- কথা বল—

A. That's all right. I have to talk to you.

A. thik ache " amar tomake kɔtokgulo kɔtha bɔlar dɔrkar ache "

ঠিক আছে । আমার তোমাকে কতগুলো কথা বলার আছে ।

25. idiom, "good enough"   beś to   বেশ তো

B. Good enough. When I come back I'll listen.

B. beś to " ami phire eśe ' śunbo "

বেশ তো । আমি ফিরে এসে শুনবো ।

26. A. When you come back, bring Nina with you.

A. phire aśbar śɔmoe ' ninake tomar śɔnge ' nie eśo "

ফিরে আস্বার সময় নীনাকে তোমার সঙ্গে নিয়ে এসো ।

27. A. She also has to hear it.

A. taro ' kɔthagulo śonar ' dɔrkar ache "

তারও কথাগুলো শোনার দরকার আছে ।

Lesson 9, part 2. Grammar.

1. The purpose of this lesson is primarily to summarize the usages of the verbal noun and past active participle forms which we had in the previous two lessons. There are two general types of usage:

1.1. As the verb in a subordinate clause, the PAP has two types of English equivalents: having done (gone, said, etc.)", and "when I (you, he, etc.) did (went, said, etc.)". For example:

a) ami'śekhane gie'boiṭa nie aśbo"

When I go there I shall take (away) the book. (i.e., I shall bring the book from there to here.)

Having gone there, I shall take (away) the book. (i.e., I shall bring the book from there to here.)

b) ganṭa śune'śe'amar kache'elo"

When he heard the song, he came to me.

Having heard the song, he came to me.

It is important to remember that in a structure of this kind, the subject of both clauses <u>must</u> <u>be</u> <u>the</u> <u>same</u>.

1.2. Note that in the English of sentence a) above, there are two semantic categories:

1. To go with the purpose of getting the book.
2. To go with some purposes, including getting the book.

It is important that these two categories, formally undistinguished in English, are formally distinguished in Bengali. The formation /ami śekhane gie .../ refers to category 1, i.e., to go with the purpose of getting the book. Category 2 cannot be expressed by the PAP. This type of expression will be dealt with in a later lesson.

1.3. As a part of a compound verb.

A compound verb in Bengali has at least two members, one of which, the second member, is a finite verb (i.e., a verb which is inflected for person and tense). The first member may be one of a number of classes of words -- nouns, adjectives, verbs -- but in the cases before us at present the first member of the compound is a past active participle. PAP + verb is in fact the commonest form of the compound verb. Also, in the cases before us, the nucleus of meaning of the compound verb is the participial form. For example:

tumi phire eśo   you come back (lit., "returning come")

tumi (eṭa) nie eśo   you bring (it) back (lit., "taking come")

In these two examples, the second member of the compound is the same, yet the meaning of the compound changes. In Bengali, as we shall see later on, this type of formation lends itself to great subtlety where by variation of one or another member of the compound, minute shades of distinction can be attained.

2. Bengali tends toward economy of expression. Note that in sentences 2 and 3, the locative case ending /-te/ on bari is not used, since there is no possibility of confusion. The use of case endings in cases of this kind is optional. We have noticed before that there are places in which the pronoun subject may be omitted also.

3. The use of /dɔrkar/, "necessity".

The form /dɔrkar/ functions as a noun, and is best considered as equivalent to the English "necessity". It does not imply compulsion or obligation; each of these types of expression has its own form in Bengali. Note that when /dɔrkar/ is used, it takes a possessive case of noun or pronoun (i.e., there is a necessity of something); in cases where the necessity is related to someone, that noun or pronoun is also in the posessive case. Bengali would phrase it this way:

> There is a necessity of me of going (i.e., it's necessary for me to go). amar jabar'dɔrkar ache"

> There is a necessity of him reading (i.e., it is necessary for him to read). tar pɔrbar'dɔrkar ache"

4. Uses of /-ke/ and /jonne/.

4.1. There are several ways of expressing an indirect object. Sentence 20 is "I shall get you the books tomorrow". The Bengali for this, depending upon the speaker's stylistic choice, can be either:

> ami tomar jonne'agamikal'boigulo nie aśbo", or,

> ami tomake'agamikal'boigulo ene dobo"

The use of the verb /de-/ in either its simple form or in a compound, permits the /-ke/ suffix denoting the indirect object. But with /de-/, the post-positional phrase with /jonne/ may be used. Thus another possibility, depending entirely on the speaker's stylistic choice, is:

> tomar jonne'boigulo ene dobo"

4.2. There are some Bengali verbs such as /ga-/ which do not take indirect objects. In "I shall sing you a song," "you" will not be translated as /tomake/. In Bengali, the expression will be either:

> ami tomar jonne'gan gaibo"
> "I shall sing a song for your benefit" (i.e., to bring you some kind of profit).

or:

> ami tomar pokkhe'gan gaibo"
> "I shall sing a song on your behalf."

4.3. Note that "to you", as in the English expression "I shall come to you" does <u>not</u> use the suffix /-ke/. Here also a post-position is required, namely /kache/, "near, in the vicinity of":

> ami'tomar kache aśbo"

5. To this point, we have had verbal nouns used only with such formations as:

> eţa kɔra'śɔkto"   It is difficult to do this.
>   (The doing of this is difficult.)

In such formations, /śɔkto, śɔmbhɔb, śɔhoj/ etc., are adjectives. In this lesson, we have another use of the verbal noun, this time as the object of the verb. Examples:

> śekhane jaoa'pochɔndo kori"   I like to go there.
>   (I like going there.)
>
> ami'baŋla pɔɽa'pochɔndo kori"   I like to read Bengali.
>   (I like reading Bengali.)
>
> ami tomake'baŋla pɔɽa śekhabo"   I will teach you to read Bengali.
>   (I will teach you reading Bengali.)
>
> apni ki take'tɔbla bajano   Will you teach him to play the tabla?
> śekhaben"   (Will you teach him playing the
>   tabla?)

6. The formation of PAP from -a final verb stems (/dæɪkha/, /bæɽa-/, etc.)

6.1. The PAP of -a final verb stems takes the high stem-vowel, except where the stem-vowel is /a/, and replaces stem-final -a by -i, thus:

	Stem	PAP	Gloss
	dæɪkha-	dekhie	showing, having shown
	bæɽa-	beɽie	wandering, having wandered
	śekha-	śikhie	teaching, having taught
	ghuma-	ghumie	sleeping, having slept
But:	jana-	janie	informing, having informed

Lesson 9, part 3. Pattern Drills.

. Pattern: sentence 1.

a. Is it necessary for you to study now?
b. Is it necessary for you to go there now?
c. Is it necessary for him to go tonight?
d. Is it necessary for them to come tomorrow?
e. Is it necessary for us to come to the office?

2. Pattern: sentence 2.

a. Yes, I have to study right away.
b. Yes, I have to go there right away.
c. Yes, it is necessary for him to go tonight.
d. Yes, it is necessary for them to come tomorrow.
e. Yes, it is necessary for you to come to the office.

3. Pattern: sentence 3.

a. When you finish, what will you do?
b. When you go there, what will you do?
c. When he arrives* there, what will he do?
d. When they come here, what will they do?
e. When I come to the office, what will I do?

4. Pattern: sentence 4.

a. I have a lot of work.
b. I have a lot of studying.
c. He has a lot of studying.
d. They have a lot of work.
e. You have a lot of work.

Pattern: sentence 5.

a. When I finish studying, I shall do that.
b. When I go there, I shall do that.
c. When he goes there, he will finish that.
d. When they come here, they will finish that.
e. When you come here, you will do that.

---

* either /poŭche/ or /poŭchie/ is possible.

5.   Pattern: sentence 6.

    a.   Will you finish studying tonight?

    b.   Will you come back home tonight?

    c.   Will he go back home tonight?

    d.   Will they come back home tonight?

    e.   Will I come back to the office tomorrow?

6.   Pattern: sentence 7.

    a.   No, I will not finish tonight.

    b.   Yes, I shall come back home tonight.

    c.   Yes, he will go back home tonight.

    d.   No, they will not come back home tonight.

    e.   Yes, you will come back tomorrow.

7.   Pattern: sentence 8.

    a.   When you finish your studying, will you meet me again?

    b.   When you come back home, will you meet me again?

    c.   When he goes back home, will he meet Lila?

    d.   When they come back home, will they meet us again?

    e.   When I come back, will I meet you here?

8.   Pattern: sentence 9.

    a.   No, I won't be able to meet you.

    b.   Yes, I will be able to meet you again.

    c.   No, he won't be able to meet her today.

    d.   No, they won't be able to meet us tomorrow.

    e.   No, you won't be able to meet me here.

9.   Pattern: sentences 10, 11, 12.

    a.   Can't you find a little time tonight? There is some need.

    b.   Can't you find a little time today? There is some need.

    c.   Can't he find a little time tonight? There is some need.

    d.   Can they find a little time today? There is some need.

    e.   Can you find a little time today? There is some need.

10. Pattern: sentence 13.

    a.   OK. In that case I'll come back this evening.

    b.   OK. In that case, I'll come back this morning.

c. OK. In that case, he'll come back tonight.

d. OK. In that case, they'll come back this evening.

e. OK. In that case, I'll come back soon.

11. Pattern: sentence 14.

a. No, come back when you have finished your studying.

b. No, come back home when you have finished your work

c. No, he'll come back when he has finished everything.

d. No, they'll come back when they have bought everything.

e. No, come back when you have bought the books.

12. Pattern: sentence 15.

a. Look, I have to meet Ram today.

b. Look, I have to meet Lila today.

c. Look, he has to meet me today.

d. Look, they have to study today.

e. Look, I have to study Bengali today.

13. Pattern: sentence 16 (use verbal nouns).

a. Why? Is he going to teach you to speak Bengali?

b. Why? Is she going to teach you to play the tabla?

c. Why? Are you going to teach him to eat Bengali sweets?

d. Why? Are they going to learn to read Bengali?

e. Why? Are you going to learn to read the language?

14. Pattern: sentence 17.

a. No, I have to take some history books from him.

b. No, I have to take some history books for her.

c. No, I have to take some new books for him.

d. No, they have to bring some new books for me.

e. No, I have to buy some Bengali books from Ram.

15. Pattern: sentence 18.

a. Go and get the history books tomorrow.

b. Go and get the history books for her tomorrow.

c. Go and bring the new books to him tomorrow.

d. Go and get the new books tomorrow.

e. Go and buy the books from Ram tomorrow.

16. Pattern: sentence 19.

    a. No, I won't be able to get them tomorrow.

    b. No, I won't be able to get them for her tomorrow.

    c. No, I won't be able to get them tomorrow.

    d. No, I won't be able to go there tomorrow.

    e. No, I won't be able to buy them tomorrow.

17. Pattern: sentences 20, 21 (note: refer to grammar, 4.1.)

    a. Then I shall get you the books tomorrow. I can go.

    b. Then I shall get the books for you tomorrow. I can go.

    c. Then I shall bring them for you tomorrow. I can go.

    d. Then I shall get you them tomorrow. I can go.

    e. Then I shall buy you them tomorrow. I can go.

18. Pattern: sentences 22, 14.

    a. In that case, I shall come back when I have finished my studying.

    b. In that case, I shall come home when I have finished my work.

    c. In that case, he will come when he has finished everything.

    d. In that case, they will come back when they have bought everything.

    e. In that case, I shall come back when I have bought the books.

Pattern: sentence 23.

    a. But I won't be able to stay here long.

    b. But I won't be able to stay with you long.

    c. But he won't be able to stay with you long.

    d. But they won't be able to stay long.

    e. But I won't be able to stay in the office long.

19 Pattern: sentence 24.

    a. That's all right. I have to give you a new sari.

    b. That's all right. I have to give you a new shawl.

    c. That's all right. I have to send* him some new books.

    d. That's all right. I have to show them some new things.

    e. That's all right. I have to tell you some good news.

Either /paṭhabar/ or /paṭhanor/ (which you will hear on the tape) is possible.

20. Pattern: general.

    a. Good. I like to get new saris.

    b. Good. I like to get new shawls.

    c. Good. He likes to get new books.

    d. Good. They like to see new things.

    e. Good. I like to hear good news.

21. Pattern: sentence 26.

    a. When you come back, bring Lila with you.

    b. When you come back, bring your daughters with you.

    c. When he comes back, he will bring his children with him.

    d. When they come back, they will bring Nira with them.

    e. When you come back, bring Sipra with you.

Pattern: sentence 27.

    a. She also has to get a sari.

    b. They also have to get new shawls.

    c. They also have to get new books.

    d. She also has to see the new things.

    e. She also has to hear the news.

Lesson 9, part 4. Sentence Drills.

Drill 1

--I must go home right away.

--Why do you have to go so soon? Do you have work there?

--Yes, a few things need to be done. When I finish my work, I shall come back.

--Good. When we have bathed and eaten, shall we take these things to Lila's house?

--Yes. I heard that she is sick.

--No, she fell on the ice this morning and broke her arm.

--Then let us bring her flowers and sweets. Then let's come back here and sleep a while.

--All right. After we have slept a while, we shall have to go to the market.

--All right. Shall I buy some fruit on my way home and bring it back?

--Yes, bring it back when you come. What else shall we bring to Lila?

--We'll buy some flowers on the way and give them to her.

--Good   Then I'll see you later.

Drill 2

--When will you go to Puri?

--Next week. I shall stay a week in Puri, and then return to Calcutta.

--Will you also go to Cattack [koṭok]?

--Yes, after I have seen the temple of Jagannath [jɔgonnath] in Puri, I shall go to Cuttack.

--There is a beautiful temple there also.

--Yes, I shall wander around Cuttack a day and then come back.

--Will you see the images?

--No, I shall not be able. I shall have to remain standing outside the temple walls.

--It will be a nice trip. What will you do after you have seen Puri and Cuttack?

--Then I shall return to Calcutta and sleep. Travelling makes me tired.

Lesson 9, part 5. Vocabulary.

misṭi	sweet (meats)	bæṛa-	wander around
murti	image	beṛie ja-	
bhromon	travelling, trip	snan kɔr-	bathe
bajar	market	can cɔr-	
bɔroph	ice	pɔṛ	fall
jiniś	thing (material goods)	poṛe ja-	
hat	hand, arm	bhaŋ-	break
ɔśukh	illness	dãṛa-	stand, wait
cãd	moon	ghuma-	sleep
kagoj	paper	(ghumie-PAP)	
deoal	wall	poũcha	arrive
lal	red	opor	on, over
nil	blue	karon	because
hɔlde	yello		
śobuj	green	ɔśukh kɔṛ	get sick (with genitive)
begune	violet	tar ɔśukh korlo	she/ne got sick
begne		bhalo kore	well
		bhalo kore śekho	learn (it) well

Analysis and Translation	Bengali
1. proper name (m.)	mɔnṭu মন্টু
"a little"	ekṭu একটু
"before, ago"	age আগে
"a little while ago"	ekṭu age একটু আগে

A. Montu, I called you on the phone a little while ago.

A. mɔnṭu ' tomake ekṭu age ' phone ḍaklam "

মন্টু , তোমাকে একটু আগে ফোনে ডাকলাম ।

A. Where were you?

A. tumi ' kothae chile "

তুমি কোথায় ছিলে ?

2. noun stem, "food"; see Grammar, 3.	khabar খাবার
PAP "eating, having eaten"	khee খেয়ে
"a little"	ekṭu একটু
high stem of verb /śo-/, "lie down"	śu- শু–
PAP "lying down, having lain down"	śue শুয়ে
to be (in a condition of) lying down	śue ach- শুয়ে আছ–

B. After I had eaten, I was lying down for a while.

B. ami khabar khee ' ekṭu śue chilam "

আমি খাবার খেয়ে একটু শুয়ে ছিলাম ।

"suddenly"   hɔṭhat হঠাৎ

PAP, "sleeping, having
slept"   ghumie   ঘুমিয়ে

high stem of verb /pɔɽ/,
"fall"   pɔɽ-   পড়-

"fall asleep"   ghumie pɔɽ-   ঘুমিয়ে পড়-

B. But suddenly I fell
asleep.   B. kintu hɔthat ' ghumie pɔɽlam "

                              কিন্তু হঠাৎ ঘুমিয়ে পড়লাম ।

3.   noun stem, "matter"   bæpar   ব্যাপার
      Note that the tense is understood by the context of the
      conversation.

A. What was the matter?   A. ki bæpar "

                                 কি ব্যাপার ?

      noun stem, "body"   śorir   শরীর
      idiom, "be feeling badly"   śorir kharap hɔ-   শরীর খারাপ হ-
      (with 3rd person verb)
      For /naki/, see Grammar,
      2.

A. Were you feeling badly?   A. tomar śorir ' kharap holo naki "

                                 তোমার শরীর খারাপ হলো নাকি ?

4.   demonstrative, "that"   ta   তা

B. No, it wasn't exactly   B. na ' thik ta nɔe "
that.
                                 না , ঠিক তা নয় ।

      "but"   tɔbe   তবে
      adjective, "whole,
      entire"   śara   সারা
      "the whole day"   śara din   সারা দিন
      adjective, "tired"   klanto   ক্লান্ত
      For the use of the verb /ach-/, see Grammar, 4.

B. But all day long I've been very tired.

B. tɔbe amɪ aɟ ' śara dɪn ' khub klanto achi "

তবে আমি আজ সারা দিন খুব ক্লান্ত আছি ।

5.   noun stem, "rest"   bissram   বিশ্রাম
   compound verb, "rest"   bissram kɔr-   বিশ্রাম কর−
                          bissram ne-   বিশ্রাম নে−

A. In that case, rest today.   A. ta hole ' aɟ bissram nao "

তা হলে , আজ বিশ্রাম নাও ।

   proper name (f.)   gita   গীতা

A. I'll come again tomorrow after seeing Gita.

A. ami gitake dekhe ' kal abar aśbo "

আমি গীতাকে দেখে কাল আবার আসবো ।

6.   "again, this time"   abar   আবার
   "what happened"   ki holo   কি হলো
   "what happened to Gita"   gitar ki holo   গীতার কি হলো

B. What happened to Gita this time?

B. gitar ' abar ki holo "

গীতার আবার কি হলো ?

7.   noun stem, "ice"   bɔroph   বরফ
   PAP, "falling, having fallen"   poɽe   পড়ে
   compound verb, "fall"   poɽe ɟa-   পড়ে যা−
   PAP of compound, "falling, having fallen"   pɔɽe gie   পড়ে গিয়ে
   noun stem, "hand, arm"   hat   হাত
   PAP of verb, /bhaŋ-/, "break"   bheŋe   ভেঙে
   to be (in a condition of) sitting   bośe ach-   বসে আছ−

A. She fell on the ice and broke her arm, and she is laid up.

A. śe ' boropher opor poṛe gie ' hat bhene ' bośe ache "

সে বরফের ওপর পড়ে গিয়ে হাত ভেঙে বসে আছে ।

8. idiom, "is that so?", an expression of concern

tai naki   তাই নাকি

B. Is that so? In that case, I'll go with you to see her and come back.

B. tai naki " ta hole ' ami tomar śonge gie ' take dekhe aśbo "

তাই নাকি ? তা হলে , আমি তোমার সঙ্গে গিয়ে তাকে দেখে আসবো ।

9. "decide"

ṭhik kɔr-   ঠিক কর-

conjunctive, "that"

je   যে

A. But I decided that I'll see her in the evening.

A. kintu ' ami ṭhik korlum je ' ami take ' śondhebæla ' dekhe aśbo "

কিন্তু আমি ঠিক করলুম যে আমি তাকে সন্ধ্যেবেলা দেখে আসবো ।

"then, at that time"   tɔkhon   তখন

PAP, "picking up, having picked up"   tule   তুলে

compound verb, "pick up a and take"   tule ne-   তুলে নে-

A. Shall I call you then and pick you up?

A. tɔkhon ' ami tomake ḍeke ' tule nebo ki "

তখন আমি তোমাকে ডেকে তুলে নেবো কি ?

10. noun stem, "car, cart"   gaṛi   গাড়ী

B. Will you take your car?

B. tumi ' tomar gaṛiṭa ' nie jabe ki "

তুমি তোমার গাড়ীটা নিয়ে যাবে কি ?

11. A. Yes, I'll take my car.

A. hæ̃ " ami ' amar gaṛiṭa ' nie jabo "

হাঁ , আমি আমার গাড়ীটা নিয়ে যাবো ।

12. B. Good. Then when you are going will you call and pick me up?

B. beś " ta hole ' jabar śɔmoe ' amake deke ' tule nebe ki "

বেশ । তা হলে যাবার·সময় আমাকে ডেকে তুলে নেবে কি ?

13. A. Yes. Shall I pick you up at seven o'clock?

A. hæ̃ " tomake śattar śɔmoe ' tule nebo ki "

হাঁ , তোমাকে সাতটার সময় তুলে নেবো কি ?

14. adjective, "ready, prepared"

"be (remain) ready"

toiri   তৈরী

toiri thak-   তৈরী থাক-

(a.)

B. All right. I shall be ready at seven o'clock.

B. beś " ami ' śattar śɔmoe ' toiri thakbo "

বেশ । আমি সাতটার সময় তৈরী থাকবো ।

(b.)

B. What time will you come back home?

B. tumi ' kɔtar śɔmoe ' baṛi phire aśbe

তুমি কটার সময় বাড়ী ফিরে আসবে ?

15. nine

nɔ, nɔe   ন , নয়

A. I'll come home at nine o'clock.

A. ami ' nɔtar śɔmoe ' baṛi phire aśbo "

আমি নটার সময় বাড়ী ফিরে আসবো ।

16. verb stem, "reach, arrive at"

PAP of stem /poŭcha-/; see Grammar, 1.

poŭcho-, poŭcha-   পৌঁছো-, পৌঁছা-

compound verb, "cause to reach"

poŭche de-   পৌঁছে দে-

For this use of /de-/, see Grammar, 5.

B. When you come back will you leave me at my house?

B. pherbar śɔmoe ' tumi amake ' barite poŭche debe ki "

ফেরবার সময় তুমি আমাকে বাড়াতে পৌঁছে দেবে কি ?

17. <u>A</u>. <u>Yes, I shall.</u>

A. hæ̃ ' dobo "

হাঁ, দোবো ।

18. PAP of verb /ken-/,
"buying, having bought"

    kine   কিনে

compound verb, "buy and
bring"

    kine an-   কিনে আন—

imperative form of stem
/an-/

    eno   এনো

<u>B</u>. <u>Look, when you come,</u>
<u>bring some flowers.</u>

B. dækho ' aśbar śɔmoe ' kichu phul '
kine eno "

দেখ , আসবার সময় কিছু ফুল কিনে এনো ।

19. <u>A</u>. <u>For whom?</u>

A. kar jonne "

কার জন্যে ?

20. For this use of the future, see Lesson 2.

<u>B</u>. <u>I want to bring Gita</u>
<u>flowérs.</u>

B. ami gitar jonne ' phulgulo ' nie
jabo "

আমি গীতার জন্যে ফুলগুলো নিয়ে
যাবো ।

21. <u>A</u>. <u>All right. Then when</u>
<u>I come, I shall bring</u>
<u>some flowers.</u>

A. accha " ta hole ' aśbar śɔmoe ' ami
kichu phul ' kine anbo "

আচ্ছা । তা হলে আসবার সময় আমি কিছু
ফুল কিনে আনবো ।

22. "afterwards, later"

    pɔre   পরে

<u>B</u>. <u>Good. Then I'll see you</u>
<u>later.</u>

B. beś " ta hole ' pɔre dækha hɔbe "

বেশ । তা হলে পরে দেখা হবে ।

23. <u>A</u>. <u>OK. See you later.</u>

A. accha " dækha korbo "

আচ্ছা , দেখা করবো ।

Lesson 10, part 2. Grammar.

1. The stem /poūcha-/ has alternative forms in the PAP, namely /poūche/ (as in sentence 16) and /poūchie/.

2. The particle /naki/.

A Bengali speaker will use the particle /naki/ to express surprise or consternation at the unexpectedness of an action that is taking place, has taken place, or will take place. There is a contrast with the simple interrogative particle /ki/:

tumi jaccho ki'	Are you going?
tumi jaccho naki"	Are you going? (i.e., I am surprised or disturbed that you are going.)

Note also the difference in intonation.

3. The form /khabar/.

The verbal noun of the stem /kha-/, "eat", is formed with the suffix /-ba/; as in sentence 2, however, there is another form /khabar/, a noun meaning "food".

4. The form /achi/, sentence 4.

In Bengali, the expression of actions or conditions originated in the past but continuing in the present necessitates a present form of the verb, even though a translation in the English present tense might not make sense. So it is in sentence 4. In this case, tiredness is a condition which originated at an earlier time, but which is still existent.

A fragment question a foreigner in Bengal will hear is:

apni'kɔto din achen"	How long have you been here?

5. The use of /de-/, sentence 16.

The use of /de-/ as an "auxilliary" in Bengali is very complex. First of all, as in this lesson, there is the sense of giving assistance to someone in doing something. Thus, using sentence 16 as an example,

tumi'baɽite poūchobe ki"	Will you reach the house?
tumi amake'baɽite poūche dɔbe ki"	Will you help me reach my house? or Will you get me to my house?

Another example:

      ami'eṭa korbo"   I shall do it.

      ami'eṭa kore debo"   I shall do it (for him, you, etc.).

There are other usages, which we shall deal with later on.

6.   The nominative form of the word "someone, anyone" is /keu/; the stem is /kau-/ before the objective suffix -ke. Thus:

      kauke'die aśbo"   I shall come and give (it) to anyone.

6.1. The negative of this formation is /kauke ... na/:

      kauke'die aśbo na"   I shall not come and give (it) to anyone, or

                                  I shall come and give it to no one.

7.   The use of the morphemes /śɔmoe/, /-khon/, and /-bar/, indicating ‡ime.

7.1. /ɔnek śɔmoe/ -- many times, much time continuously spent

      /ekṭu śɔmoe/ -- a little time, continuously spent

7.2. /ɔnek-bar/   -- many times, separated by intervals

      /kɔek-bar/   -- a few times, separated by intervals

7.3. /ɔnekkhon/   -- quite a while, quite some time (in terms of hours)

      /ekṭukkhon/ -- a little while (in terms of hours)

8. Form possible Bengali sentences:

Subj.	Clause I			Clause II	
	Obj./VM	Verb$_1$	Obj./VM	Verb$_2$	
ami	khabar	khee	tomake	ḍak-	
tumi	take	dekhe	eṭa	pher-	
tomra	śekhane	poṛe	boiṭa	phire ja-	
tara	tomar	gie		phire aś-	
	śɔnge	eśe		dekh-	
	eṭa	nie		dekhe aś-	
	tomake	ḍeke		dekhe ja-	
				ne-	
				nie aś-	
				nie ja-	
				tol-	
			Verb$_2$	tule ne-	
			de-	poũcho-, poũcha	
			die aś-	pouche de-	
			die ja-	ken-	
				kine an-	
				kine de-	
				kine nie aś-	

Lesson 10, part 3. Patterns.

1. Pattern: sentence 1.

   a. I sent you a letter a while ago. Did you receive it?
   b. I sent Robi some books a while ago. Did he receive them?
   c. I called Robi on the phone a while ago. Where was he?
   d. I saw him on the street a while ago. Where were you?
   e. I saw them in the library last night. Where were you?

2. Pattern: sentence 2.

   a. After I read it, I gave it to Das.
   b. After he got them, he put them on a table.
   c. After he had eaten, he lay down for a while.
   d. After I had studied, I lay down for a while.
   e. After I had finished my work, I lay down for a while.

a. After that, I didn't see it. (use simple past)
b. After that, I didn't see them. (use simple past)
c. After that, he fell asleep.
d. But for a long time, I didn't fall asleep. (use simple past)
e. And suddenly I fell asleep.

3. Pattern: sentence 3 (use simple past).

a. What was the matter? Didn't you show it to Gita?
b. What was the matter? Did you fall asleep?
c. What was the matter? Was he very tired?
d. What was the matter? Weren't you well?
e. What was the matter? Are you well?

4. Pattern: sentence 4.

a. No. She was very tired all day. She fell asleep.
b. Yes. All day long I was very tired. So I fell asleep.
c. Yes. All week long he's been very tired. He fell asleep.
d. Yes, but I was very tired. Sleeping was not possible.
e. Yes, but I'm a little tired. So suddenly I fell asleep.

5. Pattern: sentence 5, Lesson 9.

a. Then tell her that it's necessary that she rest today.
b. Then it's necessary that you rest today.
c. Then it's necessary that he rest today.
d. Then it's necessary that you rest this week.
e. Then it's necessary that you rest now.

a. I'll come back after seeing Ram.
b. Come back after resting.
c. Will he come back tomorrow, after resting?
d. Come back next week, after resting.
e. Rest now and come back tomorrow.

6. Pattern: sentence 6.

a. What happened to Ram?
b. What happened to Ram yesterday?
c. Yes. What will happen to him tomorrow?
d. What will happen next week?
e. All right. What will happen tomorrow?

7.   Pattern: sentence 7.

    a.   He fell from a tree and broke his arm.
    b.   He fell from a tree and broke his leg.
    c.   He will go to the library and study.
    d.   You will come to my house and study.
    e.   You will come to my house and eat.

8.   Pattern: sentence 8 (use verbal noun where possible).

    a.   Is that so? In that case, I will go with you to see him and come back.
    b.   Is that so? In that case, I will go with you to see him now.
    c.   Is that so? In that case, it will be difficult to see him tomorrow.
    d.   Is that so? In that case, it will be difficult to rest this week.
    e.   Is that so? In that case, it will be necessary to work now.

9.   Pattern: sentence 9.

    a.   I decided that I'll see him tomorrow morning.
    b.   I decided that I'll see him afterwards.
    c.   I decided that it's necessary for us to see him now.
    d.   I decided that it's necessary for you to rest this week.
    e.   I decided that it's necessary for you to rest now.

    a.   Shall I call you tomorrow morning and pick you up?
    b.   Shall I call you and take you there?
    c.   Shall I call him now and take you there?
    d.   Shall I call you next week and pick you up?
    e.   Shall I call you tomorrow and bring you here?

10.   Pattern: sentence 10.

    a.   Will you take your car tomorrow?
    b.   Will it be possible to take your car afterwards?
    c.   Will it be difficult for you to take your car now?
    d.   Will it be possible for you to take your car next week?
    e.   Will it be possible for you to take your car tomorrow?

11.   Pattern: sentence 12.

    a.   Yes. When I am going, I shall call you and pick you up.
    b.   Yes. When I reach home, I shall call you and pick you up.

c. No. When I reach home, I shall take my car and pick you up.
d. Yes. When I call you, I shall come and pick you up.
e. Yes. When you call me, I shall come and pick you up.

12. Pattern: sentence 13.

a. Will you pick me up at eight?
b. What time will you pick me up?
c. What time will you call me and pick me up?
d. What time will you come and pick me up?
e. Will you pick me up at nine sharp (i.e., "exactly nine")?

13. Pattern: sentence 14 (a).

a. Will you be ready at eight?
b. What time will you be ready?
c. Will you be ready at nine?
d. Will you be ready at ten?
e. Will you be ready before nine?

14. Pattern: sentence 14 (b).

a. Yes. Will it be possible to come home at ten sharp?
b. At six. Will you come home before nine?
c. Yes. It will be difficult to be ready before nine.
d. Yes. It will be impossible to be ready before ten.
e. Yes. It will be possible to be ready at eight.

15. Pattern: sentence 15.

a. Yes. We shall come back at ten.
b. Yes. We shall come back before nine.
c. All right. We shall come back home before ten.
d. All right. We shall come back home before eleven.
e. All right. We shall come back at nine.

Pattern: sentence 16.

a. When we come back, I shall leave you at your house.
b. On the way back we shall leave Ram at his house.
c. On the way back I shall leave you at Ram's house.
d. After coming back, I shall leave Ram at your house.
e. After leaving you, I shall leave Ram at his house.

16. Pattern: sentence 18.

    a. When you come, will you bring some flowers?
    b. When we go, shall we take some sweets?
    c. When I go to Ram's house, shall I take some flowers?
    d. When Ram comes, will he bring* some new books?
    e. When you go, will you take some things for Ram?

    Pattern: sentence 20.

    a. I want to bring Gita some flowers.
    b. I want to bring her some sweets.
    c. I want to bring him some flowers.
    d. He wants to bring me new books.
    e. I want to give Ram some new things.

17. Pattern: sentence 21.

    a. All right. When I come, I shall bring some flowers from the store.
    b. All right. When I come, I shall bring some sweets for you.
    c. All right. When we go, we shall take him some flowers.
    d. Yes. When he comes, he will bring you some new books from the store.
    e. Yes. When I go, I shall take the new things for him.

Lesson 10, part 4. Drills.

Drill 1

--Did you call me on the phone a while ago? I fell asleep.

--But what's the matter? Don't you feel well, or do you always sleep in the middle of the day?

--I don't exactly know. I've been feeling tired all week long. But let that go. What time is it?

--Almost half-past four. Are you going to class today?

--Yes. Look, will you do me a favor? When you are ready, will you pick me up? It's impossible for me to walk.

--Of course. I'll bring my car and pick you up in (i.e., "within"--use either /bhetore/ or the locative case) half an hour.

--There is one other matter. Will you buy the new books at the store and bring them to me when you come?

--That won't be possible for me. I won't go to the store today.

---

* "buy and bring"

--It doesn't matter. Will it be possible for you to leave me back here before half-past seven?

--Why? What will happen at half-past seven?

--Robi is coming. It is necessary for me to buy and cook the food before half-past eight.

--All right. I shall drop you back here by (i.e., "within") half-past seven.

Drill 2

--Will you come to the museum with me today? I'll go at about three-thirty.

--Yes, I'll certainly come. There's a Jamini Roy exhibition (i.e., "an exhibition of Jamini Roy's work"), isn't there?

--Yes. Ila likes his work very much. I told her that I would take her.

--Good. Will you take your car?

--Yes. I'll call you before I pick you up.

--Do you know Jamini Roy?

--Yes. I go to his house often. He is a wonderful man and a wonderful painter.

--People say that he is a truly Bengali painter. Is that so?

--I think so. Other painters copy European work or the work of the Mogul school. Jamini Roy copies no one.

--I hear that he paints in the manner of Bengali folk artists. Is that true?

--That's not exactly true. His colors and his forms are like Bengali folk art. But he is not a folk artist.

--How would you describe him, then?

--It is impossible to describe him. That is why he is a great artist.

Lesson 10, part 5. Vocabulary.

khabar	food	iuropio	European (adj.)
śilpo, kɔla	art	bharotio	Indian (adj.)
āka (verbal noun)	painting	cɔmotkar	wonderful
		aśol	true, genuine
śilpi	painter, artist	śotti	true
loko-śilpi	folk artist	niścoi	certainly
dhɔron	form (as in painting)	mɔto, mɔton	like, similar
		agami	next, approaching
mogol	Mogul		
ciṭhi	letter		
pa	leg, foot		

rakh-	keep, put, place	majhe, moddhe	in the middle
āk-	paint	śaṛe	half-pas
bɔrnona kɔr-	describe	śaṛe carṭe / śaṛe carṭa	half-past four
nɔkol kɔr-	copy	adn	half
ranna kɔr-	cook		
kɔtha bɔl-	converse	adh ghɔnṭa	half an hour
dækha-	show		

Idioms:

ækebare	at all
kɔṭa baje	what time is it?
tai na	isn't that so?
tai naki	is that so?
jak	
ta jete	let it go
ta chaṛo	
ar ækṭa	one more, another
tate khoti nei	there's no harm in that, that doesn't matter

Lesson 11, part 1. Conversation.

Analysis and translation	Bengali

1. "noun, "crowd"   bhir̪ ভীড়

    "crowd of people"   loker bhir̪ লোকের ভীড়

A. <u>There is a crowd of people over there.</u>   A. <u>okhane ' loker bhir̪ "</u>

          ওখানে লোকের ভীড় ।

2. high stem of verb
"be, become"   ho- হ-

    continuative suffix for
vowel stems; see Grammar, 2.   -cch- -চ্ছ-

    3rd person present
verbal ending   -e -ে

    "it is becoming"   hocche হচ্ছে

B. <u>What is happening?</u>   B. <u>ki hocche "</u>

          কি হচ্ছে ?

3. "perhaps"   bodhɔe বোধ হয়

    noun, "game"   khæla খেলা

A. <u>I don't know. Perhaps there is some game going on.</u>   A. <u>ami jani na " bodhɔe ' kono khæla hocche "</u>

          আমি জানি না । বোধ হয় কোন৹ খেলা
          হচ্ছে ।

4. **B.** <u>Will you go over and see what is happening?</u>   **B.** <u>tumi ki ' gie dekhbe ' ki hocche "</u>

তুমি কি গিয়ে দেখবে কি হচ্ছে ?

5. idiom, "think"   mone hɔ-   মনে হ-

"mutual striking"; see Grammar, 7.   maramari   মারামারি

verb, "fight" (i.e., physical combat)   maramari kɔr-   মারামারি কর-

high stem of verb "do, make"   kor-   কর-

continuative suffix for consonant stems   -ch-   -হ-

3rd person present verbal ending   -e   -ে

"(they) are fighting"   (tara) maramari korche

(তারা) মারামারি করছে

A. <u>I think that people are fighting.</u>   **A.** <u>amar mone hocche je ' lokera ' maramari korche "</u>

আমার মনে হচ্ছে যে লোকেরা মারামারি করছে ।

6. loan word, "riot"   raot   রায়ট

"beginning"   śuru   শুরু

compound verb, "be begun"   śuru hɔ-   শুরু হ-

B. <u>Do you think a riot is beginning?</u>   **B.** <u>tomar ki mone hocche je ' ækta raot ' śuru hocche "</u>

তোমার কি মনে হচ্ছে যে একটা রায়ট শুরু হচ্ছে?

7. verb stem, "flee"   pala-   পালা-

Note: for this use of the future, see Grammar, 5.

A. <u>No, if that were so, people would be fleeing.</u>   **A.** <u>na " ta hole ' lokera palabe "</u>

না , তা হলে লোকেরা পালাবে ।

noun, "crowd"   bhiṛ   ভীড়

verb, "form a crowd"   bhiṛ kɔr-   ভীড় কর-

A. <u>They wouldn't form a crowd.</u>

A. bhiṛ ' korbe na "

ভীড় করবে না ।

8. B. <u>Then who are fighting?</u>

B. ta hole ' kara ' maramari korche "

তা হলে কারা মারামারি করছে ?

9. noun, "fight" (either physical or verbal conflict)

verb, "fight"

lɔṛai   লড়াই

lɔṛai kɔr-   লড়াই কর-

A. <u>I think that little boys are fighting.</u>

A. amar mone hɔe je ' choṭo chelera ' lɔṛai korche "

আমার মনে হয় যে ছোট ছেলেরা লড়াই করছে ।

present imperative,"move"; idiomatic, "let's go"

1st person present imperative, "let's see"

cɔlo   চলো

dekhi   দেখি

A. <u>Come on, let's go see.</u>

A. cɔlo dekhi

চলো   দেখি ।

10. noun, "snake"

noun, "game"

"snake charmer's performance"

śap   সাপ

khæla   খেলা

śap khæla   সাপ খেলা

B. <u>No, I think that there's a snake charmer's performance going on.</u>

B. na " amar mone hɔe je ' śap khæla hocche "

না , আমার মনে হয় যে সাপ খেলা হচ্ছে ।

noun, "fear"

verb, "be afraid of, fear"

bhɔe   ভয়

bhɔe kɔr-   ভয় কর-

B. <u>I am afraid of snakes.</u>

B. ami śapke ' bhɔe kori "

আমি সাপকে ভয় করি ।

11.   "both"   dujon দুজন

For the /-e/ suffix, see Grammar, 6.

A. <u>All right, come on.</u>   A. accha cɔlo " dujone gie dekhi '
<u>Let's both go see</u>   ki hocche "
<u>what's happening.</u>

                                        আচ্ছা , চলো ৷ দুজনে গিয়ে দেখি
                                        কি হচ্ছে ৷

12. B. <u>No, I won't go. You go.</u>   <u>na</u> " ami jabo na " tumi jao "

                                          না , আমি যাবো না ৷ তুমি যাও ৷

13. A. <u>Why won't you go?</u>   A. kæno jabe na "

                                          কেন যাবে না

14.   high stem of verb, "see"   dekh-   দেখ-
    present continuative suf-
    fix for consonant stems   -ch-   -ছ-
    1st person present
    verbal ending   -i   -ি
    noun, "bull"   śãɽ ষাঁড

B. <u>I can see now that bulls</u>   B. ami ækhon dekhchi je ' śãɽer lɔɽai
<u>are fighting</u> (i.e., that   hocche "
<u>a bull-fight is happening).</u>

                                        আমি এখন দেখছি যে ষাঁড়ের লড়াই হচ্ছে ৷

B. <u>People are running away.</u>   B. lokera palacche

                                        লোকেরা পালাচ্ছে ৷

15. A. <u>In that case, move.</u>   A. ta hole ' cɔlo " amra o palai "
<u>Let's run too.</u>

                                        তা হলে , চলো ৷ আমরাও পালাই ৷

<u>Lesson 11, part 2. Grammar.</u>

Note that from this lesson on, there will be no mutation drills given on
the tapes. The reason for this is that by this time the student has at
his command a variety of correct ways to express a thought; the usage of
one or another form is a matter of style. All of these alternatives
cannot be given on the tape. It is expected, however, that the instructor

will continue the mutation drills in class, where allowance can be made for the student's style.

1. The use of the present continuative, as in sentences 1 ff.

1.1. The primary use of the present continuative (sometimes termed present imperfect) is indication of an action that is taking place at the time of speaking, that an action begun in the past is not completed. Bengali often uses this emphasis on continuity where English, for example, ؛ content with a simple present. A frequent Bengali phrasing is:

ami bujchi"   I understand (i.e., I am understanding)
                                     what you are saying.

1.2. Further, Bengali frequently uses the present continuative if the action is going on in the present, even if that action was originated in the distant past:

hajar bochor dhore'śãotalera ' ekháne baś korche"
Santals have been living (i.e., "are living") here for 1000 years.

1.3. A less frequent but still common usage of the present continuative is expression of action that is to take place in the immediate future. An exchange might be:

ekhane eśo'   Come here!
accha"ami aśchi"   All right, I am coming.

2. The formation of the present continuative:

2.1. The present continuative of consonant-final verb stems is formed by the high stem (except for /a/ stems) of the verb plus the suffix /-ch-/, plus the present tense personal endings. Thus:

śon	"hear"	ami śun-ch-i
		tumi śun-ch-o
		tui śun-ch-is
		apni śun-ch-en
		śe śun-ch-e
		tini śun-ch-en
khæl-	"play"	ami khel-ch-i, etc.
kɔr-	"do"	ami kor-ch-i, etc.

2.2. Consonant stems with the /a/-vowel retain their low stems, thus:

>   jan-   "know"   ami jan-ch-i, etc.

2.3. Stems with vowel final follow the same pattern: /a/-stems retain their low stem form, others take their high-stems. However, all stems of CV-shape double the /ch/ affix, thus: /-cch-/.

>   de-   "give"   ami di-cch-i, etc.
>
>   kha-   "eat"   ami kha-cch-i, etc.
>
>   hɔ-   "be,   ami ho-cch-i, etc.
>   become"

2.3.1. Stems of CVV-shape do not double the /ch/ affix:

>   ga-/gai-   "sing"   ami gai-ch-i, etc.

3. Review of formation and use of the verbal noun.

3.1. Verbal nouns of consonant-stem verbs are formed by the addition of the suffixes; /-a/ or /-ba/ to the low stem of the verb. Verbal nouns of vowel-stem verbs are formed by addition of the suffixes /-oa/ or /-ba/ to the low stem of the verb, thus:

>   de-   deoa or deba-
>   pa-   paoa or paba-
>   hɔ   hɔoa or hɔba-

3.2. The suffixes /-a/ or /-oa/ are usual when the noun is in the nominative, objective, or locative cases; the suffix /-ba-/ occurs only when the noun is in the genitive, being freely variant with /-a/ or /oa/.

3.3. Constructions with the verbal noun are very common in Bengali. For example:

Nominative:	khæla hocche"	Playing is going on.
	tar aśa'holo na"	of him coming was not (He did not come.)
Genitive:	tar aśbar / aśar śomoe'briśṭi holo"	It was raining when ne came.

234

| Objective: (rare) | baŋlae pan kɔrake' jɔl khaoa bɔle" | In Bengali, "drinking water" is called "jɔl khaoa". |
| Locative: | e kɔtha bɔlate' amra cole gelum" | On being told this, we went away. |

4. The form /maramari/ (sentences 5 ff.):

4.1. This type of reduplicated formation is frequent in Bengali, and in fact in many modern languages of India. The significance is often mutual action of some type. For example:

kaṛakaṛi	mutual snatching
laṭhalaṭhi	mutual fighting with sticks
gūtogūti	mutual pushing aside with elbows

4.2. The first vowel of the reduplicated portion of the expression (except where /a/), is the high vowel, due to the presence of the final high vowel -i.

5. Uses of the future tense, as in sentence 7.

5.1. It is not infrequent in Bengali to use the simple future to express the English conditional, as here. Another example might be:

tumi śekhane'kæno jabe"   Why should you go there?

5.2. In sentence 7, the conditional aspect of the sentence is stated in the first clause, "if that were so".

6. Use of the locative, as in sentence 11

6.1. The locative case form is frequently used in nominative constructions to indicate mutual action or reciprocity.

7. Note that sentences 9 and 14 suggest the transitive-intransitive equivalence which we have seen before. Note the distinction between:

śāṛ'lɔṛai korche"   bulls are fighting

and

śāṛer'lɔṛai hocche'   bulls are fighting (i.e., a fight of bulls is happening) or between

     chelera'loɽai korche"   boys are fighting

and

     cheleder'loɽai hocche"   boys are fighting (lit., a fight of boys is happening

7.1. The contrast is clearest in cases in which there is no case inflection. For example:

     oṭa'śuru hocche   It is beginning. (intransitive)

and

     oṭa'śuru korche"   He is beginning it. (transitive)

Lesson 11, part 3. Patterns.

Note: from this lesson on, only the first two patterns will be heard on the tape.

1. Pattern: sentences 1, 2, Grammar, 6.

    a. What is happening in that crowd of people?
    b. What are those people doing?
    c. What is he doing in that crowd of people?
    d. Are you listening to the story?
    e. Are you looking at the crowd of people?

2. Pattern: sentence 3, Grammar, 6.

    a. Perhaps there is a riot going on.
    b. Perhaps a riot is beginning.
    c. Perhaps he is starting a riot.
    d. No, I am looking at this book.
    e. No, I am listening to his reading of poetry.

3. Pattern: sentence 4.

    a. Shall we go and see what is happening?
    b. Shall we go and see what they are doing?
    c. Shall we go and listen to what he is saying?
    d. Shall we go and listen to his reading?
    e. Shall we go and see what the crowd is doing?

4.   Pattern: sentence 5.

    a. No. I think that **they are fighting.**

    b. No. I think that they are only shouting.

    c. No. I think that he is saying nothing.

    d. No. I think that I shall sit here and read.

    e. No. I think that I shall remain here and listen.

5.   Pattern: sentence 6.

    a. Do you think that some trouble is beginning?

    b. Do you think that a fight is starting?

    c. Do you think that he is starting a riot?

    d. What are you reading now?

    e. What poem is he reading now?

6.   Pattern: sentence 7.

    a. No. If that were so, everyone would be **running away.**

    b. No. If that were so, people would not be staying there.

    c. No. If that were so, everyone would be shouting.

    d. I am reading a new novel by Buddhadev ([buddhodeb]).

    e. He is reading some poems by Jibananda Das ([jibanondo das]).

7.   Pattern: sentence 8.

    a. Then what do you think is going on?

    b. Then do you think that people are fighting?

    c. Then why do you think the crowd is forming?

    d. Is Buddhadev writing another novel now?

    e. Which poems of Jibananda is he reading?

8.   a. I think that some boys are fighting.

    b. Yes, perhaps people are fighting.

    c. I think that boys are fighting; that is why the **crowd is forming.**

    d. Yes. I think that he is writing a new novel.

    e. I don't know. I am not hearing it very well.

9.   Pattern: sentence 10.

    a. Let's go see. Perhaps a snake-charmer's performance is going on.

    b. Let's go see. Perhaps there is a football game going on.

    c. Let's go see. Perhaps he is beginning a snake-performance.

    d. I see. How is that novel striking you? (use /lag-/.)

    e. Why? Are the people shouting too loudly?

10. Pattern: sentence 10.

    a. I'm not going. I'm afraid of snakes.

    b. I'm not going. I don't like football.

    c. I'm not going. I don't like snake-performances.

    d. I like it very much. He writes well.

    e. Yes. Also he is reading very softly (/cup kore/).

11. Pattern: sentence 11.

    a. Come on; let's both go and see the snake-performance.

    b. Come on; let's both go and watch the football game.

    c. Come on; let's both go and see the snake.

    d. Yes. He writes simple but very strong Bengali.

    e. Yes. It's difficult to hear. Let's go sit near him.

12. Pattern: sentence 14.

    a. No. Now I see that some boys are fighting.

    b. No. Now I see that a snake and a mongoose are fighting.

    c. No. Now I see that the snake-performance is ending.

    d. Yes. He is becoming very famous.

    e. Yes, let's go. Let's sit in front of him and listen.

13. Pattern: sentence 14.

    a. Yes. And people are becoming tired of it.

    b. Yes, and little boys are fleeing.

    c. Yes, and people are going home.

    d. These days he is writing only in colloquial Bengali ([colit bhaśal]), is he not?

    e. Yes. But now he is finishing his reading.

14. Pattern: sentence 15.

    a. In that case, let's not go.

---

* either /śap-neuler loɽai/ or /śaper ar neuler loɽai/.

b. In that case, let's go and see.

c. In that case, let's go home too.

d. Yes. He is certainly not writing literary Bengali (ĺṣạdhu bhaśạ]).

e. Yes. It is being finished. Let's go home.

Lesson 11, part 4. Sentence Drill.

Drill 1

--What are those people doing over there?

--I don't know. Let's go see.

--No, there is a lot of elbowing going on in that crowd.

--All right, then, get up on that wall and look.

--I can see now (i.e., I am seeing now).

--What is going on?

--A snake and a mongoose are fighting.

--Who is winning?

--The mongoose always wins.

--Come on, let's look.*

--No, I am afraid of snakes. Before I came to Calcutta a snake bit me.

--There is a magician there too. He is doing tricks.

--What kind of tricks is he doing?

--He is walking bare-foot (i.e., in bare feet) on a fire.

--Why is he doing that?

--Because people are giving him money.

--It's finishing now. The people are coming away (i.e., returning back).

--All right, then, let's go home. I am getting hungry.

Drill 2 When in doubt, use present continuative.

--How are you getting on?

--Fine.

--Are you studying Bengali?

--Yes, I am studying the language and the literature.

--How do you like it?

--I like it very much. But it is becoming more difficult.

--Are you studying tonight?

--No, I don't think that I will study tonight. It is getting very hot.

---

* an idiomatic possibility is /dækha jak/.

--Good. Then come to the movies with me.
--All right. When are you going?
--Right now. Come on.
--All right, I'll get (i.e., take) my coat, and be right back.

Lesson 11, part 5. Vocabulary.

jadukɔr	magician	jet-	win, conquer
jadu	trick	kamṛa	bite
pa	foot	citkar kɔr-	shout
agun	fire		
śahitto	literature	bikkhæto	famous
sinema	cinema	joralo	strong
golmal	trouble, hubbub	aste	slowly, softly
		aro	more, even more
		khali	empty, bare
		jore	loud, loudly
		cup kore	quietly, softly

Idioms:

kæmon colche	how is it going (with you), how are you getting on?
kono rɔkome colche	so-so, somehow or other it's going
gɔrom porche	it is getting hot - lit. "heat is falling"
ṭaka pɔeśa	money - lit. "rupees and lesser coins"
khide pa-	to get hungry

Lesson 12, part 1. Conversation.

	Analysis and translation	Bengali
1.	verb stem, "go"	ja- যা—
	continuative suffix with vowel stems	-cch- -চ্ছ—
	2nd person present ending	-o -ে া
	"(you) are going"	jaccho যাচ্ছ
	A. Where are you going?	A. tumi ' kothae jaccho "
		তুমি কোথায় যাচ্ছ ?
2.	proper name (Muslim)	rahim রহিম
	B. I am going to Rahim's house.	B. ami ' rohimer barite ' jacchi "
		আমি রাহিমের বাড়ীতে যাচ্ছি।
3.	A. What is happening there?	A. śekhane ' ki hocche "
		সেখানে কি হচ্ছে?
4.	noun, "birth"	jɔnmo জন্ম
	noun, "day"	din দিন
	compound noun, "birthday"	jɔnmodin জন্মদিন
	noun, "celebration"	utśɔb উৎসব
	"birthday celebration"	jɔnmodine utśɔb জন্মদিনে উৎসব

B. Rahim's son's birthday celebration is going on.

B. rohimer cheler ' jɔnmodine utɔ́ɔb ' hocche "

রহিমের ছেলের জন্মদিনে উৎসব হচ্ছে।

5.　"who"

pluralizing reduplication, "who (all)"

ke　কে

ke ke　কে কে

A. Who (all) are coming there?

A. śekhane ' ke ke aśche "

সেখানে কে কে আসছে ?

6. B. I don't know exactly. But aren't you coming?

B. ami ' thik jani na " tɔbe ' tumi ki aśchɔ na "

আমি ঠিক জানি না । তবে তুমি কি আসছো না ?

7. A. Yes, I'm also going.

A. hæ̃ " ami.o jacchi "

হাঁ , আমিও যাচ্ছি।

8.　noun, "present"

upohar　উপহার

B. Are you taking any present for him?

B. tumi ki ' tar jonne ' kono upohar ' niccho "

তুমি কি তার জন্যে কোন উপহার নিচ্ছো ?

Note: this formation, using /ache/, indicates that the present was bought some time ago, that it has been in existence for some time.

B. I have a present for him.

B. tar jonne ' amar ækṭa upohar ' ache "

তার জন্যে আমার একটা উপহার আছে ।

9.　"now"

ækhon　এখন

emphatic suffix

-o　-ে া

"even now, up until now"

ækhono　এখনো

negative past tense particle; see Grammar, 2.

ni　নি

A. As of now I have bought no present for him.

A. ami ' tar jonne ' ækhono ' kono ⏝ ar kini ni "

আমি তার জন্যে এখনো কোন উপহার কিনি নি ।

A. But before going, I am going to buy a present.

A. tɔbe jabar age ' ækṭa upohar kinchi "

তবে যাবার আগে একটা উপহার কিনছি ।

10. B. What present are you taking?

B. ki upohar niccho "

কি উপহার নিচ্ছো ?

11. noun, "story"

gɔlpo গল্প

A. I am taking a story-book.

A. ækṭa gɔlper boi ' nicchi "

একটা গল্পের বই নিচ্ছি ।

12. /je ... tar .../, see Grammar, 3.
/-khana/, qualifying suffix; see Review II, 3.2.

B. What is the name of the book which you are bringing?

B. je boikhana niccho ' tar nam ki "

যে বইখানা নিচ্ছো তার নাম কি ?

13. A. The book's name is Deśe-bideśe.

A. boitar nam ' deśe-bideśe "

বইটার নাম দেশে-বিদেশে ।

14. Present completive tense, "you have read", see Grammar, 1.

porecho পড়েছো

B. Have you read the book?

B. tumi ki ' boikhana porecho

তুমি কি বইখানা পড়েছো ?

15. negative particle, indicating past time; see Grammar, 2.

ni নি

A. No, I haven't read it.　　A. na ' poṛi ni "

না , পড়ি নি ।

present completive tense,　śunechi　শুনেছি
"I have heard"; see
Grammar, 1.

A. But I have heard that　A. tɔbe ' śunechi je ' boiṭa khub bhalo "
the book is very good.

তবে শুনেছি যে বইটা খুব ভাল ।

16.　present completive tense,　boleche　বলেছে
"he has said"; see Grammar,
1.

B. Who has said (so)?　　B. ke boleche "

কে বলেছে ?

17. A. My brother has said (so).　A. amar bhai ' boleche "

আমার ভাই বলেছে ।

A. He has read the book.　A. śe ' boiṭa poṛeche "

সে বইটা পড়েছে ।

18.　/ja ... ta .../, see Grammar, 3.
"true"　　　　　　　śotti　সত্যি

B. What he said is true.　B. ja śe boleche ' ta śotti "

যা সে বলেছে তা সত্যি ।

19. A. What present are you　A. tumi ' upohar niccho "
taking?

তুমি কি উপহার নিচ্ছ ?

20.　noun, "bird"　　　pakhi　পাখী

B. I am going to take a　B. ami ækṭa pakhi ' nie jacchi "
bird.

আমি একটা পাখী নিয়ে যাচ্ছি ।

21. noun, "color"   rɔŋ   রং

   A. <u>What color is the bird which you are taking?</u>   A. <u>je pakhiṭa ' tumi niccho ' tar rɔŋ ki "</u>

   যে পাখীটা তুমি নিচ্ছো তার রং কি ?

22. "green" (see Grammar, 4.)   śobuj   সবুজ
   noun, "parrot"   ṭiapakhi   টিয়াপাখী

   B. <u>The bird is green. It's a parrot.</u>   B. <u>pakhiṭa śobuj " oṭa ' ækṭa ṭiapakhi "</u>

   পাখীটা সবুজ । ওটা একটা টিয়াপাখী ।

23. "wonderful"   cɔmotkar   চমৎকার

   A. <u>A green colored bird! Wonderful!</u>   A. <u>ækṭa śobuj rɔŋer pakhi " cɔmotkar "</u>

   একটা সবুজ রংয়ের পাখী । চমৎকার ।

   noun, "word, story"   kɔtha   কথা
   compound verb, "talk, converse"   kɔtha bɔl-   কথা বল—

   A. <u>The parrot talks, doesn't it?</u>   A. <u>ṭiapakhiṭa ' kɔtha bɔle naki "</u>

   টিয়াপাখীটা কথা বলে নাকি ?

24. B. <u>Yes, he talks a little.</u>   B. <u>hæ̃ ' ekṭu ekṭu kɔtha bɔle "</u>

   হাঁ , একটু একটু কথা বলে ।

25. A. <u>What does he say?</u>   A. <u>ki kɔtha bɔle "</u>

   কি কথা বলে ?

26. B. <u>He only says, "Give food!"</u>   B. <u>kebol bɔle ' khabar dao "</u>

   কেবল বলে , খাবার দাও ।

Lesson 12, part 2. Grammar.

1. The formation and use of the present completive (or "present perfect") tense.

1.1. The present completive is a frequently used past tense in Bengali; it is fairly general in reference. In general, it is a fair rule of thumb to consider that any English construction which has or can have the form "has/have (read, shut, done, eaten, etc.)" will take the present completive in Bengali. The tense is frequently used where English would have a simple past, but its primary usage is to indicate an action which has been completed in the recent past but which has results which continue into the present.

1.2. The PAP forms the base of the present completive with the -oh-suffix and the present tense personal endings added to it, thus:

Stem		PAP	Suffixes	
ken-	"buy"	ami	kine-	ch-i	
		tumi	kine-	ch-o	
		tui	kine-	ch-iś	
		apni	kine-	ch-en	
		śe	kine-	ch-e	
		tini	kine-	ch-en	
khæl-	"play"	ami	khele-	ch-i	etc.
jan-	"know"	ami	jene-	ch-i	etc.
kɔr-	"do"	ami	kore-	ch-i	etc.
bojh-	"understand"	ami	bujhe-	ch-i	etc.
de-	"give"	ami	die-	ch-i	etc.
kha-	"eat"	ami	khee-	ch-i	etc.
hɔ-	"be"	ami	hoe-	ch-i	etc.

1.3. The present completive of /ja-/ "go" is irregular. The stem is /gæ- ~ gie-/ and the paradigm runs thus:

ami	gechi, giechi
tumi	gæcho, giecho
tui	gechiś, giechiś
apni	gæchen, giechen
śe	gæche, gieche
tini	gæchen, giechen

2. The past negative, as in sentence 15.

2.1. The past tenses in the negative are formed by the use of the simple present tense with **the negative particle** /ni/, thus:

ami śunechi"	I have heard.
ami śuni ni"	I have not heard.
ami'oi boiṭa poṛechi"	I have read that book.
ami'oi boiṭa poṛi ni"	I have not read that book.

2.2. An exception* to this rule is the simple past tense. The particle /na/ may optionally be used with a simple past verbal form:

ami poṛlum na	I did not read (in recent past).
ami poṛi ni	I did not read (non-definite past).

3. Relative clauses.

In Bengali, correlative constructions have the following forms:

3.1. Personal pronouns, with reference to human beings only:

3.1.1. je ... śe ... (he, she) who ... he, she ...
je aśche ' śe ke " Who is he/she who is coming?

3.1.2. jara ... tara ... (those) who ... they ...
jara'ei baṛite thake' Those who live in this house are
tara chattro" students.

3.2. Impersonal references:

ja ... ta ... (that) which ... that
ja ami dekhchi'ta ki" What is that which I see?
jegulo ami caichi'śegulo Those which I want are good.
bhalo"

3.3. Adjectival formations:

3.3.1. The relative /je/ accompanied by a noun:

je ... śe ... (that) which ... that ...
je boiṭa'tomake diechi' Where is that book which I have
śeṭa kothae" given you?

_____
*Another exception is the past habitual tense, which we have not yet met.

je chelegulo eśeche'śegulo
boŗtir chele" — The boys who have come are boys of the busti (slum).

3.3.2. jɔto ... tɔto ... — as much as ... so much ...

tomar'jɔto ţaka ache'tɔto
ţaka ami cai" — I want as much money as you have.

3.4 Other types of formations:

3.4.1. jekhane ... śekhane — where ... there ...

jekhane tumi jabe'śekhane
ami jabo" — I shall go where you go.

3.4.2. jɔkhon ... tɔkhon ... — when ... then ...

tumi jɔkhon jabe'tɔkhon ami
jabo" — When you go, I shall go.

3.4.3. jɔkhoni (jokkhuni) ...
tɔkhoni (tokkhuni) ... — the very moment ... at that moment

jɔkhoni tumi bolbe'tɔkhoni
boiţa ene dobo" — The moment you tell me (at that very moment), I'll bring the book.

3.4.4. jæmon ... tæmon ... — as ... so ...

jæmon apni bolben'tæmon ami
korbo" — As you will tell (me), so I will do.

jemni ... temni ... — just as ... just so ...

jemni apni bolben'temni ami
korbo" — Just as you will tell me, just so I will do.

3.5. Note that the correlative can be inflected, as in sentence 12. Other examples:

je aśche'tar (śe lokţir) nam ki" — What is the name of him who is coming?

jara aśche'tåder (śe lokgulor) nam ki" — What are the names of those (people) who are coming?

je chelera'śekhane bośche' taderke (śe chelederke) pɔchondo kɔro ki" — Do you like those boys who are sitting there?

je bondhura eśeche'tara ramer bondhu" — Those friends who have come are Ram's friends.

ļ 6. Drills on tape.

4. Use of adjectives of color.

4.1. Some adjectives of color have two forms, the usage of each of which is limited. For example:

holde, holud   yellow

The distribution of these forms is as follows:

pakhiṭa holde
pakhiṭa holud roṇer   The bird is yellow.

holde pakhiṭa
holud roṇer pakhiṭa   The yellow bird.

Note that these pairs are not in absolute contrast; for example, the form /holde roṇer/ is possible.

4.2. The following vocabulary items occur with or without following /roṇ/ "color".

Bengali	English
lal	red
kalo	black
śada	white
nil	blue
śobuj	green
holde	yellow
begne	violet
golapi	rosy
badami	brown
khɔeri	toast brown

4.2.1. Examples:

śaṛiṭa'lal roṇer"   The sari is of red color.
śaṛiṭa lal"   The sari is red (color).
śaṛiṭar rɔṇ'lal"   The color of the sari is red.

4.3. The following vocabulary items must be followed by /rɔṇ/ "color".

kɔmla lebu rɔṇ   orange color, or color of an orange
chai rɔṇ   ash color, or color like ash
mourkonṭhi rɔṇ   color like the peacock's neck

ghie rɔŋ	color like clarified butter
tũte rɔŋ	color like turquoise
holud rɔŋ	of turmeric color
dudhe alta rɔŋ	color of milk and <u>alta</u> mixed – a kind of red dye which women use to decorate their feet.
aśmani rɔŋ	sky color
śonali rɔŋ	golden color
rupoli rɔŋ	silvery color
koci kɔlapatar rɔŋ	color of a young banana leaf
abir rɔŋ	color of red powder used at Holi festival
sĩdur rɔŋ	vermillion

5. For purposes of the pattern drills, it is important to note the distinction between /koækjon/ and /kono kono/:

koækjon lok	a few people (a small number that can be specified)
kono kono lok	some people (indefinite number)

6. Form possible Bengali sentences:

6.1.

Possessive noun or pronoun	Post-positional phrase	Noun or pro-noun subject	Negative verb "there is not"
amar	tar jonne	upohar	nei
tomar	ramer	boi	
apnar	boner	pakhi	
tar	rohimer	ṭaka	
tãr			
amader			
cheleder			

6.2.

Correlative Clause			Relative Clause		
Pronoun/ adjective	Subject	Verb	Pronoun	Subject	Interrogative
je	boiṭa pakhiṭa cheleṭi kukurṭa beṛalṭa lokṭa	niccho kincho aśche bośche khacche	tar _ _ _ _ _	nam rɔŋ śe	ki
ja	śe	boleche poṛeche dekheche aśche	ta	śotti bhalo śɔkto śɔhoj _ _ _ _ ki	

Lesson 12, part 3. Patterns.

1. **Pattern: sentence 1.**

   a. Where are you going now?
   b. What are you reading now?
   c. Where is he going now?
   d. What are you listening to now?
   e. What are the boys doing now?

2. **Pattern: sentence 2.**

   a. I am going to class.
   b. I am reading a play.
   c. He is going to Somdeb's house
   d. I am listening to a <u>kirtan</u>.
   e. They are playing in the field.

3. **Pattern: sentence 3.**

   a. What is happening in class today?

b. What play are you reading?

c. What is happening at Somdeb's house?

d. What <u>kirtan</u> are you listening to?

e. What are they playing?

4. Pattern: sentence 4.

a. Somdeb is teaching us Bengāli.

b. I am reading Tagore's <u>Raja</u>.

c. A party is going on today.

d. I am listening to an old <u>kirtan</u>.

e. A football game is going on.

5. Pattern: sentence 5.

a. Who (all) is coming to class today?

b. Who (all) is reading in class today?

c. Who (all) is going there?

d. Who (all) is singing the <u>kirtan</u>?

e. Who (all) is playing football?

6. Pattern: sentence 6.

a. Everyone. Aren't you coming to class?

b. Somdeb. Are you coming to class today?

c. I don't know. Aren't you going there?

d. Some Vaisnavas. Aren't you listening to the song?

e. Some boys. Aren't you playing football today?

7. Pattern: sentence 7.

a. Yes, I'm coming.

b. Yes, I'm going today.

c. Yes, I'm going there.

d. Yes, I'm listening.

e. No, I'm not playing.

8. Pattern: sentence 8.

a. Do you have the books for the class?

b. Do you have the papers for the class?

c. Do you have any present for Somdeb?

d. Do you have the book for me?

e. Do you have some time for me?

9. Pattern: sentence 9.

   a. No, I do not have the books.
   b. No, I do not have the papers.
   c. No, I do not have a present.
   d. No, I do not have the book.
   e. No, I do not have any time.

   Pattern: sentence 9.

   a. Before going I am going to get (i.e., I am getting) the books.
   b. Before going I am going to get (i.e., I am getting) the work.
   c. Before going I am going to get (i.e., I am getting) a present.
   d. Before going I am going to get (i.e., I am getting) the book.
   e. Before meeting you I am going to get (i.e., I am getting) a book.

10. Pattern: sentence 10.

   a. What books are you getting?
   b. What work are you doing?
   c. What present are you buying?
   d. What book are you buying?
   e. What book are you reading?

11. Pattern: sentence 11.

   a. I am getting poetry books.
   b. I am studying Bengali history.
   c. I am buying a history book.
   d. I am buying a poetry book.
   e. I am reading a Bengali novel.

12. Pattern: sentence 12.

   a. What are the names of the books which you are getting?
   b. What are the names of the books which you are studying?
   c. What is the name of the history book which you are buying?
   d. What is the name of the poetry book which you are buying?
   e. What is the name of the novel which you are reading?

13. Pattern: sentence 13.

   a. The books' names are Balaka [bɔlaka] and Gitanjali [gitanjoli].
   b. The books are histories of Bengal.

c. The book's name is <u>Bangalir itihas</u> [baŋalir itihaś].
d. The book's name is <u>Ityadi</u> [ittadi].
e. The name of the novel is <u>Gora</u> [gora].

Pattern: sentence 14.

a. Have you read the books?
b. Have you studied history?
c. Have you read that book?
d. Have you seen that book?
e. Have you read that novel?

14. Pattern: sentence 15.

a. No, I haven't read them.
b. No, I haven't studied history.
c. No, I haven't gotten that book.
d. No, I haven't seen that book.
e. No, I haven't read that novel.

Pattern: sentence 15.

a. I have heard that they are very difficult.
b. I have heard that history is very difficult.
c. I have heard that it is very difficult to get.
d. I have heard that it is very good.
e. I have heard that it is very difficult to read.

15. Pattern: sentence 16.

a. Who has said that they are difficult?
b. Who has said that it is difficult?
c. Who has said that it is difficult to get?
d. Who has said that it is good?
e. Who has said that it is difficult to read?

16. Pattern: sentence 17.

a. My friend has said so.
b. My sister has said so.
c. My brother has said so.
d. My friends have said so.
e. My teacher has said so.

17.   Pattern: sentence 18.

    a.   What he has said is not true.

    b.   What she has said is right.

    c.   What he has said is true.

    d.   What they have said is not true.

    e.   What he has said is not correct.

    Pattern: sentences 19, 20, 21.

    a.   The books which I have read are not difficult.

    b.   The history which I have studied is difficult.

    c.   The books which I have wanted I have not found.

    d.   The book which I have read is not very good.*

    e.   The book which I have read is very easy.

18.   Pattern: sentence 18.

    a.   Then the friend who told me was not correct.

    b.   Then what she told me was correct.

    c.   Then what my brother told me was correct.

    d.   Then the friends who told me were not correct.

    e.   Then the teacher who told me is not a good teacher.

Lesson 12, part 4.   Sentence Drill.

Drill 1

--Where are you going?

--I am going to Somdev's house.

--Have you gone to the market?

--Yes, I have bought all the things that you have asked for.

--And have you finished your work and bathed?

--Yes, I have finished everything.

--All right, then, go along.   What's going on at his house?

--I don't know exactly.   I think that his brother has returned from Europe.

--I have not heard that he has returned.   I have heard that he will stay in America for two years.

The English is ambiguous; the Bengali /khub bhalo nɔe/ means that the book is good, but not _very_ good.   This construction may be used here.

--Those who leave Bengal often come back quickly. Are you coming with me?

--Yes, I'm coming. But I have not bought a present for him.

--That's all right. We will buy one on the way.

Drill 2

--Have you read the paper today?

--No, I have not seen it yet (i.e., 'even now'). What does it say?

--It says that there was a <u>hartal</u> [hɔrtal] in Bombay.

--What is happening there?

--Yesterday there was a riot, and three people were

--Is there any good news?

--Yes, the paper says that the summer will be very hot this year, and that the monsoon will be late (i.e., 'will come after').

--Has Buddadev written about my book?

--Yes, he says that it is a very bad book.

--Is that all?

--Yes, he has not written much.

--I think that I shall lie down for a while

Lesson 12, part 5. Vocabulary.

khɔbor	news	aghat pa-	get a blow, get injured
kagoj	paper		
aghat	injury; blow	ca-, cai-	want, ask for
bɔrśa, briśṭi	rain	bissram kɔr-	rest, take a rest
kal	time, season	śo-	lie down
bissram	rest nap	śue ne-	lie down
naṭoke	drama play	pa-	get, find
		khũje pa-	find after searching
beśi	much, very much	chaṛ-	leave, abandon
		śɔmmondhe, śɔmbondhe	post-position, "about, in regard to"; with genitive

Idioms:

ṭhik ache	that's all right
gɔrom kal	summer
bɔrśa kal	rainy season
bɔṛo beśi	too much

	Analysis and Translation	Bengali

1.   high stem of verb /ja-/,
   "go"   je-   যে-

       infinitive ending   -te -তে

       "to go"   jete যেতে

       For use of the infinitive, see Grammar, 1.

   A. Have you told Ram to go
   to the market?   A. ramke ' bajare jete ' bolecho ki "

                                রামকে বাজারে যেতে বলেছো কি ?

2.   alternative stem of verb
   /ja-/, "go" -- see Lesson 5   gæ-   গে-

       "he/she has gone"   gæche   গেছে

   B. Yes, I gave him two
   rupees; he has gone to
   the market.   B. hæ " du taka diechi " śe bajare
                                gæche "

                                হাঁ , দুটাকা দিয়েছি । সে বাজারে
                                গেছে ।

3. A. Has he come back from
   the market?   A. śe ki bajar theke ' phire eśeche "

                                সে কি বাজার থেকে ফিরে এসেছে ?

4.   "just now"   eimattro   এইমাত্র

   B. Yes, he has just come
   back.   B. hæ " śe ' eimattro phireche "

                                হাঁ , সে এইমাত্র ফিরে এসেছে ।

5. compound verb, "(buy and) bring"   kine an-   কিনে আন—

    A. <u>What has he brought from the market?</u>   A. śe ' bajar theke ' ki kine eneche "

সে বাজার থেকে কি কিনে এনেছে ?

6. noun, "fish"   mach   মাছ

noun, "meat"   maŋśo   মাংস

noun, "vegetables"   tɔrkari   তরকারী

    B. <u>He has brought fish, meat, and vegetables.</u>   B. śe mach ' maŋśo ' ar tɔrkari ' kine eneche "

সে মাছ , মাংস আর তরকারী কিনে এনেছে

7. high stem of verb /ken-/, "buy"   kin-   কিন—

infinitive ending   -te   —তে

"to buy"   kinte   কিনতে

past negative particle   ni   নি

    A. <u>Didn't he go to buy fruit?</u>   A. śe ki ' phɔl kinte jae ni "

সে কি ফল কিনতে যায় নি ?

8. noun, "banana"   kɔla   কলা

noun, "mango"   am   আম

noun, a small, violet-colored fruit   jam   জাম

    B. <u>Yes, he has bought bananas, mangoes, and jam.</u>   B. hæ̃ " śe kɔla ' am ' ar jam ' kine eneche "

হাঁ , সে কলা , আম আর জাম কিনে এনেছে ।

9. high stem of verb /kha-/, "eat"   khe-   খে—

infinitive ending   -te   —তে

"to eat"   khete   খেতে

258

A. Have you given Binu the bananas to eat?

A. tumi binuke ' kɔlagulo ' khete diecho ki "

তুমি বিনুকে ক্লাগুলো খেতে দিয়েছো কি ?

10. "outside"

high stem of verb /khæl-/, "play"

infinitive ending

"to play"

baire বাইরে

khel- খেল—

-te —তে

khelte খেলতে

B. No, he has gone outside to play.

B. na " śe baire ' khelte gæche "

না , সে বাইরে খেলতে গেছে ।

11. a snack taken between the two main meals (one around noon, the other in the late evening)

khabar খাবার

A. Won't he come back to have a snack?

A. śe ki ' khabar khete ' phire aśbe na "

সে কি খাবার খেতে ফিরে আসবে না ?

12. noun, "afternoon"

bikelbæla বিকেলবেলা

B. Yes, I think that he will come back home for a snack in the afternoon.

B. hæ̃ " amar mone hɔe je ' śe khabar khete ' bikelbæla ' bari phirbe "

হাঁ , আমার মনে হয় যে সে খাবার খেতে বিকেলবেলা বাড়ী ফিরবে ।

13. high stem of verb /dækh-/, "see"

infinitive ending

"to see"

verb stem, "want"

dekh- দেখ—

-te —তে

dekhte দেখতে

ca- চা—

A. Good. I want to see him. (i.e., I have never seen him before and want to meet him)

A. beś " ami oke ' dekhte cai "

বেশ । আমি ওকে দেখতে চাই ।

14.   noun, "field"   maṭh মাঠ

        compound verb, "cause
        to come by calling"   deke an- ডেকে আন-

    B. **In that case, I shall go**   B. ta hole ' ami maṭhe gie ' binuke '
       to the field and call Binu   taṛataṛi deke anchi "
       back right away.

                           তা হলে , আমি মাঠে গিয়ে বিনুকে
                           তাড়াতাড়ি ডেকে আনছি ।

Lesson 13, part 2. Grammar.

1.   The formation and use of the infinitive:

1.1.   The most frequent use of the infinitive form is as supplement to another verb, as in English:

    ami'jete cai"   I want to go.
    ami'dekhte pari na"   I cannot see; I am not able to see.
    oke'aśte bollum"   I told him to come.

1.2.   The infinitive of consonant-final stems is formed by the high stem of the verb (except where the stem-vowel is /a/) plus the infinitive ending /-te/.

ken-	buy	kinte	to buy
khæl-	play	khelte	to play
kɔr-	do	korte	to do
śon-	hear	śunte	to hear
But: jan-	know	jante	to know

1.3.   The infinitive of <u>all</u> CV- stems, regardless of stem-vowel, is formed by the high stem plus /-te/:

hɔ-	be, become	hote	to be, to become
de-	give	dite	to give
kha-	eat	khete	to eat

The stem /ja-/ is regular in this form. Its infinitive is /jete/.

1.4.   Stems of CVV- or CVCa- shape, however, preserve their low vowels:

| ga-/gai- | sing | gaite | to sing |
| bæṛa- | wander about | bærate | to wander about |

2. It should be noted that there are two ways of expressing such a phrase as "he bought (it) for me":

    a. śe'amar jonne'eṭa kineche"   He has bought it for me (but has not given it to me yet).

    b. śe amake'eṭa kine dieche"   He has bought (and given) it to me.

Note that in b., /amake/ is the indirect object of the verb /de-/. In Bengali, verbs such as /ken-/ cannot take indirect objects and require /jonne/.

3. Form possible Bengali sentences from the following:

Subj.	Ind. O.	VM	D.O.	(Int.)	V_1	V_2	Neg.
ami	ramke	bajare	mach	(ki)	jete	bɔl-	na
tumi	take	dokane	maŋśo		aste	ca-	ni
tui	bhaike	ekhane	tɔrkari		kinte	ja-	
apni	kobike	baɽite	am		nite	de-	
śe		ghɔre	khabar		khete		
tini		śɔhore			bolte		
amra		eimattro			ante		
tomra		taɽataɽi			phire		
tora		tarpɔre			nie		
apnara					kine		
tara							
tãra							
ram							
binu							

Subj.	VM	V	D.O.	(Int.)	V_1	V_2	
ami	taɽataɽi	gie	binuke	(ki)	ɖeke	an-	
tumi	ækhon	eśe	kapɔɽta		nie	aś-	
tui	eimattro	phire	amake		bole	ja-	
apni	dokane		take				
śe	maṭhe		boiṭa		dekhe		
tini			cheleke				
amra	bajar						
tomra	theke						
tora	klaśer						
apnara	theke						
tara							
tãra							
ram							
binu							

262

Lesson 13, part 3. Patterns.

1.   Pattern: sentence 1.

a. Have you told Ram to go to the river?
b. Have you told him to go to the store?
c. Have you told her to bring it here?
d. Have you told them to come back here?
e. Have you not told them to come back here?

2.   Pattern: sentence 2.

a. Yes, I gave him ten rupees and he has gone there.
b. Yes, I gave him six rupees and sent him there.
c. Yes, I gave her some money and told her that.
d. Yes, I sent them money and told them to come back here.
e. No, I have not told them to come back here.

3.   Pattern: sentence 3.

a. Has he come back from the river?
b. Has he come back from the store?
c. Has she brought it back from the market?
d. Have they come back here?
e. Have they not returned from the class?

4.   Pattern: sentence 4.

a. Yes, he has just come back.
b. No, he has just gone there.
c. Yes, she has just brought it back.
d. No, they have not come back.
e. Yes, they have just returned.

5.   Pattern: sentence 5.

a. What has he brought from the store?
b. What have you told him to bring from the store?
c. What book has she bought and brought back from the store?
d. What have you told them to bring with them?
e. What have they brought from class?

6.   Pattern: sentence 6.

a. He has brought meat and vegetables from the store.

b. I told him to bring fruit and flowers from the store.

c. She has brought several Bengali books from the store.

d. I have told them to bring many kinds of things.

e. They have brought nothing at all from class.

7. Pattern: sentence 7.

a. Didn't he go to buy fish?

b. Didn't you tell him to bring vegetables?

c. Didn't you tell her to bring English books?

d. Didn't you tell them to bring only clothes?

e. Didn't you tell them to bring me some Bengali newspapers?

8. Pattern: sentence 8.

a. Yes, he has brought <u>rui</u> and <u>hilsa</u> fish.

b. Yes, but he has bought only mangoes and berries.

c. Yes, but she has not been able to buy English books.

d. Yes, but they have not been able to bring many clothes.

e. Yes, but they have not been able to bring newspapers.

9. Pattern: sentence 9.

a. Have you given the boy the <u>hilsa</u> fish to eat?

b. Have you given the girl the mangoes to eat?

c. Have you given her the books to take back?

d. Have you given them clothes to wear?

e. Have you told them to send the newspapers to me?

10. Pattern: sentence 10.

a. No, he has not come in to eat.

b. No, she has gone to the field to play.

c. No, she has gone back to the store again.

d. No, they have said that they don't want to wear these clothes.

e. No, they have told me that they were not able to send them.

11. Pattern: sentence 11.

a. Won't he come back to eat the fish?

b. Won't she come back to eat the mangoes?

c. Won't she come back to rest?

d. Won't they go back to buy the papers?

     e.   Won't they go back to bring their clothes?

12. Pattern: sentence 12.

     a.   Yes, I think he will come back this evening.
     b.   Yes, I think that she will come back quickly.
     c.   Yes, I think that she will come back in the afternoon.
     d.   Yes, I think that they will go back to buy them.
     e.   Yes, I think that they will go back to bring them.

13. Pattern: sentence 13.

     a.   Then I want to see him.
     b.   Then I will be able to see her.
     c.   Then I will come back to see her.
     d.   I will go with them to buy them.
     e.   I will go to bring them.

Lesson 13, part 4. Sentence Drills.

Drill 1

--Have you told Tipu to buy milk at the market?

--No, I forgot to tell him that. He has brought only rice and bananas.

--Then he has already come back from the market?

--Yes, he has just come back.

--Then where has he gone? I cannot find him anywhere.

--I don't know. Perhaps he has gone to take a bath. I think he'll come back soon.

--Tell him that I want to see him. He will take this letter to Ballygunge. [baliganj].

--He cannot go today. He has not finished his work in the house.

--He can finish his work later. Go and call him.

--All right, I'll go.

Drill 2

Note: pay special attention to the order of relative clauses; see ante, Lesson 12, Grammar.

--Ram, do you want to go to the market with Tipu?

--Yes, I like to go with him. He buys me sweets.

--I don't like that. The sweets which you buy at the market are not good to eat.

--Why not? I have eaten them often. They taste good.
--Those sweets are made of bad milk. That is why Binu has gotten sick.
--But you like to drink <u>gholer śɔrbot</u>. You have not gotten sick.
--That. is another matter. I have told you what I want. Go with Tipu.

_____

--Tipu, will you buy me sweets?
--No, your mother does not want you to eat them.
--Then I shall tell her that you have bought me sweets.
--All right, then, what kind of sweets do you want to eat?
--I have not eaten the red kind before. Buy me those.

Lesson 13, part 5. Vocabulary.

gholer śɔrbot	buttermilk preparation	toiri	made, prepared make, preparation
bæpar	matter	onno	another
rɔkom	kind	jɔthesţo	enough
dudh	milk	kothao	anywhere
ciţhi	letter	age	already (previously)
		er moddhe	already (in the meantime)

pochondo kɔr-	like
kine di-	buy and give
kha-	eat, drink
par-	be able (physical ability)
bhule ja-	forget
dekhte pa-	find
khũje pa-	find (after searching)
pɔr-	wear
harie ja-	get lost
nie ja-	take (from here to there)

Idioms:

tate hɔbe na	that will not do (i.e., it is insufficient)
khete bhalo	taste good (good to eat)
khaoa bhalo	good (i.e., healthy) to eat

<u>Lesson 14, part 1.   Conversation.</u>

<u>Analysis and translation</u>	<u>Bengali</u>

1. <u>A.</u> <u>What are you going to do tonight?</u>

A. <u>tumi aj rattre ' ki korbe "</u>

তুমি আজ রাত্রে কি করবে ?

2.   compound verbal noun
stem, "studying"

pɔraśona   পড়াশোনা

verb, "study"

pɔraśona kɔr-   পড়াশোনা কর—

<u>B.</u> <u>I'm going to study tonight.</u>

B. <u>ami aj rattre ' pɔraśona korbo "</u>

আমি আজ রাত্রে পড়াশোনা করবো ।

3.   loan word, "cinema"

sinema   সিনেমা

infinitive of verb
/ja-/, "go"

jete   যেতে

verb stem, "be able"

par-   পার—

<u>A.</u> <u>Then won't you be able to go to the movies with us?</u>

A. <u>ta hole ' tumi ' amader śɔnge ' sinemate jete parbe na "</u>

তা হলে তুমি আমাদের সঙ্গে সিনেমাতে যেতে পারবে না ।

4.   verb stem, "wander around"   bæra-   বেড়া—
Note the use of the present tense /pari/; the meaning in this context is "I may be able".

<u>B.</u> <u>No, but I may be able to go about with you for a little while.</u>

B. <u>na " kintu ami ' tomader śɔnge ' kichukkhon jonne ' bærate pari "</u>

না, কি আমি তোমাদের সঙ্গে কিছুক্ষণের জন্যে বেড়াতে পারি ।

5. "studying"   pɔraśona পড়াশোনা
    post-position, "after"   pɔr, pɔre পর , পরে

    A. Good. What are you going   A. beś " pɔraśonar pɔr ' tumi ki korbe "
        to do after studying?   বেশ , পড়াশোনার পর তুমি কি করবে ?

6. variant stem of verb /ghuma-/,   ghumo- ঘুমো–
    "sleep"; see Grammar, 1.

    B. After studying, I am going   B. ami ' pɔraśonar pɔr ' ghumote jabo "
        to go to sleep.   আমি পড়াশোনার পর ঘুমোতে যাবো ।

7. A. Will you not go to eat   A. tumi ' ghumobar age ' khete jabe na '
        before sleeping (i.e.,   তুমি ঘুমোবার আগে খেতে যাবে না ?
        before going to sleep)?

8. high stem of verb /kɔr-/,   kor- কর–
    "do"

    ending for conditional   -le –লে
    conjunctive

    "if I (you, he) do (does)";   korle করলে
    see Grammar, 2.

    B. Yes, if I finish studying   B. hæ̃ " taratari ' pɔraśona śeś korle '
        quickly, I shall go to   khete jabo "
        eat.   হাঁ , তাড়াতাড়ি পড়াশোনা শেষ করলে
                                             খেতে যাবো ।

9. infinitive of verb   pɔrte পড়তে
    /pɔr-/, "study"

    A. Will Ram also go to   A. ram·o ki ' tomar śɔnge ' pɔrte
        study with you?   jabe "
                                             রামও কি তোমার সঙ্গে পড়তে যাবে ?

10. high stem of verb   pe- পে–
    /pa-/, "get"
    ending for conditional   -le –লে
    conjunctive
    "if (he) gets"   pele পেলে

B. Yes, if he gets the
time, he will come.

B. hæ̃ " śɔmoe pele ' śe aśbe "

হাঁ , সময় পেলে সে আসবে ।

11. A. But I heard that he wants
to go to the city tonight.

A. kintu ' ami śunlum je ' śe aj
rattre ' śɔhore jete cae "

কিন্তু আমি শুনলুম যে সে আজ রাত্রে
শহরে যেতে চায় ।

12. alternative stem of verb
/ja-/, "go"

ge- গে-

ending for conditional
conjunctive

-le -লে

"if (he) goes"

gele গেলে

B. In that case, if he goes
to the city, he will not
be able to come to study.

B. ta hole ' śe śɔhore gele ' pɔrte
aśte parbe na "

তা হলে , সে শহরে গেলে পড়তে আসতে
পারবে না ।

13. A. Do you know what he is
going to do tomorrow?

A. tumi ki jano ' śe agami kal '
ki korbe "

তুমি কি জানো সে আগামী কাল
কি করবে ?

14. "in the morning"

śɔkale, śɔkalbæla সকালে , সকালবেলা

noun, "picture"

chobi ছবি

verb stem, "paint"

ãk- আঁক-

B. Yes, he has told me that
he is going to the river-
bank to paint tomorrow
morning.

B. hæ̃ " śe amake boleche je ' śe kal
śɔkale ' nodir dhare ' chobi ãkte
jabe "

হাঁ , সে আমাকে বলেছে যে সে কাল
সকালে নদীর ধারে ছবি আঁকতে যাবে

noun, "noontime"

dupur, dupurbæla দুপুর , দুপুরবেলা

verb stem, "come"

aś- আস-

conditional conjunctive
ending

-le -লে

"if (he) comes"

aśle আসলে

B. If he comes back before
noon, he will come to my
house to eat.

B. śe dupurbælar age ' phire aśle '
amar barite ' khete aśbe "

সে দুপুরবেলার আগে ফিরে আসলে
আমার বাড়ীতে খেতে আসবে ।

15. noun, "afternoon"

bikel, bikelbæla   বিকেল , বিকেলবেলা

A. What will he do in the
afternoon?

A. śe bikelbæla ' ki korbe "

সে বিকেলবেলা কি করবে ?

16. loan word, "football"
(like American soccer)

phuṭbɔl   ফুটবল

variant stem of /ca-/,
"want"

cai-   চাই-

conditional conjunctive
ending

-le   -লে

"if (he) wants"; see
Grammar, 2.3.

caile   চাইলে

noun, "field"

maṭh   মাঠ

B. I don't know exactly, but
if he wants to see a football game, we shall both
go to the field.

B. ami ' thik jani na " tɔbe ' śe '
phuṭbɔl khæla dekhte caile ' amra
dujone ' maṭhe jabo "

আমি ঠিক জানি না , তবে সে ফুটবল
খেলা দেখতে চাইলে আমরা দুজনে মাঠে
যাবো ।

17. noun, "evenin~"

śondhe, śondhebæla   সন্ধ্যে , সন্ধ্যেবেলা

A. After that, will you go
to wander around in the
city in the evening?

A. tarpɔr ' tomra ki ' śondhebæla '
śɔhore bæṛate jabe "

তারপর , তোমরা কি সন্ধ্যেবেলা শহরে
বেড়াতে যাবে ?

18. high stem of verb
/hɔ-/, "be, become"

ho-   হ-

conditional conjunctive
ending

-le   -লে

"if (it) finishes"

śeś hole   শেষ হলে

B. Yes, if the game is over soon, we shall go to the city.

B. hæ̃ " taṛataṛi khæla śeś hole ' amra śɔhore jabo "

হাঁ , তাড়াতাড়ি খেলা শেষ হলে আমরা শহরে যাবো ।

19. A. Can ı come with you?

A. ami.o ki ' tomader śɔŋge ' aśte pari "

আমিও কি তোমাদের সঙ্গে আসতে পারি ?

20. B. Yes, you can come.

B. hæ̃ " tumi ' aste paro "

হাঁ, তুমি আসতে পারো ।

Lesson 14, part 2. Grammar.

1. Stems of CVCV-verbs, as in sentences 4, 6, and 7.

1.1. The verbal noun and the infinitive of this type of stem are usually formed by the addition of the infinitive or verbal noun suffix to the low stem of the verb:

Stem		Infinitive	Verbal Noun
bæka-	"bend"	bækate	bækano, bækaba-
kamṛa-	"bite"	kamṛate	kamṛano, kamṛaba-
jiro-	"rest"	jirote	jirono, jiroba-

1.2. Verb stems which have /u/ or /ou/ as the stem-vowel, however, have the alternative stem CVCo- before the suffixes /-te/, /-no/, and /-ba-/.

Stem		Infinitive	Verbal Noun
ghumo-	"sleep"	ghumote	ghumono, ghumoba-
poũcho-	"arrive.aı	poũchote	poũcnono, poũchoba-

2. ' The conditional conjunctive is formed by the addition of the suffix /-le/ to the high stem of the verb, except for verbs of shape CVC- where the vowel is /a/, and verbs of CVC- shape (1.1. and 1.2. above).

ken-	"buy"	ami kin-le	"if I buy"
		tumi kin-le	"if you buy"
		tui kin-le	"if you (inf.) buy"
		apni kin-le	"if you (hon.) buy"

		śe kin-le	"if he buys"	
		tini kin-le	"if he (hon.) buys"	
khæl-	"play"	ami khel-le	"if I play"	etc.
kɔr-	"do"	ami kor-le	"if I do"	etc.
śon-	"hear"	ami śun-le	"if I hear"	etc.
But: jan-	"know"	ami jan-le	"if I know"	etc.

Also:

de-	"give"	ami di-le	"if I give"	etc.
hɔ-	"be"	ami ho-le	"if I were"	etc.
kha-	"eat"	ami khe-le	"if I eat"	etc.
bæ̃ka-	"bend"	ami bæ̃ka-le	"if I bend"	etc.
kamṛa-	"bite"	kamṛa-le	"if I bite"	etc.
jiro-	"rest"	jiro-le	"if I rest"	etc.
ghumo-	"sleep"	ghumo-le	"if I sleep"	etc.
poũcho-	"reach"	poũcho-le	"if I reach"	etc.

2.2. Note that the conditional conjunctive is a non-finite from; it does not change with change of person or number.

2.3. CVV-stems with /a/ also preserve the low vowel in the conditional conjunctive:

ca-	"want"	caile	"if I want"	etc.
ga-	"sing"	gaile	"if I sing"	etc.

2.4. The commonest use of the conditional conjunctive is that which we have in this lesson: the expression of a condition, using English "if":

oke dekhle'ami bolbo"	If I see him, I shall tell him.
ami śunle'bujhte parbo"	If I hear (it), I shall be able to understand (it).
tumi ekhane aśle'ami taka dobo"	If you come here, I shall give (you) money.

Other usages will be seen in Lesson 15.

2.5. Note that although this is a non-finite verb form, the subjects of the two clauses may differ, as they do in the third example above. When they do differ, however, both subjects must be expressed.

3. Note that in a conditional clause, the negative particle <u>precedes</u> the verb:

> tumi na gele'ami jabo na"   If you do not go, I shall not go.
>
> briśṭi na hole'phɔśol habe na"   If there is no rain, there will be no harvest.

4. Form possible Bengali sentences.

4.1.

Subject	Verbal Modifier	(Int)	Direct Object	V_1	V_2	Neg.
ami	agami kal	(ki)	pɔṛaśona	korte	par- ja-	na
tumi	kal śɔkale		śeś		aś	ni
śe	aj rattre		kaj			
amra dujone	kichukkhon		chobi	pɔṛte	kɔr-	
ram	śondhebæla		khabar	ãkte		
			khɔborer kagoj	khete		

4.2.

Subject	Noun/Object	Conditional Conjunctive	Subject	Modifier	Finite Verb
pɔṛaśona khæla	śeś	hole korʻe	ami śe tara apnara	śekhane	ja-
śe amra tini ram apnara tomra	śɔmoe boiṭa cɔppol dapoṛṭa chobi	pele kinle becle ãkle		baṛite	ja-

Lesson 14, part 3.   Patterns.

1.   Pattern: sentence 1.

   a.   What are you going to do tonight?
   b.   Where are you going to go tonight?
   c.   Whom are you going to meet tonight?
   d.   What are you going to buy tonight?
   e.   What are you going to read tonight?

2.   Pattern: sentence 2.

   a.   I'm going to read tonight.
   b.   I'm going to sleep tonight.
   c.   I'm going to see my mother tonight.
   d.   I'm going to buy clothes tonight.
   e.   I'm going to read books tonight.

3.   Pattern: sentence 3.

   a.   Then you won't be able to go to the store with us.
   b.   Then you won't be able to come home with us.
   c.   Then you won't be able to meet my brother with us.
   d.   Then you won't be able to come to the museum with us.
   e.   Then you won't be able to come to class with us.

4.   Pattern: sentence 4.

   a.   No, but I'll be able to come home with you for a little while.
   b.   Yes, I'll be able to go with you for a little while.
   c.   No, but I'll be able to come to your house for a little while.
   d.   Yes, I'll be able to talk with you for a little while.
   e.   Yes, I'll be able to go and stay for a little while.

5.   Pattern: sentence 5.

   a.   What are you going to do when you have finished your reading?*
   b.   What are you going to do after you have finished sleeping?*
   c.   What are you going to do after coming back from the store?

---

* Either the PAP construction or verbal noun plus post-position /pɔr, pɔre/ is acceptable.

274

     d. What are you going to do after you meet your brother?

     e. What are you going to do after you meet your mother?

6. Pattern: sentence 6.

     a. After I finish reading I am going to go to sleep.

     b. After I finish sleeping I am going to go to the library.

     c. After I come back from the store I am going to Suhas's house.

     d. After I meet my brother I am going to study.

     e. After I meet my mother I am going to the store.

7. Pattern: sentence 7.

     a. Will you want to rest before sleeping?

     b. Will you want to eat before going to the library?

     c. Will you want to sleep before going to Suhas's house?

     d. Will you come to see me before studying?

     e. Will you want to wander around a little before coming back?

8. Pattern: sentence 8.

     a. Yes, if I finish reading* before nine, I shall rest a little.

     b. Yes, if I go to the library before eight, it will be good.

     c. Yes, if I come back from the store before seven, I shall sleep a little.

     d. Yes, if I come back from my brother's house before six, I shall come to see you.

     e. Yes, if I come back from my mother's house before five, I shall wander around the city.

9. Pattern: sentence 9.

     a. Will Ram also study with you tonight?

     b. Will Ram also go with you to eat?

     c. Will Ram also go with you to Suhas's house?

     d. Will Lila also come to see me?

     e. Will Sita also go with you to wander around?

10. Pattern: sentence 10.

     a. Yes, if he gets the time, he will come to study with me

     b. Yes, if he finishes writing, he will go with me.

     c. Yes, if he is able to come, he will come.

---

* Either transitive or intransitive form is acceptable.

d. Yes, if **she gets** the time, she will come.

e. Yes, if she **finishes** studying, she will come with me.

11. Pattern: sentence 11.

a. But I heard that he wants to go to Lila's house tonight.

b. But I heard that he wants to come to my house tonight.

c. But 1 heard that he wants to study tonight.

d. But I heard that she wants to paint pictures tonight.

e. But I heard that she does not want to go tonight.

12. Pattern: sentence 12.

a. If he wants to go to Lila's house, he will not be able to come with me.

b. If he wants to go to your house, he will not be able to come with me.

c. If he wants to study tonight, he will not be able to come.

d. If she wants to paint tonight, she will not be able to come.

e. If she does not want to go to the city, then she will not go.

13. Pattern: sentence 13.

a. Do you know what Lila wants to do tomorrow?

b. Do you know what he will do tomorrow morning?

c. Do you know what he wants to do on Saturday?

d. Do you know what she will do tomorrow night?

e. Do you know what she wants to do tomorrow night?

14. Pattern: sentence 14a.

a. Yes, she has told me that she is going to the office to work.

b. Yes, he has told me that he is going to start writing another novel.

c. Yes, he has told me that he is going to see a movie.

d. Yes, she has told me that she is going to meet Probhas.

e. Yes, she has told me that she is going to meet Lila.

Pattern: sentence 14b.

a. If she comes back quickly, she will study.

b. If he feels tired, (use /klanto bodh kɔr-/) he will go to paint.

c. If he comes back before night, he will come to my house.

d. If they eat before ten, they will come to my house.

e. If they come to the city, they will come to my house.

15. Pattern: sentence 15.

    a. Do you know what she will do tomorrow night?

    b. Do you know what he will do in the evening?

    c. Do you know what he will do in the morning?

    d. Do you know what they will do tomorrow morning?

    e. Do you know what they will do on Sunday?

16. Pattern: sentence 16.

    a. If she wants to go to the movies, we shall both go.

    b. If he wants to go to Ram's house, we shall both go.

    c. If he wants to go to the city, we shall both go.

    d. If they want to study in the library, we shall all go.

    e. If they want to eat, we shall all go to eat.

Pattern: sentence 18.

    a. And if she wants to go walking (use /bæṛate/), I shall go with her.

    b. And if he wants to begin work, we shall both work.

    c. And if he wants to stay at home, I shall stay with him.

    d. And if they want to rest, we shall stay here.

    e. And if they want to begin writing, we shall all work.

Lesson 14, part 4. Sentence Drills.

Drill 1

--Will you be able to come to the movies with us tonight?

--No, I am going to work tonight. Perhaps I'll be able to come for a little while.

--We are going to see Pather Pancali [pọther pãcali]. You'll be able to finish your studying after the movie.

--No, it's a long picture. I won't be able to go.

--We are going to eat something after the picture is over. Will you be able to come with us then?

--Yes, I like to eat a little before going to sleep.

--Then if we come back soon, will you come with us?

--Yes. Is Ram going with us too?

--No, he is going to see Lila this evening. He won't be able to come.

--What is he going to do tomorrow?

--He said that he is going to look at pictures in the museum in the morn-
   ing. But he'll come to my house to eat tomorrow night.
--Good. Can I come to see (i.e., "to meet") him then?
--Yes, you can come.

Drill 2

--Ila, will you be able to come with me to the movies tonight?
--No, my mother does not want me to go with you. She doesn't like you.
--Then if you come, don't tell her. Why doesn't she like me?
--You don't have any money. My mother says that if you work you can make
   money.
--I have not begun to work. After I get my degree, I shall make lots
   of money.
--Then after you take your degree, I'll be able to go to the movies with
   you.
--After the movie we'll go dancing.
--No, I am going to study tonight. After I have finished studying, I am
   going to sleep.
--And after dancing, we'll go to listen to some music.
--No, I am going to work. What music?
--There is a good singer of folk-songs here. We'll go to hear his songs.
--Can you come at eight sharp?

Lesson 14, part 5. Vocabulary.

chobi	picture (i.e., either painting or motion picture)
polli-giti	village-song (i.e., "folk song")
gaeok	singer
pɔther pācali	name of a novel and a motion picture
śɔnge dækha kɔr-	meet with, visit a person (with genitive of person)
śuru kɔr-	begin (i.e., "make a beginning")
arɔmbho kɔr-	begin
lag-	begin (with infinitive), a colloquial usage
i.e.,	
śe porte lage	"he begins to read"
śe kaj korte lage	"he begins to work"

beśi	very much	tɔkhon	then
kɔm	less		
bɔro	big	ae	revenue, income
choṭo	small	ṭaka pɔeśa	
moṭa	fat, plump	ae kɔr-	make money
roga	lean	uparjon	earning, gain
lɔmbe	tall	uparjon kɔr-	earn
bẽṭe	short	upae kɔr-	earn
cɔora	wide		
śoru	narrow, thin		
klanto	tired		

Lesson 15, part 1. Conversation.

Analysis and translation	Bengali

1. noun, festival of the goddess Durga, which takes place in early October

durga pujo   দুর্গা পুজো

   conditional particle, "if"; see Grammar, 2.

jodi   যদি

   "if I go"

ami jodi jai   আমি যদি যাই

   A. If I go to my village house for Durga-puja, will you be able to go with me?

A. দুর্গা পুজোর সময় আমি যদি গ্রামের বাড়ীতে যাই তা হলে তুমি কি আমার সঙ্গে যেতে পারবে ?

durga pujor śɔmoe ' ami jodi '
gramer barite jai ' ta hole ' tumi
ki ' amar śɔnge ' jete parbe "

2. alternative stem of verb /ja-/, "go" see Grammar, 1.

ge-   গে—

   conditional conjunctive ending

-le   —লে

   B. If you go, I'll go with you.

B. তুমি গেলে আমি তোমার সঙ্গে যাবো ।

tumi gele ' ami ' tomar śɔnge '
jabo "

3. pronoun "self, one's self"

ãtto   আত্ম

   noun, "that which is related to one's self, a relative"

ãttio   আত্মীয়

   nominal plural, "relatives"

ãttiora   আত্মীয়রা

"if relatives come" āttiora jodi aśen আত্মীয়রা যদি আসেন

negative prefix, "not in-, un-" ɔ- অ-

"convenience" śubidhe, śubidha সুবিধে , সুবিধা

"inconvenience" ɔśubidhe, ɔśubidha অসুবিধে , অসুবিধা

A. If my relatives come, will that be an inconvenience for you?

A. আমার আত্মীয়রা যদি আসেন তা হলে তোমার অসুবিধে হবে কি ?

amar āttiora ' jodi aśen ' ta hole ' tomar ɔśubidhe hɔbe ki "

4. Note the position of the negative particle, before the verb in the conditional clause; see Grammar, 3.

adjective, "any" kono কোন

"none at all" kono ... na কোন....না

B. If it is no inconvenience for you, it will be no inconvenience for me at all.

B. তোমার অসুবিধে না হলে আমার কোন অসুবিধে হবে না ।

tomar ɔśubidhe ' na hole ' amar ' kono ɔśubidhe ' hɔbe na "

5. noun, "end" śeś শেষ

loan word, "mile" mail মাইল

PAP of verb stem /hāṭ-/, "walk" hēṭe হেঁটে

compound verb, "walk, go by walking" hēṭe ja- হেঁটে যা-

'if we walk' amra jodi hēṭe jai আমরা যদি হেঁটে যাই

A. If we walk the last five miles of the way, will you be able to walk with us?

A. আমরা যদি পথের শেষ পাঁচ মাইল হেঁটে যাই , তা হলে তুমি কি আমাদের সঙ্গে হাঁটতে পারবে ?

amra jodi ' pɔther ' śeś pāc mail ' hēṭe jai ' ta hole ' tumi ki ' amader śɔnge ' hāṭte parbe "

6. "cart, wheeled vehicle" gaṛi গাড়ী

"motor-car, automobile" moṭor gaṛi মোটর গাড়ী

"arrangements" bæbostha ব্যবস্থা

"make arrangements" bæbostha kɔr- ব্যবস্থা কর-

B. No. But if you make arrangements for a car, I
can go with you.

B. না । কিন্তু একটা মোটর গাড়ীর ব্যবস্থা
করলে আমি তোমাদের সঙ্গে যেতে পারি ।

na " kintu ' ækta motor garir '
bæbostha korle ' ami ' tomader
sɔnge jete pari "

7.   Note position of negative particle.

A. All right. If we are not
able to make arrangements
for a car, then what?

A. আচ্ছা । আমরা যদি মোটর গাড়ীর
ব্যবস্থা করতে না পারি , তা হলে ?

accha " amra jodi ' motor garir
bæbostha korte na pari ' ta hole

8.   "bullock"   goru   গোরু
     "bullock cart"   gorur gari   গোরুর গাড়ী

B. If you make arrangements
for a bullock cart, I'll
go with you.

B. তোমরা একটা গোরুর গাড়ীর ব্যবস্থা
করলে আমি তোমাদের সঙ্গে যাবো ।

tomra ' ækta gorur garir '
bæbostha korle ' ami' tomader
sɔnge jabo "

9.   negative prefix,
     "non-, in-, un-"   nir-   নির-
     "flesh, fish, meat"   amiś   আমিষ
     "vegetarian (food)"   niramiś   নিরামিষ
     "if we eat vegetarian food"   amra jodi niramiś khai

     আমরা যদি নিরামিষ খাই

A. If we eat vegetarian food
during the Durga-puja, then
will you also eat vegetarian
food?

A. আমরা যদি দুর্গাপূজোর সময় নিরামিষ
খাই , তা হলে তুমিও কি নিরামিষ
খাবে ?

amra jodi ' durga pujor sɔmoe '
niramiś khai ' ta hole ' tumi.o
ki ' niramiś khabe "

10.   "certainly"   niścoi   নিশ্চয়ই

B. Certainly. If you eat vegetarian food, so shall I.

B. নিশ্চয়ই । তোমরা নিরামিষ খেলে আমিও নিরামিষ খাবো ।

niścoi " tomra niramiś khele ' ami·o ' niramiś khabo "

11. adjective, "the whole"
verb stem, "be awake, stay awake"
"if we are awake"

śara   সারা

jag- জাগ−

amra jodi jagi   আমরা যদি জাগি

A. And if we are awake the whole night, then will you stay awake the whole night?

A. আর আমরা যদি সারা রাত জাগি , তা হলে তুমিও কি সারা রাত জাগবে ?

ar ' amra jodi ' śara rat jagi ' ta hole ' tumi ki ' śara rat jagbe "

12. B. Yes. If you stay awake the whole night, I shall also stay awake the whole night.

B. হাঁ , তোমরা সারা রাত জাগলে আমিও সারা রাত জাগবো ।

hæ " tomra ' śara rat jagle ' ami·o ' śara rat jagbo "

13. nour, "fast"
verb, "fast, make a fast"
"if we fast"

upoś, upobaś   উপোস , উপবাস

upoś kɔr-, upobaś kɔr-   উপোস কর

amra jodi upoś kori

আমরা যদি উপোস করি

A. And if we fast on Durga-puja day, then will you also fast?

A. আর আমরা যদি দুর্গাপূজোর দিন উপোস করি , তা হলে তুমিও কি উপোস করবে ?

ar amra jodi ' durga pujor din ' upoś kori ' ta hole ' tumi·o ki ' upoś korbe "

14. B. If you fast, I shall also fast.

B. তোমরা উপোস করলে আমিও উপোস করবো ।

tomra upoś korle ' ami·o ' upoś korbo "

15 "Wednesday"

budhbar   বুধবার

A. Good. In that case, we
shall go on Wednesday.

A. বেশ । তা হলে আমরা বুধবার দিন যাবো

beś " ta hole ' amra budhbar din '
jabo "

16. "before"
adjective, "prepared"
"if you are ready"

age আগে
toiri তৈরী
tumi jodi toiri hɔo

তুমি যদি তৈরী হও

B. All right. If you are
ready before (then),
will you call me?

B. আচ্ছা । তুমি যদি আগে তৈরী হও ,
তা হলে আমাকে ডাকবে কি ?

accha " tomi jodi ' age toiri
hɔo ' ta hole ' amake dakbe ki "

17. A. All right. If I am
ready before (then)
I shall call you.

A. আচ্ছা । আমি আগে তৈরী হলে
তোমাকে ডাকবো ।

accha " ami age ' toiri hole '
tomake dakbo "

Lesson 15, part 2. Grammar.

1. The verb stem /ja-/, "go", is irregular in the conditional conjunctive.
The stem of the conditional conjunctive is /ge-/.

2. Note that there are two ways of forming a conditional sentence.

2.1. The first is that which we have already covered in Lesson 14: the
use of the non-finite conjunctive in the conditional clause, with an
indicative verb of appropriate tense in the main clause. Remember that
the conditional clause always stands first in the sentence.

2.2. The second type of formation uses the form /jodi/, "if, when".
The position of /jodi/ can be either first in the sentence or following
the subject, depending upon style. Note that when /jodi/ is used in the
conditional clause, the main clause is usually introduced by /ta hole/.

3. The position of the negative particle in conditional clauses, as in
sentences 4 and 7.

In a conditional clause, whether formed with /jodi/ or by the conditional conjunctive, the negative particle always stands <u>before</u> the verb

tumi'śekhane na gele ami jabo na"   If you do not go there, I shall not go.

tumi jodi'śekhane na jao'ta hole' ami jabo na"   If you do not go there, I shall not go.

4. There are various ways of making negative nouns and adjectives in Bengali. Two of the most common are represented in sentences 3 and 9.

4.1. /ɔ/: śɔmbhɔb   "possible"   ɔśɔmbhɔb   "impossible"
          jana   "known"   ɔjana   "unknown"
          śustho   "healthy"   ɔśustho   "ill"

This prefix takes the form /ɔn-/ before vowels:

          acar   "conduct"   ɔnacar   "bad conduct"
          abośśɔk   "necessary"   ɔnabośśɔk   "unnecessary"
          aeaś   "labor"   ɔnaeaś   "without labor, easily"

4.2. /ni-/:rog   "disease"   nirog   "free of disease"

This prefix takes the form /nir-/ before vowels and voiced consonants except /r/. Examples:

          jɔn   "people, man"   nirjɔn   "without people, alone"
          akar   "form"   nirakar   "formless"

Such forms, however, are mostly found in the <u>śadhu-bhaśa</u>. They are found in the <u>colit-bhaśa</u> only as loans.

5. Form possible Bengali sentences

5.1.

	Clause I			Conj.		Clause II	
Subject	Cond.	Verbal Modifiers	Verb	Conj.	Subject	Modifiers	Verb
ami		oi dine	hẽṭe ja-		ami	amader	hẽṭe ja-
tumi		durga pujor dine	ghumote ja-		tumi	tomader śɔnge	kha-
apni	jodi	gramar barite	khete ja-		śe		bɔś-
śe		śara rat		ta hole	tini	śara rat	bɔl-
tini		age	hãṭ-		amra	tɔkhon	ja-
amra		śekhane	ghuma-			sei śɔmoe	aś-
		śɔhore	kha-			śekhane	beṛa-
		nodir dhare	bera-			gramer taṛite	
		ei pɔthe	ghor-				
			jag-				

5.2.

	Clause I				Clause II		
Subject	Modifiers/Object	(Neg.)	Verb	Subject	Modifiers	Verb	(Neg.)
ami	śekhane	(na)	gele	ami	amar śɔnge	thak-	(na)
tumi	śara rat		korle	tumi	tomar śɔnge	bɔs	
apni	baṛite		jagle		amader śɔnge	jag-	
śe	age		aśle		ekhane	dãṛa-	
tini	pɔre		bośle		śekhane	kɔr-	
amra	baire		ghumale		bhetore	ja-	
tomra			dile			de-	
	khabar		khele		khabar	kha-	
	niramiś				niramiś	ne-	

Lesson 15, part 3. Patterns.

1.   Pattern: sentence 1.

   a.   If I go home tomorrow, will you be able to go with me?

   b.   If I come back tomorrow, will you be able to come with me?

   c.   If I do not go home next week, will you be able to stay with me?

   d.   If I am not able to come back tonight, will you come to my house?

   e.   If you do not stop on the way to India, will you get there before Durga-puja?

2.   Pattern: sentence 2.

   a.   If you go home tomorrow, I'll go with you.

   b.   If you come back tomorrow, I'll come back with you.

   c.   If you don't go home, I'll stay here with you.

   d.   If you cannot come back tonight, I'll come to your house.

   e.   If I do not stop on the way, I'll get there before Durga-puja.

3.   Pattern: sentence 3.

   a.   If my mother and father are there, will that be an inconvenience for you?

   b.   If my relatives come with us, will that be an inconvenience for you?

   c.   If my brothers also stay with us, will that be an inconvenience for you?

   d.   If my friend wants to come with you, will that be an inconvenience for you?

   e.   If you do not get there before Durga-puja, will that be an inconvenience for you?

4.   Pattern: sentence 4.

   a.   If it is no inconvenience for them, it will be no inconvenience for me.

   b.   If it is no inconvenience for your relatives, it will be no inconvenience for me.

   c.   If it is no inconvenience for them, it will certainly be no inconvenience for me.

   d.   If he will be ready before eight, it will be no inconvenience at all.

   e.   If I do not get there before Durga-puja, it will be a great inconvenience for me.

5.   Pattern: sentence 5.

a. If they cannot walk, will you be able to take your car?
b. If we walk, will you be able to walk with us?
c. If they cannot take their car, will you be able to pick them up?
d. If he cannot be ready before eight, will he be able to come?
e. If you get there before <u>Durga-puja</u>, will you be able to go to my village?

6.   Pattern: sentence 6.

a. No, but if you make arrangements for a car, I can pick them up.
b. No, but if you make arrangements for a car, I can go with you.
c. No, but if I can make arrangements for a bullock-cart, they will be able to come.
d. No, but if you can make arrangements for a car, he can come later.
e. No, if you cannot make arrangements for a car, I shall not be able to go?

Pattern: sentence 7.

a. If you cannot make arrangements for that, I shall not go.
b. If you cannot make arrangements for a car, I shall not be able to go.
c. If I can make arrangements for that, they can come afterwards.
d. If you cannot make arrangements for that, he will not be able to come.
e. If you cannot make arrangements for that, I shall stay in Calcutta.

7.   Pattern: sentence 9.

a. If we eat Indian food, will you be able to eat it?
b. If my relatives eat vegetarian food, will that be an inconvenience for you?
c. If we do not eat vegetarian food, will you be able to eat with us?
d. If we eat meat, will you also be able to eat meat?
e. If they eat only vegetarian food, will you also eat only vegetarian food?

8.   Pattern: sentence 10.

a. If you give me Indian food, I shall eat it.
b. If you do not give me meat, I shall eat vegetarian food.
c. If you do not give me vegetarian food, I shall not eat anything.

    d.   If you do not give me vegetarian food, I shall eat meat.

    e.   If they give me only vegetarian food, I shall eat it.

9.   Pattern: sentence 11.

    a.   If we talk the whole night long, will you be able to stay awake?

    b.   If we sing the whole night long, will you be able to stay awake?

    c.   If we dance the whole night long, will you also dance?

    d.   If we sing the whole night long, will you also sing?

    e.   If they stay awake all day and all night long, will you be able to stay awake?

10. Pattern: sentence 12.

    a.   If you talk the whole night long, I also shall talk the whole night long.

    b.   If you sing the whole night long, I also shall sing the whole night long.

    c.   If you dance the whole night long, I also shall dance the whole night long.

    d.   If you sing the whole night long, I shall stay awake easily.*

    e.   If they dance and sing the whole day and night, I shall stay awake easily.

Lesson 15, part 4. Sentence Drills:

Use conditional conjunctive and /jodi/ constructions alternatively.

Drill 1

--If I go home at the end of next month, will you be able to come with me?

--If your wife says that it is all right, I'll go with you. If it is an inconvenience for her, I won't come.

--If you don't come, it will be an inconvenience for her. She expects you.

--If she is expecting me, then of course I shall come. How shall we go?

--If I can make arrangements for a car, then we shall go by car.

--If you cannot make arrangements for a car, then what?

--Then we shall go by train.

--If you go by train, I'll meet you there. I do not like trains.

--If you do not go by train, how will you go?

---

* Either /śɔhɔje/ or /ɔnaeaśe/.

--I shall go by plane. If I go by train, I shall not be able to sleep
  the whole night.

--All right. Then we shall go at the end of next month.

--Good. If you are ready to go before that, will you call me?

--All right. When I get ready, I shall call you.

Drill 2

--If you come to India, will you come to Calcutta?

--Yes, if I come to India, I shall come first to Calcutta.

--When you come to Calcutta, will you visit us?

--All right. If I stay with you, will it cause you an inconvenience?

--If you stay with us, it will not be an inconvenience. It will be a
  pleasure for us.

--If I want to stay in Calcutta for a long time, where will I live?

--If you want to live in old Calcutta, you can live on Citpur Road.

--But if I don't want to live in old Calcutta, what then?

--If you want to live in the new city, you can live in Ballygunge.

--If I decide to live in Ballygunge, will I be able to find a house?

--Yes. But if you want to live in North Calcutta, it will be difficult
  to find a house.

Lesson 15, part 5. Vocabulary.

ʈren	train	notun	new
rel gaʈi	train	śukhi	happy
śukh	happiness	śara	whole, complete
ɔpekkha	waiting	purono	old
maŋśo	meat	bharotio	Indian (adj.)

kiśe	
ki kore	how, by what means.

Idioms:

ɔpekkhae ach-	be in a state of expectation (with genitive)
ɔpekkha kɔr-	wait (with /jɔnno/, "for", and preceding genitive)
--śɔŋge dækha kɔr-	visit with
ʈhik kɔr-	decide; fix
ɔnek din	many days, a long time

Lesson 16, part 1. Conversation.

Analysis and translation	Bengali

1.
adjective, "past"	gɔto গত
"last month"	gɔto maś গত মাস
PAP of verb /ja-/ "go", base of past completive tense	gie- গিয়ে—
past completive tense suffix	-chil- —ছিল—
2nd person ordinary past tense ending	-e —ে
"(you) did go"	giechile গিয়েছিলে

A. <u>Robi, where did you go last month?</u>

A. রবি , তুমি গত মাসে কোথায় গিয়েছিলে ?

robi ' tumi gɔto maśe ' kothae giechile "

2.
| noun, "vacation" | chuṭi ছুটি |

Note: conditional conjunctive plus /-i/ emphatic suffix can mean "just as, as, since"

"as it began"	śuru holei শুরু হলেই
PAP of verb /ja-/, "go", base of past completive tense	gie- গিয়ে—
past completive tense suffix	-chil- —ছিল—
1st person past tense suffix	-um —ুম
"(I) did go"	giechilum গিয়েছিলুম

B. As I began my vacation last month, I went to Delhi.

B. গত মাসে ছুটি শুরু হলেই আমি দিল্লীতে গিয়েছিলুম ।

    gɔto maśe ' chuṭi śuru holei ami dillite giechilum "

3. PAP of verb /śon-/, "hear" base of past completive tense

    śune-   শুনে-

   past completive tense suffix

    -chil-   -ছিল-

   1st person past tense suffix

    -um   -ুম

   "I heard"

    śunechilum   শুনেছিলুম

A. I heard that you went home to Calcutta.

A. আমি শুনেছিলুম যে তুমি কলকাতাতে তোমার বাড়ী গিয়েছিলে ?

    ami śunechilum je ' tumi kolkatate ' tomar bari giechile "

4. Note: the conditional conjunctive plus /-o/ emphatic suffix means "even though" or in some circumstances "even if".

   "even though they stay"   tara thakleo   তারা থাকলেও

B. No, even though my mother and father live in Calcutta, I went to wander around Delhi and Agra.

B. না , আমার মা-বাবা কলকাতায় থাকলেও আমি দিল্লী আর আগ্রাতে বেড়াতে গিয়েছিলুম ।

    ṇa " amar ma-baba ' kolkatae thakleo ' ami dilli ar agrate ' bærate giechilum "

5. PAP of verb /bæṛa-/, "wander about, visit", base of past completive tense

    beṛie-   বেড়িয়ে-

   particle, "then, so, if that be so"

    ta   তা

A. Then what various places did you visit in Delhi?

A. তা , তুমি দিল্লীতে কোথায় কোথায় বেড়িয়েছিলে ?

    ta ' tumi dillite ' kothae kothae ' beṛiechile "

6. "(it) fell"   pɔrlo   পড়লো

   idiom: "get hot"   gɔrom pɔr-   গরম পড়-

"suddenly"   hɔṭhat হঠাৎ

idiom: "no more"   ar · · · na আর ... না

B. Suddenly it got very hot in   B. হঠাৎ দিল্লীতে খুব গরম পড়লো ,
Delhi, and so I did not   তাই আমার আর বেশী বেড়ানো
wander around much any more.   হল না ।

                                          hɔṭhat ' dillite ' khub gɔrom
                                          pɔrlo ' tai amar ' ar beśi
                                          bæṛano holɔ na "

7.   PAP of verb /dækh-/, "see"   dekhe- দেখে–

A. Still, which places in   A. তবু , তুমি দিল্লীতে কোন কোন
Delhi did you see?   জায়গা দেখেছিলে ?

                                          tobu ' tumi dillite ' kon kon
                                          jaega ' dekhechile "

8   noun, a carriage drawn
      ʃ one horse   tɔŋga টঙ্গা

      "in, by"; for this usage,   kore করে
      see Grammar, 4.

      PAP of verb /ghor-/,   ghure- ঘুরে–
      "tour, visit"

B I only toured Delhi for   B. আমি কেবল একদিন টঙ্গা করে দিল্লী
one day in a tɔŋga.   শহর ঘুরেছিলুম ।

                                          ami kebol ækdin ' tɔŋga kore
                                          dilli śɔhor ' ghurechilum "

9. A. Did you see the Birla   A. দিল্লীতে বিড়লা মন্দির দেখেছিলে কি ?
Temple in Delhi?

                                          dillite ' birla mondir '
                                          dikhechile ki "

10.   "enough"   beśi বেশী

      idiom: "have time"   hate śɔmoe ach-   হাতে সময় আছ –

      B. NO, I did not have enough   B. না . হাতে বেশী সময় ছিল না ।
time.

                                          na " hate ' beśi śɔmoe chilo na "

"hour"	ghɔnṭa ঘণ্টা
post-position, "within"	moddhe মধ্যে
"within two hours"	du ghɔnṭar moddhe দু ঘণ্টার মধ্যে
"mosque"	mośjid মসজিদ

B. So I saw the Delhi Fort and the Jumma Masjid within two hours.

B. তাই দু ঘণ্টার মধ্যে দিল্লী ফোর্ট আর জুম্মা মসজিদ দেখেছিলুম।

tai ' du ghɔnṭar moddhe ' dilli phorṭ ar jumma mośjid ' dekhechilum "

11. "other" onno অন্য

A. What did you do on all the other days?

A. অন্য সব দিন কি করেছিলে ?

onno śɔb din ' ki korechile "

12. "remaining" baki বাকী।

B. On all the remaining days, I sat in the house and read a book.

B. আমি বাকী সব দিন বাড়ীতে বসে একটা বই পড়েছিলুম।

ami ' baki śɔb din ' barite bośe ' ækṭa boi ' porechilum "

13. A. How many days were you in Agra?

A. তুমি আগ্রাতে কতদিন ছিলে ?

tumi agrate ' kɔtodin chile "

14. B. I was in Agra only two days.

B. আমি মাত্র দু দিন আগ্রাতে ছিলুম।

ami ' mattro du din ' agrate chilum "

15. A. What did you see in Agra?

A. তুমি আগ্রাতে কি দেখেছিলে ?

tumi agrate ' ki dekhechile "

16. B. In Agra I saw the Taj Mahal and the Agra Fort.

B. আমি আগ্রাতে তাজমহল আর আগ্রা ফোর্ট দেখেছিলুম।

ami agrate ' taj mohol ar agra phorṭ ' dekhechilum "

17. A. How did you like the Agra Fort?

       A. তোমার আগ্রা ফোর্ট কেমন লেগেছিলো ?

          tomar ' agra phort̪ ' kæmon legechilo "

18.   "extreme, extremely"   beś বেশ
      "good, well"   bhalo ভাল
      emphatic suffix   -i –ই
      "very much indeed" bes bhaloi বেশ ভালই

    B. I liked the Agra Fort very much indeed.

       B. আমার আগ্রা ফোর্ট বেশ ভালই লেগেছিলো ।

          amar ' agra phort̪ ' beś bhaloi legechilo "

19. A. And the Taj Mahal?

       A. আর তাজমহল ?

          ar taj mohol "

20. B. Wonderful!

       B. চমৎকার ।

          c̪omotkar "

Lesson 16, part 2. Grammar.

1. The formation and use of the past completive.

1.1. The most frequent use of the past completive tense is to refer to an action which has been completed before the time stipulated in the context of the utterance. A rule of thumb for the use of the tense is that whatever is expressed in English with the use of the auxilliary "had" is expressed in Bengali by the past completive, as:

    śe baṛite giechilo"   he had gone home
    śe kaj śeś korechilo"   he had finished his work

1.2. The past completive is also used to designate an action completed in the distant past:

    śe baṛite giechilo"   he went home (a long time ago)
    pãe bochor age śe   he came to Calcutta five years ago
    kolkatae eśechilo"

1.3. The past active participle forms the base of the past completive tense. To this base are added the past suffix /chi-/, the past tense sign /-l-/, and the past tense personal endings.

ami kine-chi-l-um	I bought, I had bought
tumi kine-chi-l-e	you (ord.) bought, you had bought
apni kine-chi-l-en	you (hon.) bought, you had bought
śe kine-chi-l-o	he (ord.) bought, he had bought
tini kine-chi-l-en	he (hon.) bought, he had bought

2. Additional uses of the conditional conjunctive, as in sentences 2 and 4.

2.1. The conditional conjunctive plus the emphatic suffix /-i/ can mean, as it does in sentence 2, "as", "just as", "just when", or "since". The conditional conjunctive plus this /-i/ suffix can also mean "if only", as:

tumi'śekhane jete parlei' tar śɔŋge dækha hɔbe"	If only you could go there, you would meet him.

-or-

As soon as you can go there, you will meet him.

ami'car ṭaka pete parlei' boiṭa kinbo"	If only I could get four rupees, I would buy the book.

2.1.1. The infinitive plus the emphatic suffix /-i/ is in some circum-stances used in this same way, to mean "as" or "just as". The infinitive plus /-i/, i.e., /hotei/ could also have been used in sentence 2.

2.2. The conditional conjunctive plus the emphatic suffix /-o/ carries the meaning "even if", as:

śe ekhane aśleo'ami take'kichu debo na"	Even if he comes here, I shall give him nothing.

2.2.1. If the conditional with /jodi/ is used, the emphatic suffix can be added to the verb form with the same result:

jodi śe aseo ' ta hole take'kichu debo na"	Even if he comes, I shall give him nothing.

2.2.2. If, however, the emphatic /-o/ is added to the /jodi/ particle

the meaning is "even though he comes (i.e., in spite of the fact that he comes ...)":

> jodio'śe ekhane ase'   Even though he comes here,
> ami take'kichu dii na"   I give him nothing.

2.2.2.1. The morpheme /jodio/ meaning "even though" can be thought of as entirely different from the conditional morpheme /jodi/, "if". An indication that this is grammatically sound is that the negative particle <u>follows</u> the verb when /jodio/ is used, while it precedes the verb in a clause with /jodi/:

> śe jodio jae ni'ami   Even though he didn't go, I went.
> giechilum"
>
> śe jodi na jae'ami   If he doesn't go, I won't go.
> jabo na"

3. Verb stems of shape CVCa- form their verbal nouns by the addition of the suffix /-no/. The most common of these include:

> bæṛa-no   wander about
> hara-no   defeat; be lost
> lapha-no   leap
> douṛo-, douṛa-no   run
> poũcho-, poũcha-no   reach, arrive at
> ghumo-, ghuma-no   sleep
> bæ̃ka-no   bend
> kamṛa-no   bite

4. The use of the PAP /kore/ in sentence 8.

4.1. The PAP /kore/ is frequently used to form a phrase expressing means, particularly means of transportation. Other examples:

> śe nouko kore'eśechilo"   He came by boat.
> ami moṭor kore'eśechi"   I have come by car.

4.2. The locative ending with this usage is optional; you will find both /nouko kore/ and /noukote kore/ or /noukoe kore/.

4.3. Other PAPs are also used in the same way. For example:

> śe'rasta dhore'jae"   He goes along the path.

ṡe take'churi die'   He killed him by means of a knife.
merechilo

4.4. Another usage of /kɔrə/ should be mentioned here, though it will be mentioned again later. That is the so-called adverbial formation, noun or adjective + /kore/:

ṡɔkto kore   firmly
ṡe'ṡɔkto kore'dhɔre"   He holds it firmly.

jor kore   forcibly
ṡe oṭa'jor kore'kere nilo" He snatched it away forcibly.

4.4.1. In certain circumstances the adverbial function of a word is defined only by its position in the order of words in the sentence:

tumi'kharap gan'gao"   You sing bad songs.
tumi gan'kharap gao"   You sing badly (habitually).

The use of /kore/ may alter the meaning of the sentence:

tumi gan'kharap kore'gao" You sing badly (on this particular occasion; i.e., you have the capacity to sing well, but are not doing it).

Lesson 16, part 3. Patterns.

1.   Pattern: sentence 1.

    a. Robi, where did you stay last week?
    b. Robi, where did you go last month?
    c. Robi, where did you go in India?
    d. Robi, what did you see in the village?
    e. Robi, what did you buy at the store?

2.   Pattern: sentence 2.

    a. As I began work last week, I went to Calcutta.
    b. As I finished my work last month, I went on my vacation.
    c. As I finished seeing Agra, I went to Delhi.
    d. As I came to the village in Asvin [aṡṡin], I saw the Durga-pu
    e. As I arrived there late, I was not able to buy anything.

298

3. Pattern: sentence 3.

   a. I heard that you did not stay in Delhi.
   b. I heard that you had gone to Delhi.
   c. I heard that you also went to Bengal.
   d. I heard that you had lived in a village before.
   e. I heard that you had bought a new car.

4. Pattern: sentence 4.

   a. Yes. Even though I live in Delhi, they sent me to Calcutta.
   b. No, even though I live in Calcutta, I went there this time.
   c. Yes, even though I didn't go to Calcutta, I saw Bengal.
   d. No, even though I lived in India, I always lived in cities.
   e. No, even though I want a new car, I have never been able to buy one.

5. Pattern: sentence 5.

   a. What things did you like in Calcutta?
   b. What people did you meet in Calcutta?
   c. What places did you go in India?
   d. What cities have you visited in India?
   e. What other things did you see at the store?

6. Pattern: sentence 6.

   a. Nothing. Suddenly it got very hot in Calcutta, and I wasn't able to rest.
   b. No one. Suddenly it got very hot in Calcutta, and my travelling about was hampered.
   c. Nowhere. Suddenly it got very hot in May, and my travelling was stopped.
   d. Many. It gets very cool in Delhi, and I always went there in winter.
   e. Many things. But I had no money, and I was not able to buy.

7. Pattern: sentence 7.

   a. Still, did you see any places in the city?
   b. Still, did you meet any people there?
   c. Still, did you go to many places in Bengal?
   d. But did you go to the mountains in the summer?
   e. But did you not go to the bank?

8.   Pattern: sentence 8.

    a.   Yes, I went around the Hugli one day by boat.
    b.   Yes, I went around the city one day by taxi and saw people.
    c.   Yes, I went to Konarok in Orissa by bullock-cart.
    d.   Yes, I went to the mountains by train.
    e.   Yes, I went to the bank by tram this morning.

9.   Pattern: sentence 9.

    a.   Did you see the Kali temple in Kalighat?
    b.   Did you meet any painters or writers?
    c.   Did you see the temple at Puri?
    d.   Did you go to Dehra Dun?
    e.   Did you get some money there?

10.   Pattern: sentence 10.

    a.   Yes, I had time to see that.
    b.   No, I did not have time to meet them.
    c.   No, I did not have time to go there.
    d.   Yes, I went to Dehra Dun and Mussoorie [muśuri].
    e.   No. The bank was closed, and I had no time to wait.

11.   Pattern: sentence 11.

    a.   What did you do on the other days?
    b.   Where did you go on the other days?
    c.   What did you do for the remaining time?
    d.   What did you do in Dehra Dun?
    e.   Where did you go after that?

12.   Pattern: sentence 12.

    a.   The remaining days I sat on my veranda and slept.
    b.   The remaining days I sat in my chair and read.
    c.   The remaining days I went and looked at paintings.
    d.   I rested and talked with people.
    e.   I went and looked in some book shops.

13.   Pattern: sentence 13.

    a.   How many weeks were you in Calcutta?
    b.   How many months were you in Bengal?
    c.   How long were you in India?
    d.   How many years were you in India before?

    e. How long were you in India before?

    f. How long were you in the book shops?

14. Pattern: sentence 14.

    a. I was in Calcutta only five weeks.

    b. I was in Bengal exactly two months and three days.

    c. I was in India five months.

    d. I was in India almost five years before.

    e. I was in the shops about two hours.

15. Pattern: sentence 17.

    a. How did you like the trip?

    b. How did you like Bengal?

    c. How did you like India?

    d. How did you like coming home?

    e. How did you like the shops?

16. Pattern: sentence 18.

    a. I liked the trip very well.

    b. I didn't like Calcutta at all.

    c. I liked the country very well.

    d. I liked coming home.

    e. I didn't like the shops very well.

Lesson 16, part 4.   Sentence Drills.

Drill 1

--I did not see you last month. were you not in the city?

--No, I went to Calcutta.

--I thought perhaps you had gone there. Did you see your brother and sister there?

--No, even though they live there, I did not have time enough to see them.

--Did you see many places in the city?

--No if only I get my vacation next month, I shall go back and wander around the city.

--Did you like it, then?

--Yes, I liked it very much. But it got very hot in the city and I could not wander around very much.

-Were you able to see the Jain temple?

--No. I had heard about it, and I wanted to go. But I did not have the time.

--What did you do there, then?

--When it was not too hot, I worked. When I could not work, I stayed in my room and read a book.

--How many days were you there?

--I stayed there only three days. Then I went on to Cuttack.

Drill 2

--Did you go to a village for Durga-puja?

--Yes, I went to the house of a friend of mine in a village near Bankura.

--How did you like it?

--Wonderful. The people were very open-hearted and took good care of me, even though I was a foreigner.

--What did you do?

--In the morning and the evening we went to the temple. In the afternoon we often went for a walk.

--There is a Santal village nearby, isn't there? Did you see the Santals?

--Yes, there is a village there in the jungle. One night we went there to see a dance.

--And did you hear any Baul songs?

--Yes, one afternoon a Baul came and sang for us. Even though he was very old, he sang beautifully.

--If only I could collect those Baul songs, people would be able to hear their sweetness.

--Rabindranath did collect a few. They are beautiful.

Lesson 16, part 5. Vocabulary.

bideśi	foreigner	śɔŋgraho kɔr-	collect
madhurjo, miṣṭota	sweetness		
buṛo, briddho	old man	biśeś	special, especially
ador	love, ffection	prankhola	open-hearted
śit kal	winter	pran	heart
pɔrbot	mountain	khola	open, frank, candid
jɔŋgol	jungle	ɔpurbo	unprecedented, very wonderful
ebar, eibar	this time	bɔndho	hindered, stopped, closed

302

śɔmmondhe   post-position, "in regard to", with genitive

Idioms:

--ke odor jɔtno kɔr-   to take good care of, to treat
                                   with great kindness

hate beśi śɔmoe ach-   to have enough time
śɔmoe pa-
tai na   is it not so? (note intonation)

Analysis and translation	Bengali
1. stem of verb "remain"	thak- থাক–
past habitual tense suffix	-t- –ত
2nd person ordinary past tense ending	-e –ে
"(you) used to remain/ live"	thakte থাকতে

A. <u>Where did you used to live?</u>

A. তুমি আগে কোথায় থাকতে ?

    <u>tumi age ' kothae thakte</u> "

2.   past habitual tense suffix   -t- –ত

    1st person past tense ending   -um –ুম

    "(I) used to remain/ live"   thaktum থাকতুম

B. <u>I used to live in Syam-bazar before. Now I live in Bhowanipur.</u>

B. আমি আগে শ্যামবাজারে থাকতুম ।
এখন ভবানীপুরে থাকি ।

    <u>ami age ' śambajare thaktum</u> "
    <u>ᵊkhon ' bhᴐbanipure thaki</u> "

3.   high stem of verb /pᴐɽ-/, "study"   poɽ- পড়–

    past habitual tense suffix   -t- –ত

    2nd person ordinary past tense ending   -e –ে

    "(you) used to study"   porte পড়তে

"university'   biśśobiddalɔe বিশ্ববিদ্যালয়

A. Did you used to study   A. তুমি ক্লকাতা বিশ্ববিদ্যালয়ে পড়তে কি ?
at Calcutta University?

           tumi ' kolkata biśśobiddalɔe '
           porte ki "

4. "study for the B.A."   bi.e pɔr- বি.এ. পড়-

B. Yes, 1 studied for the   B. হাঁ , আমি ক্লকাতা বিশ্ববিদ্যালয়ে
B.A. at Calcutta   বি.এ. পড়েছিলুম ।
University.

           hæ " ami ' kolkata biśśobiddalɔe '
           bi.e porechilum "

5. loan word, "university" iunibharśiṭi ইউনিভার্সিটি

A. At which college of the A. তুমি ইউনিভার্সিটির কোন কলেজে
University did you used   পড়তে ?
to study?

           tumi ' iunibharśiṭir ' kon kɔleje '
           porte "

6. name of a college of
Calcutta University,
"City College"   siti kɔlej সিটি কলেজ

name of a college of
Calcutta University,
"Presidency College"   presidensi kɔlej প্রেসিডেন্সী কলেজ

B. First I used to study at B. আমি প্রথমে সিটি কলেজে , তার পরে
City College, after that   প্রেসিডেন্সী কলেজে পড়তুম ।
at Presidency College.

           ami prothome ' siti kɔleje ' tar
           pɔre ' presidensi kɔleje ' portum "

7. A. Did you used to go to A. তুমি কি ক্লকাতায় খুব ফুটবল খেলা
see many football games   দেখতে যেতে ?
in Calcutta?

           tumi ki kolkatae ' khub phuṭbɔl
           khæla ' dekhte jete "

8.   "often"   prae   প্রায়

        emphatic suffix   -i   -ই

        "very often"   praei   প্রায়ই

        B. Yes, when friends went with me, I used to go to watch the game very often.

        B. হাঁ , বন্ধুরা আমার সঙ্গে গেলে আমি প্রায়ই খেলা দেখতে যেতুম ।

        hæ̃ " bondhura ' amar sɔŋge gele ' ami praei ' khæla dekhte jetum "

9.   loan word, "coffee house"; there are several in Calcutta, very popular with students and intellectuals

                                         kɔphi hauʃ   কফি হাউস

        "conversation, gossip"   gɔlpogujob   গল্পগুজব

        A. And did you used to go to the coffee house to talk very often?

        A. আর তুমি কি প্রায়ই গল্পগুজব করতে কফি হাউসে যেতে ?

        ar tumi ki praei gɔlpogujob korte ' kɔphi hause ' jete "

10.   "between"   majhe   মাঝে

        "from time to time"   majhe majhe   মাঝে মাঝে

        B. When I had no more studying, I used to go there from time to time.

        B. পড়াশোনা না থাকলে আমি মাঝে মাঝে সেখানে যেতুম ।

        pɔraʃona na thakle ' ami majhe majhe ' ʃekhane jetum "

11.   "vacation, day off"   chuʈi   ছুটি

        A. What did you used to do on your days off?

        A. ছুটির দিনগুলোতে তুমি কি করতে ?

        chuʈir dingulote ' tumi ' ki korte "

12.   "field", a large common in the middle of a city like Calcutta   mɔedan   ময়দান

B. When my sister used to
come to see me, I used
to take her for a walk
on the maidan.

B. আমার বোন দেখা করতে এলে , তাকে আমার সঙ্গে নিয়ে ময়দানে বেড়াতে যেতুম

amar bon ' dækha korte ele ' take '
amar ʃɔŋge nie ' mɔedane bærate
jetum "

13. "heat, hot season"   grísśo গ্রীষ্ম

A. What did you used to do
in the long summer
vacation?

A. গ্রীষ্মের লম্বা ছুটিতে তুমি কি করতে ?

grísśer lɔmba chuṭite ' tumi ki
korte "

14. "body"   śorir শরীর
"be in good health"   śorir bhalo thak- শরীর ভাল থাক-
hill station in   śimla সিমলা
North India

B. When my mother and father
were in good health, we
used to go to visit Simla.

B. আমার মা-বাবার শরীর ভাল থাকলে সিমলাতে বেড়াতে যেতুম ।

amar ma-babar ' śorir bhalo thakle'
śimlate bærate jetum "

15. idiom: "didn't you?,   tai na তাই না
isn't that so?"

A. You used to write poetry
in college, didn't you?

A. তুমি কলেজে কবিতা লিখতে , তাই না ?

tumi kɔleje ' kobita likhte ' tai
na "

16. noun, "journal", a common
name of journals   potrika পত্রিকা
compound verb, "be
published, come out"   bar hɔ- বার হ-

B. Yes, my poetry used to be
published in the college
journal very often.

B. হাঁ , আমার কবিতা কলেজ পত্রিকাতে প্রায়ই বার হতো ।

hæ " amar kobita ' kɔlej potrikate '
praei bar hoto "

17. <u>A.</u> <u>You used to do other</u>
<u>things in college,</u>
<u>didn't you?</u>

<u>A.</u> তুমি কলেজে আর কিছু করতে নাকি ?

<u>tumi kɔleje ' **ar ki.chu** korte '
naki "</u>

18. <u>B.</u> <u>Yes, I used to play tennis</u>
<u>when I got a little time,</u>
<u>and I used to play cricket</u>
<u>often.</u>

B. হাঁ , আমি একটু সময় পেলে টেনিস
খেলতুম আর প্রায় সময় ক্রিকেট খেলতুম ।

<u>hæ̃ " ami ek.tu **śɔmoe** pele ' teniś
kheltum ' ar prae śɔmoe ' kriket
kheltum "</u>

19. "job"

"games"

compound verb stem,
"give up, leave"

cakri চাকরী

khæladhulo খেলাধুলো

cheɹe de- ছেড়ে দে-

<u>B.</u> <u>But now I have a job.</u>
<u>That is why I have</u>
<u>given up games.</u>

B. কিন্তু এখন আমার চাকরী আছে । তাই
খেলাধুলো ছেড়ে দিয়েছি ।

<u>kintu ækhon ' aᵐar cakri ache " tai
khæladhulo cheɹe diechi "</u>

Lesson 17, part 2. Grammar.

1. Formation and use of the past habitual:

1.1. The most common use of the past habitual is that which we have seen
in this lesson -- reference to action which was customary in the past;
the tense can be used wherever English can use the phrase "used to".

1.2. The formation of the past habitual is by the <u>high</u> <u>stem</u> of all verbs
except verb stems of (C)VC- shape where the vowel is /a/, and stems of
CVCa- shape. These two types of stems preserve their low vowels. The
sign of the past habitual is /-t-/, which is affixed to the verb stem.
To the tense sign /-t-/ are then added the past tense personal endings.

ken-	"buy"	ami kin - t - um
		tumi kin - t - e
		tui kin - t - iś
		apni kin - t - en
		śe kin - t - o
		tini kin - t - en

	khæl-	"play"	ami khel - ṭ - um, etc.
	kɔr-	"do"	ami kor - ṭ - um, etc.
	śon-	"hear"	ami śun - ṭ - um, etc.
But:	jan-	"know"	ami jan - ṭ - um, etc.
	bæṛa-	"wander about"	ami bæṛa - ṭ - um, etc.

----

	de-	"give"	ami di - ṭ - um, etc.
	hɔ-	"be"	ami ho - ṭ - um, etc.
	kha-	"eat"	ami khe - ṭ - um, etc.

The verb stem /ja-/ is regular, having the stem /je-/ in the past habitual.

1.3. This tense and the simple past are the only tenses which permit the formation of the negative with /na/:

> I used to play   kheltum
> I did not used to play kheltum na

2. As in sentence 4, the Bengali usage is to make /bi·e/ the direct object of /pɔṛ-/, "study (or "read") B.A.", where English usage will be "study for the B.A."

Lesson 17, part 3. Patterns.

1. Pattern: sentence 1.

    a. Where did you used to go?

    b. Where did she used to live?

    c. Where did they used to meet you?

    d. Where did you (pl.) used to study?

    e. Where did he used to live?

2. Pattern: sentence 2.

    a. I used to go often to Kalighat (/kalighaṭ/) before.

    b. She used to live in Ballygunge before.

    c. They used to come to my house, a long time ago.

    d. We used to study in that room.

    e. He used to live in Calcutta.

3. Pattern: sentence 5.

    a. What part of Kalighat did you used to go to see?
    b. In what part of Ballygunge did she used to live?
    c. In what part of the city did they used to live?
    d. In what field of study did you (pl.) used to work?
    e. In what part of the city did he used to live?

4. Pattern: sentence 6a.

    a. I used to go to see the Kali temple.
    b. She used to live near Gariahat (/goɽiahaʈ/).
    c. They used to live in Citpur Road (/citpur roḍ/).
    d. We used to study Bengali literature.
    e. He used to live near the river.

    Pattern: sentence 6b.

    a. After that I used to walk along the river.
    b. After that she used to live near the lake.
    c. After living there for ten years, they went to Poona.
    d. After that we began to study Sanskrit (/śɔŋśkrit/).
    e. After that he used to live with me most of the time.

5. Pattern: sentence 7.

    a. Did you used to see many boats on the river?
    b. Did she used to be able to see the lake from her home?
    c. Did they used to be able to come back to Calcutta?
    d. Did you used to be able to read Sanskrit well?
    e. Did you (pl.) used to meet Sipra often?

6. Pattern: sentence 8.

    a. Yes, when my friends went with me, we used to go in a boat to Shalimar.
    b. Yes, when she lived in that house, she used to see the lake very clearly (/śpɔśʈo/).
    c. No, when they went there, they didn't used to come back often.
    d. Yes, when we were studying, we used to read very well.
    e. Yes, when my friend went with me, I used to go to her house often.

7.   Pattern: sentence 9.

    a.   Did you (pl.) used to go in the boat often?

    b.   Did she used to go to the lake often?

    c.   Did you used to see them very often?

    d.   Did you (pl.) used to read kavya (/kabbo/)?

    e.   Did you used to meet her parents often?

8.   Pattern: sentence 10.

    a.   When I had no more studying, we used to go from time to time.

    b.   When she had no more studying, she used to walk there.

    c.   When we had the time, we used to go to see them.

    d.   When we had learned enough, we used to read kavya.

    e.   When we went there, her parents always used to be there.

9.   Pattern: sentence 11.

    a.   What did you used to do on the trip?

    b.   Where did she used to walk there?

    c.   Where did you used to stay in Poona?

    d.   Where did you (pl.) used to study Sanskrit?

    e.   What did her father used to do?

10. Pattern: sentence 12.

    a.   When we used to go on the river, we used to read and sleep all the time.

    b.   When she used to walk there, she used to walk along the lake shore.

    c.   When we used to go to Poona, we used to stay with my sister.

    d.   When we studied Sanskrit, we used to study with a pandit (/pondit/ -- see vocabulary).

    e.   When we knew him, her father used to write poetry.

Lesson 17, part 4. Sentence Drills.

Drill 1

--Have you been to Calcutta?

--Yes, I used to live in Calcutta, a few years ago. I used to study at Calcutta University.

--At ,at college of the University did you used to study?

--I studied for the B.A. at Presidency College. Then I studied for the M.A. at St. Xavier's College.

--Did you like the city?

--Yes. When I had no studying, I used to walk through the maidan (/mɔedaner bhetor die/) and along the bank of the river.

--Did you used to stay in Calcutta during the summer also?

--No, when my friends would go with me, I used to go to Darjeeling. We also used to go to Puri from time to time.

--You used to play cricket in college, didn't you?

--Yes, I used to play cricket when I got the chance, but usually I had too much studying.

--Did you used to go to the movies very often?

--No, not often. From time to time I used to take my sister there.

--Did your sister used to live in Calcutta too?

--No, she lived in Delhi. But she used to come to Calcutta often to see me.

Drill 2

--We used to be able to buy a seer of rice for four annas. Do you remember?

--Yes, I remember. Prices are not what they used to be (i.e., what price was, now that is not).

--And we used to be able to buy ɹilk sari for fifteen rupees.

--Yes, When we used to live in   village, things were much cheaper.

--We used to sit on the veranda, in our village house, and people used to come and talk.

--Yes, the old men used to gossip incessantly.

--They used to say that the old days were good, and that modern times are bad.

--They used to tell stories from the Ramayana (/ramaeon/) and Mahabharata (/mɔhabharot/).

--Yes, I used to like those stories. But in the village we did not used to be able to go to the movies.

Lesson 17, part 5. Vocabulary.

bibhag	department, division
śujog	chance, opportunity
cal	rice (husked rice)
jiniśpɔttro, jiniśpɔttor	things (in general)
jiniś	thing
pɔttro, pɔttor	suffix, "and such"
kagojpɔttro, kagojpɔttor	papers and other such things
cithipɔttro, cithipɔttor	letters and other such things
gɔlpo	story

bɔrtoman (sɔmoe)	present (time)
nouko	boat
lek, dighi	lake
bhromon	trip
ser	seer (about two pounds weight)
baś kɔr-	live (make dwelling)
gɔlpo bɔl-	tell a story
gɔlpo kɔr-	gossip
mone rakh-	remember
purono din	olden times
śpɔśṭo, pɔśṭo	clear, clearly
śɔsta	cheap
kɔek	a few, several
pɔnero	fifteen
śɔb śɔmoe	all the time, incessantly
praei	usually, very often
ponḍiter kache	with a pandit (scholar)
baeṛate (gie)	(going) on the trip
æk śer cal	a seer of rice

Lesson 18, part 1. Conversation.

Analysis and translation	Bengali

1.   high stem of verb
/pɔṛ-/, "read"   pɔṛ- পড়–

         past tense suffix   -chil- –িছল–

         2nd person ordinary
past tense ending   -e   –ে

         past continuative,
"you were reading"   pɔṛchile   পড়িছলে

     A. <u>John, what book were
you reading?</u>   A. জন , ত‍ুমি কি বই পড়িছলে ?

                                      <u>jɔn ' tumi ' ki boi pɔṛchile</u> "

2.   noun, "novel"   uponnaś   উপন‍্যাস

         high stem of verb
/dækh-/, "see"   dekh-   দেখ–

         past tense suffix   -chil-   –িছল–

         1st person past
tense ending   -um   –‍ুম

         past continuative,
"I was looking at"   dekhchilum   দেখিছল‍ুম

     B. <u>I was looking at a
Bengali novel.</u>   B. আমি একটা বাংলা উপন‍্যাস দেখিছল‍ুম ।

                                        <u>ami ækṭa ' baṇla uponnaś '
dekhchilum</u> "

3.   interrogative pronoun
stem, "who"   ka-   ক–

         "whose, of whom"   kar   কার

         verb stem, "write"   lekh-   লেখ–

314

verbal noun/adjective
"writing, written"   lekha   লেখা
"written by whom"   kar lekha   কার লেখা

A. Who wrote the novel you   A. কার লেখা উপন্যাস দেখেছিলে ?
were looking at?

                                                             kar lekha uponnaś ' dekhchile "

4.   name of a 19th century
Bengali novellist   boŋkim   বঙ্কিম
name of a Bengali novel   anondomɔth   আনন্দমঠ

B. It was Anandamath, writ-   B. তোমাদের বঙ্কিমবাবুর লেখা আনন্দমঠ ।
ten by your Bankim-babu.

                                                             tomader boŋkim babur lekha '
                                                             anondomɔth "

5.   "is it not so?"   naki   নাকি

A. You read Bengali books,   A. তুমি বাংলা বই পড় নাকি ?
don't you?

                                                             tumi ' baŋla boi pɔro naki "

6.   a stem of irregular
verb "go" (/ja-/)   gɔ-   গ—
an adjectival suffix   -to   —ত
"gone, past"   gɔto   গত
high stem of verb,
"learn"   śikh-   িশখ—

B. Yes, in the past two years B. হাঁ , আমি গত দু বছর একটু বাংলা
I have been learning a   ভাষা িশখছিলুম ।
little Bengali.

                                                             hæ̃ " ami ' gɔto du bɔchor ' ektu
                                                             baŋla bhaśa ' śikhchilum "

1st person present of   dekhi   দেখি
stem /dækh-/ "see";
"I see" or "let me see"
question marker   ki   িক
negative   na   না
"whether or not"   kina   িকনা

B. So I thought, "Let me see whether or not I can read the writing of Bankim-babu."

B. তাই ভাবলুম যে দেখি বঙ্কিমবাবুর লেখা পড়তে পারি কিনা ?

tai ' bhablum je ' dekhi ' boŋkim babur lekha ' porte pari kina "

7. untranslatable particle which transmits a feeling of condition or doubt on the part of the speaker

to তো

"strike, or seem or be difficult (for)"

śɔkto lag- (with genitive)

শক্ত লাগ–

A. I think that his writing will be a little difficult for you.

A. আমার তো মনে হচ্ছে যে তাঁর লেখা তোমার একটু শক্ত লাগবে ।

amar to ' mone hocche je ' tãr lekha ' tomar ' ektu śɔkto lagbe "

8. B. Why do you say that?

B. কেন বলো তো ?

kaeno bɔlo to "

9. "because"
"Sanskrit"
noun, "word"
noun, "use"
compound verb, "use"

karon   কারণ
śɔŋśkrito   সংস্কৃত
śɔbdo   শব্দ
bæbohar   ব্যবহার
bæbohar kɔr-   ব্যবহার কর্–

A. Because at the time when Bankim was writing, almost all the writers were using Sanskrit words.

A. কারণ যে সময়ে বাঙ্কিম লিখছিলেন সে সময়ে প্রায় সব লেখক সংস্কৃত শব্দ ব্যবহার করছিলেন ।

karon ' je śɔmoe ' boŋkim likhchilen ' śe śɔmoe ' prae śɔb lekhɔk ' śɔŋśkrito śɔbdo ' bæbohar korchilen "

10. B. That is why I was finding the book so hard.

B. তাই বইটা আমার এত শক্ত লাগছিলো ।

tai ' boiṭa ' amar æto śɔkto ' lagchilo "

11. adjective, "current"

name for colloquial
Bengali language

adjective, "pure"

name for literary
Bengali language

"or"

colit চলিত

colit bhaśa   চলিত ভাষা

śadhu   সাধু

śadhu bhaśa   সাধু ভাষা

na, ba   না , বা

A. <u>When you were learning
Bengali, were you learn-
ing the colloquial or
the literary language?</u>

A. তুমি যখন বাংলা ভাষা শিখছিলে তখন তুমি কি চলিত ভাষা শিখছিলে না সাধু ভাষা শিখছিলে ?

<u>tumi jɔkhon ' baŋla bhaśa śikhchile '
tɔkhon ' tumi ki ' colit bhaśa
śikhchile ' na śadhu bhaśa
śikhchile "</u>

12. "two, both"

emphatic suffix

dui দুই

-i -ই

B. <u>I was learning both the
colloquial and the
literary language.</u>

B. আমি চলিত ও সাধু ভাষা দুই শিখছিলাম ।

<u>ami ' colit o śadhu bhaśa ' duii
śikhchilum "</u>

13. A. <u>Look, if you learn a
little Sanskrit it will
be very expedient for you.</u>

A. দেখ , তুমি যদি একটু সংস্কৃত শেখ তা হলে তোমার বড় সুবিধে হবে ।

<u>dækho ' tumi jodi ' ektu śɔŋskrito
śekho ' ta hole tomar ' bɔro
śubidhe hɔbe "</u>

14. noun, "India"

stem of verb, "go"

past tense suffix
(with vowel-stem verbs)

1st person past suffix

"I was going"

"another"

adjective, "cultivated"

"person"

"gentleman"

bharɔt, bharotbɔrśo   ভারত , ভারতবর্ষ

ja-   যা—

-cchil-   -চ্ছিল—

-um   -ুম

jacchilum   যাচ্ছিলাম

ar æk   আর এক

bhɔddro .   ভদ্র

lok   লোক

bhɔddrolok   ভদ্রলোক

317

"that"   ta   তা

"that (emphatic)"   ta.i   তাই

B. <u>When I was going to India last year, another Bengali gentleman told me the same thing.</u>

B. গত বছর আমি যখন ভারতবর্ষে যাচ্ছিলুম তখন আর একজন বাঙালী ভদ্রলোক তাই বলিছিলেন ।

gɔto bɔchor ' ami jɔkhon ' bharotbɔrśe jacchilum ' tɔkhon ' ar ækjon baŋali bhɔddrolok ' ta.i bolchilen "

15. A. <u>Why were you going to India last year?</u>

A. তা তুমি গত বছর ভারতবর্ষে যাচ্ছিলে কেন ?

ta tumi ' gɔto bɔchor ' bharotbɔrśe jacchile kæno "

16.   "speech, address"   boktrita   বক্তৃতা

B. <u>To give speeches in your country.</u>

B. তোমাদের দেশে বক্তৃতা দিতে ।

tomader deśe boktrita dite "

17. post-position, "concerning" (preceding genitive optional)   biśɔe   বিষয়ে

A. <u>To give speeches about America?</u>

A. আমেরিকার বিষয় বক্তৃতা দিতে কি ?

amerikar biśɔe ' boktrita dite ki "

18. stem of verb, "read"   pɔr-   পড়-

causative stem of verb "read" (i.e., "teach")   pɔra-   পড়া-

past suffix (with vowel stems)   -cchil-   -চ্ছিল-

1st person past suffix   -um   -ুম

"I was teaching"   pɔracchilum   পড়াচ্ছিলুম

"connection, relation"   śɔmmondho   সম্বন্ধ

post-position "in regard to, about" (preceding genitive optional)   śɔmmondhe   সম্বন্ধে

B. Yes. I was teaching
(about) American
literature.

B. ইাঁ , আমি আমেরিকান সাহিত্য সম্বন্ধে পড়াী লম্ ।

hæ̃ " ami ' amerikan śahitto śɔmmondhe ' pɔracchilum "

19. "wish, desire"   icche ইচ্ছে
    "government"   śɔrkar সরকার

B. That is why the government's wish was that I
give a speech about that.

B. তাই সরকারের ইচ্ছেছিল আমি এ বিষয়ে বক্তৃতা দিই ।

tai ' śɔrkarer icche chilo ' ami oi biśoe ' boktrita dii "

20. "whereabouts, in which
different places"   kothae kothae কোথায় কোথায়

A. In which different places
in India were you giving
speeches?

A. তুমি ভারতবর্ষে কোথায় কোথায় বক্তৃতা দিচ্ছিলে ?

tumi bharot bɔrśe ' kothae kothae ' boktrita dicchile "

21. "the greatest, the most"   beśi বেশী
    "of the greatest"   beśir বেশীর
    "part, portion"   bhag ভাগ
    "the majority, the
    greatest part"   beśir bhag বেশীর ভাগ

B. The greatest part of the
time I was giving speeches
in Calcutta itself.

B. আমি বেশীর ভাগ সময় কলকাতাতেই বক্তৃতা দিচ্ছিলম্ ।

ami ' beśir bhag śɔmoe ' kɔlkatatei ' boktrita dicchilum "

22. A. How did you like Bengal?

A. তা তোমার বাংলা দেশ কেমন লাগছিলো ?

ta tomar ' baŋla deś ' kæmon lagchilo "

23. "extremely"   bhari ভারী
    "special, particular"   biśeś বিশেষ
    function word; see
    Grammar, 3.   kore করে

"especially"   biśeś kore   বিশেষ ন্বরে

B. I think that Bengal is an   B. আমার মনে হয় যে বা'লা দেশ ভারী সন্দর
extremely beautiful place,   জায়গা । বিশেষ করে কলকাতা শহর ।
especially Calcutta city.

amar mone hɔe je   banla deś ' bhari
śundor jaega ' biśeʃ kore ' kɔlkata
śɔhor "

24.   "mouth"   mukh   মুখ

A. I like very much to hear   A. তোমার মুখ থেকে এ কথা শুনে আমার
this (word) from your   ভারী ভাল লাগছে ।
mouth.

tomar mukh theke ' ɛ kɔtha śune '
amar bhari bhalo laɡche "

Lesson 18, part 2. Grammar.

1. The formation and use of the past continuative.

1.1. The use of the past continuative (sometimes termed past imperfect)
is to indicate that an action had begun in the past and was continuing at
the past time referred to by the speaker. A rule of thumb is that
wherever the form "was/were ...ing" is used in English, the past continuative is used in Bengali. Thus:

        śunchilum   "I was listening"
        dekhchile   "you were looking"
        khelchilo   "he was playing", etc.

1.2. The tense is formed by the addition of the past tense suffix and
past personal endings to the high stem of the verb, except where the
stem-vowel is /a/ or the shape of the stem is CVCa-. Where the stem-
vowel is /a/ and where the shape of the stem is CVCa-, the low stem is
retained. Thus:

        śon-   "hear"   ami śun-chil-um
                                tumi śun-chil-e
                                tui śun-chil-i
                                apni śun-chil-en
                                śe śun-chil-o

                                    tini śun-chil-en

    phæl-   "drop"   ami phel-chil-um, etc.

    bɔś-   "sit"   ami boś-chil-um, etc.

/a/-stems retain their low forms:

    jan-   "know"   jan-chil-um, etc.

as do CVCa-stems:

    jana-   "cause to   jana-chil-um, etc.
              know"

    śona-   "cause tc   śona-chil-um, etc.
              hear"

1.3. CV-stems follow this same pattern: all stems are high except where
the stem-vowel is /a/. CV-stems, however, also double the /-c-/ of the
/-chil-/ suffix:

    ne-   "take"   ami ni-cchil-um, etc.

    hɔ-   "become"   ami ho-cchil-um, etc.

    ja-   "go"   ami ja-cchil-um, etc.

2. Formation of verbal adjectives, as in sentence 3.

2.1. Verbal adjectives may be identical in form with verbal nouns; only
their syntactical function separates the two classes. Some examples of
verbal adjectives:

    e'amar hate lekha boi"   this is my hand-written book (this book
                                is written by my hand (i.e., in my hand-
                                writing))

    akaś kalo kɔra dhõa"   the smoke making the sky black (i.e., the
                                sky-black-making smoke; /akaś kalo kɔra/
                                is an adjectival complex modifying
                                /dhõa/.)

    oʈa'kharap lekha boi"   that is a badly written book (extremely
                                colloquial)

    eʈa'bhalo āka chobi"   that is a well painted picture (extremely
                                colloquial)

2.2. It should be mentioned that there is another type of verbal
adjective, which functions somewhat differently syntactically. This

second type of formation is much less frequent (except in certain stylized idioms) than the one above. Note the śadhu-bhaśa vocabulary in the following examples:

e boi'amar hɔsto <u>likhito</u>"   this book is <u>written</u> by my hand

o boiṭa'mondobhabe <u>likhito</u>"   that book is badly <u>written</u>

2.2.1. This form is called in traditional grammars "past passive participle"; it should be noted that the construction /akaś kalo kɔra dhõa/ cannot be transformed in this way; "past passive participles" form a limited class in modern spoken Bengali.

3. Function word /kore/, as in sentence 23.

3.1. It should be noted that in this situation, as in that mentioned in lesson 16, the form /kore/, while it has the same form as the PAP of the stem /kɔr-/, "do", does not act in the same way. A PAP has a verbal function in a sentence:

śe kaj kore'gælo"   He did the work and went.

śe baṛite phire'boślo" He returned home and sat down.

The function word /kore/ occurs either in immediate relation as a noun:

śe nouko kore'aśe"   He comes by boat.

or, as in the present case, as an adjective:

śe biśeś kore'śɔhorṭa' pɔchondo kɔre"   He especially likes the city.

śe śɔkto kore'dhɔre"   He holds it firmly.

<u>Lesson 18, part 3. Patterns.</u>

1. Pattern: sentence 1.

a. What picture were you looking at?
b. What song were you listening to?
c. What stories were you reading?
d. What songs were they singing?
e. What novels was he reading?

2. .Pattern: sentence 2.

    a.   ⊥ was looking at a picture by a Bengali painter.

    b.   I was listening to a song by a Bengali writer.

    c.   I was reading some Bengali short stories.

    d.   They were singing some Bengali songs.

    e.   He was reading some Bengali novels.

3. Pattern: sentence 3.

    a.   Who painted the picture you were looking at?

    b.   Who wrote the song you were listening to?

    c.   Who wrote the stories you were reading?

    d.   Who wrote the songs they were singing?

    e.   Who wrote the novels he was reading?

4. Pattern: sentence 4.

    a.   It was a picture painted by Jamini Roy.

    b.   It was a song written by Rabindranath.

    c.   They were stories written by different people.

    d.   They were songs written by kaviwallas (/kobioala/).

    e.   They were novels by Saratcandra (/śɔrotcɔndro/).

5. Pattern: sentence 5.

    a.   You like Bengali pictures, don't you?

    b.   You like Rabindranath's songs, don't you?

    c.   You have studied Bengali a lot, haven't you?

    d.   You listen to all kinds of folk songs, don't you?

    e.   You can read that kind of Bengali, can't you?

6. Pattern: sentence 6.

    a.   Yes, for the past ten years I have been studying Indian painting.

    b.   Yes, for the past few years I have been listening to many Indian songs.

    c.   Yes, for the past six years I have been studying Bengali.

    d.   Yes, for the past twenty years I have been listening to folk songs.

    e.   Yes, for the past several months I have been learning to read <u>śadhu-bhaśa</u>.

Pattern: sentence 6.

a. So I thought, "Let me see whether or not I like Bengali painting."

b. So I thought, "Let me see whether or not I can like Rabindranath's songs."

c. So I thought, "Let me see whether or not I can read short stories easily."

d. So I thought, "Let me see whether or not I can understand kaviwalla songs."

e. So I thought, "Let me see whether or not I can read Saratcandra's writing."

7. Pattern: sentence 7.

a. I think that you will like Bengali painting very much.

b. I think that you will like Rabindranath's songs very much.

c. I think that you will read these short stories easily.

d. I think that these songs will be a little hard for you to understand.

e. I think that his writing will be very difficult for you to read.

8. Pattern: sentence 8.

a. Why do you think that?

b. Why do you do that?

c. Why do you say that?

d. Why do you say they will be difficult?

e. Why do you say that it will be hard to read?

9. Pattern: sentence 9.

a. Because at the time when modern painters were learning, many painters were using folk art.

b. Because when Rabindranath was writing songs, he liked folk songs very much.

c. Because when writers write short stories, they often use colit-bhaśa.

d. Because the poets who wrote those songs were not often educated people.

e. Because when Saratcandra was writing, many writers were using difficult language.

10. Pattern: sentence 10.

a. I like folk art. That is why, when I was looking at the picture, I liked (i.e., "was liking") it very much.

b. I like folk songs. That is why, when I was listening to Rabindranath's songs, I liked them very much.

    c. That is why, when I was trying to read the stories, I was finding (use /lag-/) them so easy.

    d. That is why, when I was listening to the songs, I was not able to understand the language.

    e. That is why, when I was looking at the books, I was finding (use /lag-/) them hard to read.

11. Pattern: sentence 11.

    a. When you were studying painting, were you studying ancient or modern painting?

    b. When you were studying folk songs, were you studying Indian or European folk songs?

    c. When you were studying Bengali, were you studying the colloquial or the literary language?

    d. When you were learning Bengali, what kind of Bengali were you learning?

    e. When you were studying śadhu-bhasa, whose writing were you studying?

12. Pattern: sentence 12.

    a. I was studying ancient and modern painting.

    b. I was studying both Indian and European folk songs.

    c. I was studying both the colloquial and the literary language?

    d. I was studying only the literary language.

    e. I was studying Bankim-candra.

13. Pattern: sentence 13.

    a. If you learn a little about Indian sculpture, it will be very helpful to you.

    b. If you learn a little about Indian classical music, it will be very helpful to you.

    c. If you are studying the śadhu-bhaśa, learning a little Sanskrit will be very helpful to you.

    d. If you are studying the colit-bhaśa, speaking the language will be very helpful to you.

    e. If you want to learn the literary language, studying a little Sanskrit will be helpful to you.

14. Pattern: sentence 14.

    a. When I was in Calcutta last year, my professor said the same thing to me.

    b. When I was studying music, my teacher said the same thing to me.

    c. When I was living in Bengal, my friends said the same thing to me

d. When I was going to India, many people said the same thing to me.

e. When I was studying Bengali, other people said the same thing to me.

15. Pattern: sentence 15.

a. What were you doing in Calcutta last year?
b. Where were you studying Indian music?
c. Where were you living in Bengal?
d. When were you going to India.
e. Why were you studying Bengali?

16. Pattern: sentence 16.

a. The government was sending me there to teach at the University.
b. The government was sending me to Madras to study music.
c. The government was sending me; therefore I was living on Park Street.
d. The government was sending me to India last year.
e. The government was sending me to study; also, I wanted (i.e., was wanting) to read Bengali literature.

17. Pattern: sentence 17.

a. To teach about folk art?
b. To teach about folk music?
c. The government sent you to study the language?
d. They were sending you to learn Bengali?
e. They were sending you to study only Bengali?

18. Pattern: sentence 18.

a. Yes, I was teaching a little about folk art.
b. Yes, I was also learning to play the vina (/bina/).
c. Yes, I was studying the language and the literature.
d. Yes, I was also teaching a little.
e. No, I was studying other languages also.

19. Pattern: sentence 20.

a. In what different places were you teaching?
b. What other instruments were you learning to play?
c. In what various places were you living in Bengal?
d. In what various places were you teaching in India?

    e. What other different languages were you studying?

20. Pattern: sentence 21.

    a. The greatest part of the time I was teaching in Calcutta itself.

    b. The greatest part of the time I was learning to play the vina itself.

    c. The greatest part of the time I was living right in Calcutta.

    d. The greatest part of the time I was teaching in Calcutta itself.

    e. The greatest part of the time I was studying Bengali; I was learning a little Hindi also.

21. Pattern: sentence 22. (use past continuative)

    a. How did you like Calcutta?

    b. How did you like playing the vina?

    c. How did you like living in Calcutta?

    d. How did you like teaching in India?

    e. How did you like learning Indian languages?

22. Pattern: sentence 23.

    a. I think that Calcutta is a wonderful city, especially at night.

    b. I think that all Indian instruments are beautiful, but especially the vina.

    c. I think that all Bengal is beautiful, but especially Calcutta.

    d. I think that teaching is wonderful, especially in India.

    e. I think that learning all languages is hard, but especially Indian languages.

Lesson 18, part 4. Sentence Drills.

Drill 1

--What were you doing when you went to India last year?

--I was studying Indian languages, especially Bengali.

--Before going, were you studying Bengali in the United States?

--Yes, I was studying Bengali for about two years before going.

--Where were you living for most of the time when you were in India?

--I was living most of the time in Calcutta, though I was able to go from time to time to other parts of the country.

--Which parts of the country did you like particularly?

--I particularly liked Bengal. I was able to speak with people in

Bengali and to read the literature.

--With whom were you studying?

--I was studying with Professor Sen, at Calcutta University.

--How long were you working with Professor Sen.

--About a year. I was learning a great deal, and I was having wonderful fun, but then I became ill.

--Why? Were you eating bad food?

--Perhaps. Whatever other people were eating, I ate. Maybe that is why I became ill.

Drill 2

--What were you doing when I came in?

--I was working on my book.

--What book are you writing?

--I am writing a book about religion in India, especially Bengal.

--You were doing work on the Saktas (/śakto/) when you were in Bengal, weren't you?

--Yes, but I was also reading the biographies of Caitanya (/coitɔnno/) and the Vaisnava padaboli (/boisnɔb pɔdaboli/).

--I have heard people say that Vaisnavism (/boisnɔb ɗhɔrmo/) ruined Bengal. What do you think of that?

--I have also heard people say that Vaisnavas are too peace-loving. People say that those who do not eat meat, etc., do not fight well.

--Do you think that this is true?

--I don't know People say that the terrorist movement against the British was the work of the Saktas.

--But I do not think that anyone has ever proved that, is that not so?

--I do not know whether or not anyone has tried to prove it. But until someone does, we will not know for certain.

Lesson 18, part 5. Vocabulary.

markin jukto raśtro	United States of America	sthapotto	sculpture
		ūccaŋgo śongit	classical music
majhe majhe, sɔmoe sɔmoe	from time to time	śikkha	education
		śikkhito	educated
bibhinno	different, various	dhɔrmo	religion
		jiboni	biography
onno	other, different	śantippric	peace-loving
		andolon	movement

328

Idioms:

ɔnek kichu	a great deal
jɔkhono porjonto, jɔtokkhon	until
niścito bhabe	for certain, certainly

śɔntraśbad	terrorism
śɔntraśbad	terrorist
pɔdaboli	Vaiṣṇava religious lyrics
dhɔŋśo kɔr- nɔśṭo kɔr-	(to) ruin
proman kɔr-	prove
ceśṭa kɔr-	try
bhab-	think
biruddhe	post-position, "against"

<u>Lesson 19, part 1. Conversation.</u>

<u>Analysis and Translation</u>	<u>Bengali</u>

1. "worthless, rotten, insignificant" baje বাজে

Note: when refering to "your city", "your country", etc., the plural of "your" is always used.

<u>A. Amiyababu, your Calcutta is a very miserable city.</u> A. অমিয়বাবু , আপনাদের কলকাতা বড় বাজে শহর ।

ɔmiobabu ' apnader kolkata ' bɔro baje śɔhɔr "

2. stem of verb, "come" aś- আস—

past conditional suffix -t- —ত

honorific personal ending -en —েন

"if you had come" jodi aśten যদি আসতেন

"such" æmon এমন

high stem of verb /bɔl-/, "say" bol- বল—

past conditional suffix -t- —ত

honorific personal ending -en —েন

"you would have said" bolten বলতেন

<u>B. Mr. Smith, if you had come to Calcutta fifteen years ago, you would not have said such things.</u> B. স্মিথসাহেব , আপনি যদি পনের বছর আগে কলকাতায় আসতেন তা হলে এমন কথা বলতেন না ।

śmithśaheb ' apni jodi ' ponero bɔchor age ' kolkatae aśten ' ta hole ' æmon kɔtha bolten na "

3. noun or form of address,
"gentleman" or "sir"   mɔśae মশায়

  "even if I had come"   ami aśleo আমি আসলেও

A. No sir, even if I had come A. না মশায় , পনের বছর আগে কলকাতাতে
to Calcutta fifteen years   আসলেও এ লোকের ভীড় দেখতুম ।
ago, I would have seen
that same crowd of people.

           na mɔśae ' ponero bɔchor age '
           kolkatate aśleo ' oi loker bhir
           dekhtum "

  "rotten, putrid, sticky" pɔca পচা

A. And this sticky heat   A. আর এই পচা গরম থাকতো ।
would have been here.

           ar ei pɔca gɔrom ' thakto "

4. loan word, "partition" parṭiśan পার্টিশন
  "be partitioned"   parṭiśan hɔ- টিশন হ-
  Note the position of the negative particle in the conditional
clause.

B. No sir. If the country B. না স্যার , দেশ যদি পার্টিশন না হতো
had not been partitioned,   তা হলে এত লোকের ভীড় দেখতেন না ।
you would not see such
crowds of people.

           na sar " deś jodi ' parṭiśan na
           hoto ' ta hole ' æto loker bhir'
           dekhten·na "

5. loan word, "refugee" rephiuji রেফিঞ্জী

A. Then is that crowd all A. তা হলে এ ভীড় কি সব রেফিজীদের ?
of refugees?

           ta hole ' oi bhir ki ' śɔb
           rephiujider "

6. "thousand"   hajar হাজার
  "thousands and thousands" hajar najar হাজার হাজার
  noun, "refuge"   assrɔe আশ্রয়
  "take refuge"   assrɔe ne- আশ্রয় নে-

B. Yes, when the country was
   partitioned, thousands and
   thousands of refugees came
   to Calcutta and have taken
   refuge here.

B. হ্যাঁ , দেশ পার্টিশন হলে হাজার হাজার
   রেফিউজী কলকাতাতে এসে আশ্রয় নিয়েছে ।

hæ̃ " deś partiśan hole ' hajar
hajar rephiuji ' kolkatate eśe '
assrɔe nieche "

7. "then, in that case"   ta hole   তা হলে
   emphatic suffix   -o   -ও
   "even then"   ta holeo   তা হলেও
   "that kind, in that way"   oi rɔkom   এ রকম
   "filthy"   noŋra   নোংরা
   "so filthy"   oi rɔkom noŋra   এ রকম নোংরা

A. But sir, even if the refugees had not come, your
   city would be so filthy.

A. কিন্তু মশায় , রেফিউজীরা যদি না আসতো
   তা হলেও আপনাদের শহর এ রকম নোংরা
   থাকতো ।

kintu mɔśae ' rephiujira jodi n
asto ' ta holeo ' apnader śɔhor
oi rɔkom noŋra ' thakto "

8. "how"   ki kore   কি করে

B. How can you say that?

তা কি করে বলছেন ?

ta ' ki kore ' bolchen "

B. If there were not such a
   crowd of people, Calcutta
   would not be so filthy.

B. এত লোকের ভীড় না হলে কলকাতা ?
   নোংরা হতো না ।

ækto loker bhiɽ na hole ' kolkata
śɔhor ' æto noŋra hoto na "

9. honorific imperative,
   "look, please look"   dekhun   দেখুন
   "habit"   obbheś obbhæś   অভ্যোস , অভ্যাস
   "perhaps"   hɔeto   হয়তো
   "more, in addition"   ar   আর
   "a little more"   ar ekʈu   একটু
   "clean"   poriśkar   পরিষ্কার

Note here the use of /apnader/ indicates that the speaker wants
to be considered remote from the hearer's concern; students
should be wary of using such a form.

A. Look, if your Bengalis did A. দেখুন , আপনাদের বাঙালীদের কতকগুলো
not have so many bad habits, খারাপ অভ্যাস যদি না থাকতো তা হলে
perhaps the city would be ছমতো শহরটা একটু পারিস্কার হতো ।
a little cleaner.

dekhun ' apnader banalider
kɔtokgulo kharap obbhæs ' jodi na
thakto ' ta hole hɔeto ' sɔhorta '
ar ektu poriskar hoto "

10.   "only"   śudhu   শুধু

B. Why only Bengalis?   B. শুধু বাঙালীরা কেন ?

śudhu banalira kæno "

noun, "state, place"   prodeś   প্রদেশ
verb stem, "abandon,
leave"   char-   ছাড়-

B. If people of other places   B. অন্য প্রদেশের লোকেরা যদি তাদের খারাপ
would abandon their bad   অভ্যাসগুলো ছাড়তো তা হলে শহরটা
habits, the city would   আরো পারিস্কার থাকতো ।
become cleaner.

onno prodeśer lokera ' jodi tader
kharap obbhæsgulo ' charto ' ta
hole ' sɔhorta ' aro poriskar '
thakto "

11.   "street"   rasta   রাস্তা
        "bull"   śāṛ   ষাঁড়
        verbal noun, "walking,
        moving"   cɔla   চলা
        noun, "prevention,
        hindrance"   bɔndho   বন্ধ
        compound verb,
        "prevent, stop"   bɔndho kɔr-   বন্ধ কর-
        "genteel, civilized"   bhɔddro   ভদ্র

A. Still, sir, if you would prevent the wandering of bulls about the streets, the city would become a little civilized.

A. তুবে , মশায় , আপনারা যদি রাস্তাতে ষাঁড়ের চলা বন্ধ করতেন তা হলে শহরটা একটু ভদ্র হতো ।

tɔbe mɔśae ' apnara jodi ' rastate śārer cɔla ' bɔndho korten ' ta hole ' śɔhorṭa ' ektu bhɔddro hoto "

12. noun, "side" — paś পাশ
"side by side" — paśapaśi পাশাপাশি
negative prefix — ɔ- অ-
"uncivilized" — ɔbhɔddro অভদ্র

B. Look, we don't consider that walking side by side with bulls in the street is uncivilized.

B. দেখুন , আমরা ষাঁড়ের সঙ্গে রাস্তায় পাশাপাশি চলা অভদ্র মনে করি না ।

dekhun ' amra ' śārer śɔnge ' rastae paśapaśi cɔla ' ɔbhɔddro mone kori na "

13. "can you say, can you imagine" — bolte paren বলতে পারেন
generalizing nominative suffix — -e -ে
"people (in general)" — loke লোকে
"bulls (in general)" — śāṛe ষাঁড়ে

A. Can you imagine, if bulls wandered about the streets of New York or Paris, what people would say?

A. বলতে পারেন , ষাঁড়ে যদি নিউইর্ক বা প্যারিসের রাস্তাতে ঘুরে বেড়াতো তা হলে লোকে কি বলতো ?

bolte paren ' śāṛe jodi ' niuiork ba pæriser rastate ' ghure bærato ' ta hole ' loke ki bolto "

14. B. I don't know what people would say, sir.

B. লোকে কি বলতো জানি না , সার ।

loke ki bolto ' jani na sar "

noun, "gentleman" — śaeb, śaheb সায়েব , সাহেব
noun, "European lady" — mem মেম
compound noun, "ladies and gentlemen" — śaeb-mem সায়েব-মেম

verb stem, "run"	choṭ-	ছোট-
verb stem, "flee"	pala-	পালা-
compound verb, "run to escape"	chuṭe pala-	ছুটে পালা-

B. <u>But I think that if they saw a bull in New York, the ladies and gentlemen would run to escape.</u>

B. তবে আমার মনে হয় যে সায়েব-মেমেরা নিউইয়র্ক শহরে ষাঁড় দেখলে ছুটে পালাতো

<u>tɔbe ' amar mone hɔe je ' śaeb-memera ' niuiork śɔhore ' śaঁṛ dekhle ' chuṭe palato "</u>

verb stem, "stand, stand around"	dãṛa-	দাঁড়া-
noun, "fun, amusement"	mɔja	মজা
compound verb, "be amused, look on with amusement"	mɔja dækh-	মজা দেখ-

B. <u>And in Paris, the people would probably stand around and be amused.</u>

B. আর প্যারিসে ছাতো লোকেরা দাঁড়িয়ে মজা দেখতো ।

<u>ar pæriśe hɔeto ' lokera dãṛie ' mɔja dekhto "</u>

Lesson 19, part 2. Grammar.

1. Formation and use of the past conditional tense.

1.1. The past conditional is formed by the addition of the sign /-t-/ to the <u>high stem</u> of verbs except verbs of CaC- and CVCa- shapes. The personal endings are identical with those of other past tenses

Stem	Gloss	Past conditional
ken-	"buy"	kin - t - um
		kin - t - e
		kin - t - iś
		kin - t - en
		kin - t - o
		kin - t - en
khæl-	"play"	khel - t - um, etc.
śon-	"hear"	śun - t - um, etc.

kɔr-	"do"	kor - t - um, etc.
de-	"give"	di - t - um, etc.
pa-	"get"	pe - t - um, etc.

But:

jan-	"know"	jan - t - um, etc.
jana-	"cause to know"	jana - t - um, etc.
dækha-	"show"	dækha - t - um, etc.
khæla-	"cause to play"	khæla - t - um, etc

1.2. The past conditional is identical in form with the past habitual tense, but functions differently. It is used to express past action which was not realized:

> If you had come before,　　apni jodi'age aśten'ta hole'ami
> I would not have gone.　　jetum na"

1.3. The past conditional may be used on two types of constructions:

1.3.1. When the conditional clause of the sentence includes the conditional particle /jodi/. When /jodi/ is used, the past conditional is used in **both** clauses of the sentence; the second clause of the sentence is introduced by /ta hole/:

> If he had given me the book,　　śe amake'jodi boiṭa dito'
> I would have read it.　　ta hole'ami'ota porṭum"

1.3.2. When the conditional aspect of the sentence is expressed by the non-finite conditional conjunctive stem-<u>le</u>. Since the conditional conjunctive is non-finite, the tense of the sentence is carried wholly by the finite past conditional verb in the second clause.

> If he had given me the book,　　śe amake'boiṭa dile'ami oṭa
> ᵀ would have read it.　　porṭum"

2. Form possible Bengali sentences:

2.1.

	Clause I			Clause II		
	Subject	Modifier	Conditional		Object	Verb
	ami	śohore	jodi (na) ást-	ta hole	amon kɔtha	bolt- (na)
	tumi	śekhane	jet-		take	dekht-
	apni	ekhane	thakt-		oʈa	śunt-
	tãra				gan	hot-
	śe				kobita	jant-
	apnara	poŕaśona	śeś hoto korten		ɔśuśtho	jete part-
		kajta	śeś hoto korten		klanto	
					eśɔb	
					tar śɔnge	

2.2.

Conditional		Verb
aśleo	aśle	bolt-
geleo	gele	dekht-
thakleo	thakle	śunt-
holeo	hole	hot-
korleo	korle	kort-
		jant-
		jete part-

Lesson 19, part 3. Patterns.

1. Pattern: sentence 1.

    a. Your city is a very beautiful place.
    b. Your Bengali conversation is very good.
    c. The habits of Bengalis are very good.
    d. Your room is very dirty.
    e. Your country is very uncivilized.

2. Pattern: sentence 2.

    a. If you had not come in the summer time, you would not have said such things.
    b. If you had heard me in class today, you would not have said such things.
    c. If you had lived in Calcutta, you would not have said such things.
    d. If my wife had cleaned it today, you would not have said such things.
    e. If you had come before the partition, you would not have said such things.

3. Pattern: sentence 3.

    a. Even if I had come in the winter time, I would have liked the city.
    b. Even if I had heard you in class, I would have liked your Bengali conversation.
    c. Even if I had lived in Calcutta, I would like Bengalis.
    d. Even if she had cleaned it today, it would have been dirty.
    e. Even if I had come before partition, I would have thought (use /bhab-/) it uncivilized.

4. Pattern: sentence 4.

    a. No, sir. If you had come in the winter, you would have been very cold.
    b. No, sir. If you had come to class, you would have heard very bad Bengali.
    c. No, sir. If you had lived there, you would have seen the bad habits of Bengalis.
    d. No, sir. If she had cleaned it, it would not be so filthy.
    e. No, sir. If you had come at that time, you would not have seen the city so dirty.

5. Pattern: sentence 5.

   a. Then is the place so cold in the winter?

   b. Then why is your Bengali so good out of class?

   c. Then are the habits of Bengalis so bad?

   d. Then are your habits so good?

   e. Then is the dirt the fault of the refugees?*

6. Pattern: sentence 6.

   a. Yes, when it gets cold, people stay in their houses.

   b. When I speak Bengali to you, I speak more easily.

   c. Yes, when you go to Bengal, you will see.

   d. Yes, when you come to see me again, you will see.

   e. Yes, when the refugees came, the city became dirty.

7. Pattern: sentence 7.

   a. But even if I had not come in the summer, I would not have been cold.

   b. But even if you had not learned to speak, your Bengali would be good.

   c. But even if I had not known so many Bengalis, I would have liked then.

   d. But even if your wife had cleaned, you smoke (/kha-/) cigarettes.

   e. But even if the refugees had not come, the bulls would be in the streets.

8. Pattern: sentence 8.

   a. How can you say that? If it were not so cold in the winter, more people would like the city.

   b. How can you say that? If I had not learned to speak Bengali, I would not know the language well.

   c. How can you say that? If you have not gone to Bengal, how can you know Bengalis? ____

   d. That is true. If I did not smoke so many cigarettes, perhaps my room would be neater.

   e. How can you say that? If there were not so many people the city would be clean.

9. Pattern: sentence 9.

   a. Look, if people did not like the place, they would not come here.

---

* a possible construction is /ta hole noṇra rephiuji der dośe hoeche/.

b. Look, if people do not learn to read Bengali, they do not know the language.

c. Look, if there were not so many Bengalis here, I would not know them so well.

d. Yes. If you did not smoke so many cigarettes, your room would be cleaner.

e. Look, if people would abandon their bad habits, the city would be cleaner.

10. Pattern: sentence 11.

a. Still, if we could prevent people from coming here in the winter, we would do so.

b. Still, if we could prevent people from learning only reading, we would teach them better Bengali.

c. Still, if Bengalis would stop talking of Bengal, they would be more popular.

d. If I would stop my cigarette smoking, my wife would be happier.

e. If you would tell us how to prevent people from sleeping on the streets, we would be very happy.

11. Pattern: sentence 12.

a. I don't consider that coming here in the winter is so bad.

b. I don't consider that speaking a language is enough.

c. I don't consider that speaking of one's own country is so bad.

d. I don't consider that smoking cigarettes is good.

e. I don't consider that stopping people sleeping on the street is enough.

12. Pattern: sentence 14.

a. Can you imagine, if someone from Ceylon came here in the winter, what he would say?

b. Can you imagine, if someone could not speak a language, what people would say?

c. Can you imagine, if you talked only about your country, what people would say?

d. Can you imagine, if you smoked cigars, what your wife would say?

e. Can you imagine, if people slept on the streets of New York, what people would say?

Lesson 19, part 4. Sentence Drills.

--Nareshbabu, your Calcutta is a very beautiful city.

--Mr. Jones, if you had lived in Citupr Road or in Sealdah (/śealda/),
you would not have said that.

--Even if I had lived in those places, people would have taken care of me.

--If you had not lived in Park Street, you would certainly have become
ill.

--Even though I lived in Park Street, I became ill.

--Then why do you think that Calcutta is such a pleasant place?

--Even if I had found it ugly, I would have liked it.

--But there are so many people. If there were not so many people, the
city would be cleaner.

--If the city were cleaner, it would not be such an interesting place.

--Mr. Jones, you are a strange American.

Drill 2

--That is a big old house.

--Yes, Rabindranath Tagore and his family used to live in that house.

--Really? If we had lived fifty years ago, perhaps we would have come
to see him there.

--Yes, if we had lived in those days, perhaps we would have been
invited to meet him.

--I have heard that there used to be two hundred people in his family.

--Yes, and they all lived here. We would have been very fortunate, if
we had been born into that family.

--Why would we have been so fortunate?

--Because we would have grown up **among** writers and painters and
musicians.

--But is is not always good to be surrounded by great men.

--Why do you say that? If we had lived in this house, we would
ourselves be great writers or painters.

--Perhaps not. If our friend Satyen (/śɔtten/) had not been the son of
a great painter, perhaps he would be a better painter today.

Lesson 19, part 5. Vocabulary.

jaega	place	gire thak-	
śilpi, kɔlaśilpi	artist	poribeṣṭito thak-	be surrounded
śɔŋgitoggõ	musician	jɔnma-	be born
		bɔṛo hɔ-	grow up
ɔśukh	illness	gɔṛe oṭh-	be built up
noŋra	dirt, filth	bhab-	consider
dos	fault	śigaret kha-	smoke cigarettes

śundor	beautiful	nimontrito	invited
ɔśusthɔ	ill	amontrito	
ɔdbhut			
ajob	strange		
mɔhot	great		
bhaggoban	fortunate, lucky		
śotti	really, truly		
śɔb śɔmoe	always		

Note.

He becomes ill.   tini ɔśustho hɔn
                   tãr ɔśukh kɔre

Lesson 20, part 1. Conversation.

Analysis and translation	Bengali

1. high stem of verb
   /de-/, "give"   di- দি-

   2nd person singular
   imperative ending   -o -ও

   future imperative, "give";
   see Grammar, 1.   dio দিও

   A. When you go to Calcutta, give this money to my brother.

   A. তুমি কলকাতাতে গিয়ে আমার ভাইকে এই টাকাগুলো দিও ।

   tumi ' kolkatate gie ' amar bhaike ' ei takagulo ' dio "

2. Note that /hole/ is not conditional here. The conditional conjunctive can be translated by "when", depending on context.

   B. All right. And when I meet your brother, shall I tell him anything?

   B. আচ্ছা , আর তোমার ভাইয়ের সঙ্গে দেখা হলে তাকে কিছু বলবো কি ?

   accha " ar tomar bhaier śɔnge ' dækha hole ' take kichu ' bolbo ki "

                           (a)

3. A. No, just give the money to him.

   A. না , কেবল তাকে টাকাগুলো দিও ।

   na ' kebol take ' takagulo dio "

   variant stem of verb
   /ne-/, "take"   na- না-

   2nd person singular
   imperative ending   -o -ও

   present imperative "take"   nao নাও

verb stem, "place, guard, keep"	rakh- রাখ–
2nd person present imperative, "guard"	rakho রাখো
"carefully"	śabdhane সাবধানে

(b)

A. Take the money in a box and guard it carefully.

A. তুমি টাকাগুলো কোন বাক্সতে নাও আর সাবধানে রাখো ।

tumi ṭakagulo ' kono bakśote nao ' ar śabdhane rakho "

conjunctive, "that, lest"; see Lesson 21, Grammar, 2.	jæno যেন
verb stem, "be lost"	hara- হারা–

(c)

A. See that it doesn't get lost (i.e., keep it carefully lest it get lost).

A. দেখ যেন হারায় না ।

dækho jæno ' harae na "

4.

high stem of verb /kha-/, "eat"	khe- খে–
2nd person singular imperative ending	-o –ও
future imperative, "eat"	kheo খেও
"how, how about that?"	kæmon কেমন

B. All right. But before I leave the country, come to my house and eat one day. How about it?

B. আচ্ছা । কিন্তু আমার দেশ ছাড়ার আগে তুমি আমার বাড়িতে এসে একদিন খেও , কেমন ?

accha " kintu ' amar deś charar age ' tumi amar baṛite eśe ' ækdin kheo " kæmon "

5.

"instead"	bɔroŋ বরং

A. No, instead, you eat with us tomorrow.

A. না , তুমি বরং , আগামী কাল আমাদের সঙ্গে খেও ।

na ' tumi bɔroŋ ' agami kal amader śɔŋge ' kheo "

344

A. I am going now, OK?

A. এখন চলি , কেমন ?

ækhon coli ' kæmon "

6. noun, "rain"

high stem of verb
/ja/, "go"

2nd person singular
future imperative, "go"

briśṭi বৃষ্টি

je- যে-

jeo যেও

B. No, don't go home in
this rain.

B. না , এই বৃষ্টিতে বাড়ী যেও না ।

na ' ei briśṭite ' baṛi jeo na "

B. Instead stay here today.

B. এখানে বরং আজ থাকো ।

ekhane bɔroŋ ' aj thako "

7. verb stem, "stop"

compound verb stem,
"come to a stop"

tham- থাম-

theme aś- থেমে আস-

A. Look, the rain outside
has almost stopped.

A. দেখ , বাইরে বৃষ্টি প্রায় থেমে এসেছে ।

dækho ' baire ' briśṭi prae '
theme eśeche "

"umbrella"

"easily (without
difficulty)"

chata ছাতা

ɔnaeaśe অনায়াসে

A. Only give me an umbrella,
then I'll be able to get
home easily.

A. আমাকে কেবল একটা ছাতা দাও , তা হলেই
আমি অনায়াসে বাড়ী যেতে পারবো ।

amake kebol ' ækṭa chata dao '
ta holei ' ami ɔnaeaśe ' baṛi
jete parbo "

8. B. I have no umbrella.

B. আমার তো কোনো ছাতা নেই ।

amar to ' kono chata nei "

"raincoat"

bɔrśati বর্ষাতি

B. <u>Take my raincoat instead.</u>

B. তুমি বরং আমার বর্ষাতিটা নিয়ে যাও ।

tumi bɔroŋ ' amar bɔrśatiṭa ' nie jao "

9. A. <u>Good. In that case,</u>
<u>give me your raincoat.</u>

A. বেশ । তা হলে তোমার বর্ষাতিটা দাও ।

beś " ta hole ' tomar bɔrśatiṭa dao "

A. <u>I shall return it</u>
<u>tomorrow morning.</u>

A. কাল সকালে আমি ফেরত দোবো ।

kal śɔkale ' ami pherot dobo "

10. high stem of verb
/ken-/, "buy"

kin-   কিন-

2nd person singular fu-
ture imperative, "buy"

kino   কিনো

B. <u>All right. Before you</u>
<u>come tomorrow, buy these</u>
<u>things for me, OK?</u>

B. আচ্ছা । কাল আসবার আগে আমার জন্যে এই জিনিসগুলো কিনো , কেমন ?

accha " kal aśbar age ' amar jonne ei jiniśgulo ' kino " kæmon "

11. A. <u>Look, tomorrow I will</u>
<u>not have the time.</u>

A. দেখ , আমার তো কাল সময় হবে না ।

dækho ' amar to kal ' śɔmoe hɔbe na "

"self"; see Grammar, 4.

nije, nijei   নিজে , নিজেই

high stem of verb
/an-/, "bring, fetch"

-en   এন-

2nd person singular
future imperative,
"bring, fetch"

eno   এনো

A. <u>Instead, go and get</u>
<u>them yourself.</u>

A. তুমি বরং নিজে গিয়ে কিনে এনো ।

tumi bɔroŋ ' nije gie kine eno "

12. B. <u>All right. Then I</u>
<u>shall go myself.</u>

B. আচ্ছা , তা হলে আমি নিজেই যাবো ।

accha " ta hole ' ami nijei jabo "

Lesson 20, part 2. Grammar.

1. Formation and use of the future imperative. As there is no future imperative in English, both present and future imperatives in Bengali have only one translation.

1.1. The future imperative of the 2nd person ordinary of all verbs is formed by the addition of the 2nd person imperative ending /-o/ to the high stem, thus:

Stem	Gloss	Future Imperative
ken-	buy	kin-o
dækh-	see	dekh-o
kɔr-	do	kor-o
śon-	hear	śun-o
jan-	know	jen-o
de-	give	di-o
ja-	go	je-o
dækha-	show	dekhi-o

1.2. The future imperative in the honorific form is identical with the simple future honorific:

    ken-   buy   kinben

1.3. The future imperative is used to indicate that a command or wish is to be carried out at some future time, thus:

    After eating, read this.   khabar pɔr'eṭa pɔṛo
    When you get there, call him.   śekhane poŭche'take ḍeko"

1.4. Be wary of the use of negatives with imperative expressions. The negative imperative will be treated in Lesson 21.

2. The formation of "adverbs" in Bengali.

2.1. The class of words called "adverbs" by western grammarians is sometimes paralleled in Bengali by a formation consisting of a noun or adjective with the suffix /-e/ or the suffix /bhabe/. Of the former type we have two examples in this lesson:

carefully, care	śabdhan
carefully, (in care)	śabdhane
easy, ease	śɔhoj
easily, in ease	śɔhoje

2.2. The suffix /-bhabe/ means "in the condition of". Therefore:

| silence, silent | mouno |
| silently, (in a con-dition of silence) | mounobhabe |

This /-bhabe/ formation is more frequent in śadhu-bhaśa or literary Bengali than it is in the colloquial language. Note that the two morphs, /-e/ and -/bhabe/, are not always substitutable for one another.

3. The partical /to/.

3.1. The particle /to/ has a great variety of uses. It sometimes implies doubt on the part of the speaker. But perhaps the most common use is a purely stylistic one: the particle is used in the sentence simply because it sounds good to the ear of the speaker. There has been much speculation on the use of this particle, some people feeling that it is used to lengthen a breath-group to proper portions. But it seems as if all that can be said about it is that it has an esthetic rather than a semantic value. Thus, its use is difficult to teach. The student will simply have to listen to enough Bengali to allow his ear to become sufficiently adjusted to the rythms of the language to tell him when the particle should be used.

3.2. It should be noted, however, that in some cases /to/ does have definite assignable semantic value. For example, it can have the force of the English expressions "so, at any rate, whatever else happens", as:

So you'll go anyway.	apni to jaben"
So you'll go whether anyone else else goes or not.	
So you're well?	apni bhalo achen to"
You're well, aren't you?	

Take careful note of the intonation of the above expressions.

3.3. The particle may have the force of "since, but, although" relating to the previous and subsequent utterances in the discourse.

An example of this is in sentence 8.

> But/since I have no umbrella,   amar to'kono chata nei'bɔroŋ amar
> take my raincoat instead   bɔrśatita nao"

3.4. The particle may also function for /ta hole/:

> If you will come tomorrow,   tumi jodi'kal aśo'to bhalo hɔe"
> that will be good.

4. The use of /nije/.

The form /nije/, "self", is uninflected for person (though it agrees in case with its noun or pronoun, as we shall see), and can be used with all nouns or pronouns:

> I myself shall go.   ami nije jabo"
> You yourself buy it.   tumi jije oṭa keno"

Lesson 20, part 3. Patterns.

1. Pattern: sentence 1.

   a. If you go to Delhi, take this letter to my sister.
   b. If you go to Calcutta, take this book to my father.
   c. If you go to Calcutta, send these things to my brother.
   d. If you go to Delhi, tell my brother that I am well.
   e. If you go to Calcutta, tell my brother that I shall come home soon

2. Pattern: sentence 2.

   a. When I meet your sister, what should I tell her?
   b. When I take the book to your father, shall I take him anything else?
   c. When I send them to your brother, shall I send him a letter also?
   d. When I meet your brother, shall I give him anything from you?
   e. When I meet your brother, shall I ask him to send you anything?

3. Pattern: sentence 3(a).

   a. Nothing. Just take the letter to her.
   b. No, just take the book to him.
   c. No, but bring back a letter from him.
   d. No, just tell him that he must write soon.
   e. No, just go and meet him.

Pattern: sentence 3(b).

a. Take the letter with you and guard it carefully.

b. It is a valuable book; guard it carefully.

c. Bring the letter carefully; see that it doesn't get lost.

d. Tell him that I want a letter from him; see that he understands.

e. Tell him that I will write him soon.

4. Pattern: sentence 4.

a. All right. But before I go to Delhi, come to my house and see me.

b. All right. But before I leave Delhi, come to my house and bring the book.

c. All right. But before I go to Calcutta, go and tell Ram that I want to see him.

d. All right. But before I reach Delhi, call your brother and tell him that I am coming.

e. All right. But before I leave here, come and give me your brother's address.

5. Pattern: sentence 5.

a. No, instead, you come to my house. Now I have to go home.

b. All right. I shall come tonight. Now I have to go home.

c. No, instead you go and see Ram. Now I have to go home.

d. No, instead you call him when you reach Delhi. Now I have to go home.

e. No, instead you come to my house. Now I have to go home.

6. Pattern: sentence 6.

a. No, don't go outside in this rain. Stay here for a while.

d. No, don't come tonight. Come and stay tomorrow night.

c. No, don't go outside in this heat. Stay here today.

d. No, don't go outside without a hat. Take my hat.

e. No, don't go home now. Stay here tonight.

7. Pattern: sentence 7.

a. Look, the rain has stopped. Only give me a little money, and I'll be able to get home on the tram.

b. Look, I must come tonight. Only give me your key, and I will come and wait for you.

c. Look, the heat outside is not so bad. Only give me your hat, and I'll be able to get home easily.

350

    d. Look, the sun is not hot. Only give me a piece of cloth and I'll be able to get home easily.

    e. Look, I have to go now. Only give me your address, and I'll be able to come back easily.

8. Pattern: sentence 8.

    a. I have no money. Walk instead.

    b. I have no key. Come tomorrow night instead.

    c. I have no hat. Take my umbrella instead.

    d. I have no cloth. Take my hat instead.

    e. I have no pencil. You write it down instead.

9. Pattern: sentence 9.

    a. In that case, give me your umbrella. I will return it tomorrow night.

    b. In that case, give me your brother's key. I will return it tonight.

    c. In that case, give me your umbrella. I will return it tomorrow.

    d. In that case, give me your umbrella. I will return it soon.

    e. In that case, give me your pen. I will return it immediately.

10. Pattern: sentence 10.

    a. All right. Before you come tomorrow, call me at the office.

    b. All right. Before you come back, call my brother and tell him.

    c. All right. Before you return it, call me at home.

    d. All right. Before you come back, buy these things for me.

    e. All right. Before you write, shake the pen.

11. Pattern: sentence 11.

    a. No, I will not have the time. Call me yourself.

    b. No, I will not be able to. Call him yourself.

    c. No, I will not be able to call. Call me yourself.

    d. No, I will not have the time. Buy them yourself.

    e. No, shake it yourself.

Lesson 20, part 4. Sentence Drills.

Drill 1

--When you come to my house tomorrow, bring your sitar with you.
--All right. Shall I also return the book you gave me?

--No, I don't want the book. Just bring the sitar. We'll listen to
  some music.

--All right. You bring the food tomorrow night, and I'll bring my
  instrument.

--When you get home, ask Mathur whether or not he will come.

--I won't see him tonight. He has gone to a movie.

--Then ask him when you see him in class tomorrow.

--All right. Come and eat with me tomorrow night, before the party.

--No, I can't. My friends are coming. You come and eat with us instead.

--Perhaps. I'll tell you tomorrow.

--All right. Tell me tomorrow.

Drill 2

--Tipu, when you finish cooking, shine my shoes.

--Yes, saheb, when I finish cooking, I shall shine your shoes.

--When you finish shining my shoes, go to the market. And when you go,
  don't put any money in your own pocket.

--Yes, saheb, I shall go to the market. I shall not steal any money.

--When you get back from the market, clean the room.

--Yes, Saheb, when I get back, I shall clean the room.

--When you finish cleaning the room, make some <u>luci</u>.

--Yes, saheb, I shall make some <u>luci</u> for you.

--After that, I want you to clean the brassware.

--Yes, saheb, I shall clean the brassware.

--All right. Have you anything to say?

--Yes, saheb, starting tomorrow, find another bearer.

Lesson 20, part 5. Vocabulary.

ranna	cooking
paliś	shine, polish
kãśar-baśon	brassware
thikana	address
roddur	heat (of day), sunshine
ṭupi	hat
ṭram (gaṛi)	tram
cabi	key
ækkhana kapoṛ	piece of cloth
kɔlom	pen

352

dami	valuable
poriśkar kɔr-	clean
jhar	shake (an object)
pherot de	return (an object)
kal theke	from tomorrow

Analysis and translation	**Bengali**

1. Note the use of /amader/ without a noun or post-position; substitutable would be /amader śɔŋge/, /amader baṛite/, etc.

   The negative particle /na/ with present imperative: "why dont you ..."

   | "why don't you stay ..." | thako na   থাকো না |

   A. Bob, why don't you stay here with us today ?

   A. বব , আজ আমাদের এখানে থাকো না ?

   bɔb ' aj amader ekhane ' thako na "

2. "objection"   apotti   আপত্তি

   B. Look, Faruk, I have no objection, but do you know ...

   B. দেখ ফারুক , আমার তো কোন আপত্তি নেই । তবে কি জানো ...

   dɛkho pharuk ' amar to ' kono apotti nei " tɔbe ki jano ...

3. | noun, "matter, trouble" | bæpar   ব্যাপার |
   | "why don't you tell ..." | bɔlo na   বলো না |
   | emphatic | bɔloi na   বলোই না |

   A. Why don't you say what the trouble is?

   A. কি ব্যাপার বলোই না ?

   ki bæpar ' bɔloi na "

4. | "again and again" | barbar   বারবার |
   | "ever"; see Grammar, 2. | jæno abar   যেন আবার |
   | "village" | gã   গাঁ |

   The negative particle /na/ with future imperative = negative imperative, "Do not ...".

"Do not stay ..."   theko na   থেকো না

B. Mr. Dunn has said again
and again, "Do not ever
stay in a village at
night.

B. মিস্টার ডান বারবার বলে দিয়েছেন
'রাতে যেন আবার গাঁয়ে থেকো না ।'

mistar dan ' barbar bole diechen '
rate ' jæno abar ' gãe theko
na "

5. A. Why is that?

A. কেন বলো তো ?

kæno bɔlo to "

6.   "very great" (emphatic
of /bɔro/)   bɔddo   বড্ডো
noun, "inconvenience"   ɔsubidhe   অসুবিধে
"apart from that"   ta chaṛa   তা ছাড়া

B. He was saying, "In the
village there is very
great difficulty of
food and accomodation,
and apart from that ...

B. তিনি বলেছিলেন , 'গাঁয়ে থাকা খাওয়ার
বড্ডো অসুবিধে ,' তা ছাড়া ...

tini bolchilen ' gãe thaka
khaoar ' bɔddo ɔsubidhe " ta
chaṛa ...

7.   Note the word order. The place of the pronoun subject is
matter of style.

A. What did he say apart
from that?

A. তা ছাড়া আর কি বলেছেন তিনি ?

ta chaṛa ' ar ki bolechen tini "

8.   "snake"   śãp   সাপ
"snakes and other
such things"   śãp-khop, śãp-ṭap   সাপখোপ সাপ-টাপ
"very much" (used with
quantities measurable
but not countable)   bejae   বেজায়
noun, "trouble, danger,
disturbance"   upodrob   উপদ্রব

B. He was saying that in the village there is lots of trouble with snakes and such.

B. তিনি বলছিলেন যে গাঁয়ে সাপ-খোপের বেজায় উপদ্রব ।

tini bolchilen je ' gãe ' śāp-khoper ' bejae upodrob "

9. "perhaps"

hɔeto ছয়তো

A. Look, perhaps he's right about that.

A. দেখ , তা তিনি ছয়তো ঠিকই বলেছেন ।

dækho ' ta tini hɔeto ' thiki bolechen "

A. But still, we live among the snakes and such.

A. তবে আমরা তো সাপ-খোপের মাঝেই বাস করছি ।

tɔbe amra to ' śāp-khoper majhei ' baś korchi "

10. B. That's true. But do you know ...

B. তা ঠিক । তবে কি জানো ...

ta thik " tɔbe ki jano ...

11. reflexive pronoun, "one's self" Note agreement with noun or pronoun.

nije নিজে

A. I understand -- you your-self will be greatly in-convenienced, isn't that it?

A. বুঝেছি — তোমার নিজের খুব অসুবিধে হবে , তাই না ?

bujechi " tomar nijer ' khub ɔśubidhe hɔbe ' tai na "

12. For uses of /kɔtha/, see Grammar, 3.

B. No, no, I'm not thinking about inconvenience.

B. না , না , আমি অসুবিধের কথা ভাবছি না ।

na na ' ami ' ɔśubidher kɔtha ' bhabchi na "

13. compound verb stem, "spend (time)"

katie ja-, kata- কাটিয়ে যা- , কাটা-

A. <u>In that case, why don't</u>
<u>you spend the night here</u>
<u>with me?</u>

A. তা হলে , রাতটা আমার এখানে কাটিয়ে
যাও না ?

ta hole ' ratta ' amar
ekhane ' katie jao na "

14. "true, honest"

aśol   আসল

B. <u>All right, Faruk; in that</u>
<u>case, let me tell you the</u>
<u>true story.</u>

B. দেখ ফারুক . তা হলে আসল কথাটা বলি ।

dækho pharuk " ta hole ' aśol
kɔthaṭa boli "

15. A. <u>What's the matter then?</u>

A. কি ব্যাপার বলো তো ?

ki bæpar bɔlo to "

16. "belly, stomach"
     "today, these days'

peṭ   পেট
aj   আজ

B. <u>My stomach is very</u>
<u>bad these days.</u>

B. আমার পেটটা আজ বেজায় খারাপ ।

amar peṭṭa ' aj bejae kharap "

B. <u>And do you know what the</u>
<u>doctor said to me?</u>

B. আর ডাক্তার আমাকে কি বলেছে , জানো ?

ar ' ḍaktar amake ' ki boleche
jano "

17. A. <u>What did the doctor say?</u>

A. ডাক্তার কি বলেছে ?

ḍaktar ' ki boleche "

18. Note use of /jæno/; see Grammar, 2.
     "this and that"--
     derogatory feeling

ja-ta   যা-তা

B. <u>The doctor told me, "Look,</u>
<u>don't go into a village</u>
<u>and eat this and that."</u>

B. ডাক্তার বলে দিয়েছে , 'দেখ . গাঁয়ে গিয়ে
যেন যা-তা খেও না ।'

ḍaktar bole dieche ' dekho '
gãe gie jæno ' ja-ta kheo na "

19.   "only" (Persian)   sreph   স্রেফ

      "liquid curry"   jhol   ঝোল

      "curry and rice"   jhol-bhat   ঝোল-ভাত

   A. Why will you eat "this   A. যা-তা খাবে কেন ? আমার বাড়ীতে স্রেফ
      and that"? In my house   ঝোল-ভাত খাবে ।
      you eat only curry and
      rice.   ja-ta khabe kæno " amar barite '
                                      sreph jhol-bhat ' khao "

20.   For this use of /abar/, see Grammar, 4.

   B. But won't you be incon-   B. কিন্তু আমার জন্যে তোমাদের আবার
      veniencing yourselves   অসুবিধে হবে তো ?
      on my account?
                                     kintu amar jonne ' tomader abar
                                      ɔsubidhe ' hɔbe to "

21.   exclamation of about the   are   আরে
      strength of "Good heavens!"

   A. Good heavens, no. Don't A. আরে না , না । ও সব কথা ভেবো না ।
      consider such things.
                                     are ' na na " o śɔb kɔtha bhebo na "

   A. It will be no inconve-   A. আমার কোন অসুবিধে হবে না ।
      nience for me.
                                     amar ' kono ɔśubidhe hɔbe na "

22. B. OK, in that case,   B. বেশ , তা হলে চলি ।
      let's go.
                                     beś " ta hole ' cɔlo "

   B. Let's spend tonight   B. তোমার বাড়ীতে আজ রাত্তা কাটিয়ে যাই ।
      at your house.
                                     tomar barite ' aj ratta ' katie
                                      jai "

23.   idiom, "pay attention to"
      (lit. "give ear to")   kan de-   কান দে-

      "so much"   oto   অত

A. Look, Bob, don't pay so much attention to Mr. Dunn's stories.

A. দেখ বব , ডান সাহেবের কথায় অত কান দিও না ।

dækho bɔb ' ḍan śaheber kɔthae ' ɔto kan dio na "

A. Listen to me a minute.

A. আমার একটা কথা শোনো ।

amar ækṭa kɔtha ' śono "

24. B. What is it?

B. কি কথা বলো তো ?

ki kɔtha bɔlo to "

25. For this use of /kɔtha/, see Grammar, 3.

"east"

"know this for sure, believe me"

purbo, pub পূর্ব , পূব

e kɔtha jeno এ কথা জেনো

A. Believe me, it's important that you spend a little time in an East Bengal village.

A. এ কথা জেনো যে তোমার পূর্ব বাংলার গাঁয়ে কিছুকাল কাটানো দরকার ।

e kɔtha jeno je ' tomar ' purbo baṇlar gãe ' kichukal kaṭano ' dɔrkar "

26. B. Why?

B. কেন বলো তো ?

kæno bɔlo to "

27. "exactly, perfectly"

"exactly, perfectly"

ṭhik ঠিক

ṭhikbhabe ঠিকভাবে

A. Because you want to know East Bengal thoroughly.

A. কারণ তুমি তো পূর্ব বাংলাকে ঠিকভাবে জানতে চাও ।

karon ' tumi to purbo baṇlake ' ṭhikbhabe jante cao "

28. B. Right.

B. তুমি যা বলছো তা ঠিক ।

tumi ja bolcho ' ta ṭhik "

B. But I'm not coming here again in the rainy season.

B. তবে বর্ষাকালে আর এখানে আসছি না ।

tɔbe ' bɔrśa kale ' ar ekhane ' aśchi na "

29. <u>A</u>. <u>OK, next time come in the cool season.</u>   A. বেশ , তা হলে , পরের বার শীত কালে এসো ।

beś ' ta hole ' pɔrer bar ' śit kale ' eśo "

    <u>A</u>. <u>And bring your wife then too.</u>   A. আর তখন তোমার স্ত্রীকেও এনো ।

ar tɔkhon ' tomar strikec ' eno "

30. <u>B</u>. <u>Yes, I'll bring her then.</u>   B. হাঁ , তাই আনবো ।

hæ̃ ' tai anbo "

31. <u>A</u>. <u>Good. Then let's go to my house now.</u>   A. বেশ । তা হলে এখন আমার বাড়ীতে চলো ।

beś " ta hole ' ækhon ' amar barite cɔlo "

    loan word, "train"   ṭren ট্রেন
    loan word, "ticket"   ṭikeṭ টিকেট

    <u>A</u>. <u>Buy the train ticket tomorrow instead.</u>   A. কাল বরং ট্রেনের টিকেটটা কিনো ।

kal bɔroṇ ' ṭrener ṭikeṭṭa ' kino "

32. <u>B</u>. <u>Let's go.</u>   B. চলো যাই ।

cɔlo jai "

<u>Lesson 21, part 2. Grammar.</u>

1. Negative imperatives.

1.1. It was noted in Lesson 20 that the future imperative (high stem plus imperative endings) can be used to indicate an action that is to be carried out at some future time. Imperatives both present and future can be used with the negative particle /na/; in such cases, however, the logic of English grammar cannot be applied. The situation is as follows:

1.2. A negative form of the future imperative indicates a prohibition in <u>either</u> present or future time. Examples are sentences 4, 18, 21, 23; other examples:

ʈake'kichu dio na"   Don't (ord.) give him anything.
ʈar kachtheke'kichu kino na" Don't (ord.) buy anything from him.

1.3. The use of the negative particle /na/ with the present imperative indicates a <u>positive</u> request, which mught be translated by the English "Why don't you ..."; for example:

oʈa dao na"   Why don't you give it (to me)?
śɔndeśʈa khao na"   Why don't you eat the śandeś (i.e., please eat it)?

1.4. The same situation holds for the honorific imperative:

kichu khan na"   Why don't you eat something?
kichu khaben na"   Don't eat anything (with intonation of command).

1.5. Pay special attention to the taped drills. It will be clear that intonation helps to make clear the distinction between command and request.

1.6. The form /khabe na/ can be used to specify a future negative ordinary; but the same distinction exists between /kheo na/ and /khabe na/ as in English between "do not do something" and "you will not do something", the latter being a command made in the form of a statement. Such a form can be used only in certain situations, as when speaking to a subordinate in rank.

2. The form /jæno/, as in sentence 4.

/jæno/ as used here is a difficult form to translate. The significance is, in sentence 4, "see that you don't have to stay ...", "take care lest you stay ...". Another example:

ʈake khɔborʈa'jæno deoa na   (Take care) lest he be given the news.
hɔe"   (See that) he is not given the news.

See also Lesson 20, part 1, sentence 3.

3. The form /kɔtha/:

Again, the word varies rather widely in terms of lexical meaning.

3.1. It can mean "about, relating to", and in such cases can be replaced by /biśɔe/ or /śɔmmondhe/. Sentence 12 could read, without change of meaning:

ami'ɔśubidher biśɔe'bhabchi na"

3.2. It can mean, literally, "story" or "word", as in sentence 14. Another example:

śotti, śottikɔtha   truth, (lit. "true word")

3.3. It can mean, as a noun, "matters" (or as in the general sense in English, "things"); see for example sentences 21, 25.

4. You will have realized by this time that there are in Bengali a large number of what might be called "filler words" which sometimes have definable lexical meaning and sometimes not. A Bengali speaker will sometimes say in regard to these words that there is a slight emotional content which is lent to the utterance by their use, but that this content is very difficult to specify. In other words, by leaving them out, literal meaning is not changed, but some suggestive element is lost. Such words are /to/, which we have met frequently before, and, as in sentence 4 here, /abar/. By omitting /abar/ in sentence 4, the meaning of the utterance would remain the same, but an overtone would be lost. It is difficult, if not impossible, to teach students when to use these forms. Their use has to do with the natural rhythm of the language, a sense of which can be gained only by listening to Bengali speakers over a long period of time.

5. Any word in Bengali can be reduplicated, the second part beginning with /ʈ/. Examples:

boi-ʈoi   "books and such"
dækha-ʈækha   "looking around and so on"
ãttio-ʈãttio   "relatives and such"

Frequently this type of reduplication indicates a slightly derogatory or informal attitude on the part of the speaker.

5.1. There are more polite and formal ways to express "and such"; polite forms of the above would be:

dækha-śakha   "looking around and so on"
ãttio-śɔjon   "relatives and such"

Lesson 21, part 3. Patterns.

1. Pattern: sentence 1.

   a. Why don't you spend the night here with us?

   b. Why don't you spend some time in Bengal with us?

   c. Why don't you spend the week there with them?

   d. Why don't you rest here a while with us?

   e. Why don't you come and live with us?

2. Pattern: sentence 2 and 4.

   a. I have no objection; but my father has said, "See that you do not stay out tonight."

   b. I have no objection; but my instructions are: "See that you do not stay too long in one place."

   c. I have no objection; but my father has said, "See that you do not go to their house."

   d. I have no objection; but my mother has said: "See that you do not delay at all."

   e. I have no objection; but my father has said: "See that you do not stay outside the hostel."

3. Pattern: sentence 5 and 8.

   a. Why is that? Does he think there are dangers here?

   b. Why is that? Does he think that there are lots of dangers in Bengal?

   c. Why is that? Does he think that there will be trouble at their house?

   d. Why is that? Does she think that there is inconvenience to us?

   e. Why is that? Does he think that there is danger in staying outside the hostel?

4. Pattern: sentence 9.

   a. Yes, and perhaps he's right. You live among snakes and other such things.

   b. Yes, and perhaps he's right. There are lots of dangers of snakes and such.

   c. Yes, and perhaps he's right. They live in the middle of a constant uproar.

   d. Yes, and perhaps he's right. You live with all kinds of relatives and such.

   e. Yes, and perhaps he's right. There are dangers from robbers and such.

5. Pattern: sentence 11.

    a. I understand. He thinks that you yourself will be greatly inconvenienced; isn't that it?

    b. I understand. He thinks that we ourselves will be inconvenienced; isn't that it?

    c. I understand. He doesn't think that they themselves will be inconvenienced, does he?

    d. I understand. She thinks that we ourselves will be inconvenienced; is that it?

    e. I understand. He doesn't think that we ourselves will be inconvenienced, does he?

6. Pattern: sentence 12.

    a. No, he's not thinking about my own inconvenience.

    b. No, he's not thinking about inconvenience at all.

    c. No, he's not thinking about their own inconvenience.

    d. No, she's not thinking about your own inconvenience.

    e. No, he's not thinking about anyone's inconvenience.

7. Pattern: sentence 13.

    a. In that case, why don't you stay here with us?

    b. In that case, why don't you spend some time in Bengal with us?

    c. In that case, why don't you stay with them?

    d. In that case, why don't you stay here a while?

    e. In that case, why don't you stay here; there are no dangers.

8. Pattern: sentence 14, 16, 18.

    a. All right. Let me tell you the true story. My stomach is very bad. The doctor told me: "Don't eat this and that."

    b. All right. Let me tell you the true story. My health is bad, and the doctor told me: "Don't stay in hot places."

    c. All right. Let me tell you the true story. My health is bad, and the doctor told me: Don't go where there is trouble."

    d. All right. Let me tell you the truth. My mother is angry, and she told me: "Don't go to Kabir's house."

    e. All right. Let me tell you the truth. My father doesn't like you; he told me: "Don't go and stay with them."

9. Pattern: sentence 19.

    a. Why will you eat this and that? You will eat good food.

    b. Why does he say that? In Bengal the weather will not be hot.

364

 c. Why does he say that? There will be no trouble at his house.

 d. Why does she say that? In my house we will feed you well.

 e. Why does he say that? In our house perhaps you will be very happy?

10. Pattern: sentence 20.

 a. But won't you be inconveniencing yourselves on my account?

 b. But you should not inconvenience yourselves on my account.

 c. But they should not inconvenience themselves on my account.

 d. But don't inconvenience yourselves on my account.

 e. But you will inconvenience yourselves on my account.

11. Pattern: sentence 21.

 a. Don't even consider such things.

 b. There will be no inconvenience for us; don't even consider it.

 c. Don't worry about all that.

 d. Don't even talk about it.

 e. Don't even mention such things.

Pattern: sentence 23.

 a. Don't pay so much attention to the doctor's stories.

 b. Don't pay so much attention to his stories.

 c. Don't pay so much attention to his stories; listen to me a minute.

 d. Don't pay any attention to such things.

 e. Don't pay any attention to such stories.

12. Pattern: sentence 25.

 a. Believe me, I know it's important for me to spend some time in a Bengal village.

 b. Believe me, I think it's necessary for me to spend some time in Bengal.

 c. Believe me, I know it's necessary for me to spend a little time there

 d. Believe me, you know I want to spend a little time with you.

 e. Believe me, you know that I think it's necessary for me to spend a little time in a village.

Pattern: sentence 27.

 a. I want to know Bengal thoroughly.

 b. I want to know one part of India thoroughly.

c. I want to know them well.

d. I want to know you better.

e. I want to know village life thoroughly.

Lesson 21, part 4. Sentence Drills.

Drill 1

--Don't take all those things to India. You won't need them.

--But everyone says: "Do take that with you," or "Won't you take this to my friend in Bombay."

--Tell them that you cannot. Don't tell them that you are going to Bombay.

--What shall I take, then?

--Take only what you need. Many things you will be able to buy cheaply in India.

--What shall I eat in India?

--Do not eat uncooked things or drink water. Drink tea instead.

--But if someone says, "Why don't you eat this," what shall I do?

--Say that you are ill and cannot eat all those things.

--How shall I get a servant in India?

--After you reach India, write a letter to a friend of mine. He will give you the name of a good servant.

--If someone comes to the door, should I give him a job?

--No. Give a job only to someone whom you know.

--Where shall I live in Calcutta?

--Decide that after you reach there.

Drill 2

--What are you studying at the university?

--I'm studying Bengali literature.

--Have you read the poems of Candidas? If not, do read them. They are very beautiful.

--Tell me the names of some other well-known Bengali writers.

--Read Rabindranath, of course. But don't read his work in English translation. Read it in Bengali.

--What other writers of that period should I read?

--Read Bankim-candra. Read Sarat-candra only afterwards.

--What writers of the older period should I read?

--Read Bharat-candra's Bidya-sundar (bidda-sundor). But don't expect it to be a religious poem.

--Should I read the Vaisnava writers also?

--Yes, their poetry is very sweet. But don't read Dina Candidas now.

--Why not?

--His poetry is very difficult. Read it after reading other Vaisnava
  poets.

Lesson 21, part 5. Vocabulary.

lɔrkar proeojon	need, necessity	śɔsta	cheap
		ɔśustho	ill
cakor	servant	namkɔra	well-known
cakri	job	modhur	sweet
ciʈhi	letter	ɔśeddo	uncooked
dɔrja	door	khuśi	happy
dhɔrmer kobita	religious poem		
nirdeś	instruction	aśa kɔr- cinta kɔr-	(to) hope, expect
hosʈel	hostel, dormitory	deri kɔr-	(to) delay
jhamela jhɔnjhaʈ muśkil	trouble		
āttio-śɔjon (polite) āttio-tāttio	relatives and such	bɔroŋ tar bɔdole	instead
ɖakat-ʈakat	robbers and such		

Idioms:

agekar śɔmoe	older times
rege ache/en	is angry
hɔʈʈogoler majhkhane	in the middle of constant uproar

Lesson 22, part 1. Conversation.

| | Analysis and translation | Bengali |

Note: the conversation is between two women.

1. verb stem, "eat" — kha- খা-

causitive suffix for vowel-stems; see Grammar, 1. — -oa- -ওয়া

causative stem, "feed" — khaoa- খাওয়া-

verbal noun suffix — -ba- -বা-

"feeding" — khaoaba- খাওয়াবা-

A. I heard that you have made arrangements to feed many people at Minu's wedding.

A. আমি শুনলুম যে তোমরা মিনুর বিয়েতে অনেক লোকজন খাওয়াবার ব্যবস্থা করেছো ।

ami śunlum je ' tomra ' minur biete ' ɔnek lokjon ' khaoabar bæbostha ' korecho "

2. 3rd person nominative honorific pronoun; the reference here is clearly to the speaker's husband. — uni তিনি

alternative form of causative verbal noun stem, "feeding"; see Grammar, 1. — khaoano- খাওয়ানো-

verb stem, "bring" — an- আন-

causative form of PAP, "causing/having caused to bring" — anie আনিয়ে

"he has caused to be brought"; see Grammar, 1.3. — aniechen আনিয়েছেন

B. <u>Yes, he has had many kinds</u>
<u>of food and sweets brought</u>
<u>from Calcutta to feed the</u>
<u>people.</u>

B. হাঁ , তুঁনি কুলকাতা থেকে অনেক রকম
খাবার ওমিষ্টি লোকজন খাওয়ানোর জন্যে
আনিয়েছেন ।

<u>hæ̃ ' uni kolkata theke ' ɔnek rɔkom</u>
<u>khabar o miṣṭi ' lokjon khaoanor</u>
<u>jonne ' aniechen "</u>

3.   type of śaṛi made in   benarośi   বেনারসী
     Benares

     verb stem, "wear"   pɔr-   পর-

     causative verb stem,   pɔra-   পরা-
     "dress, cause to wear"

     "you will dress"   pɔrabe   পরাবে

A. <u>In which Benares śaṛi</u>   A. মিনুকে বিয়ের রাত্রে কোন বেনারসীটা
<u>will you dress Minu on</u>   পরাবে ?
<u>her wedding night?</u>

<u>minuke ' bier rattre ' kon</u>
<u>benarośiṭa pɔrabe "</u>

4.   "the other day"   śe din   সে দিন

     "aunt" -- mother's sister   maśi   মাসী

     verb stem, "send"   paṭha-   পাঠা-

     "(she) has sent"; see   paṭhieche   পাঠিয়েছে
     Grammar, 1.3.

     verb stem, "see"   dækh-   দেখ-

     causative verb stem,   dækha-   দেখা-
     "show"

     causative PAP, "showing,   dekhie   দেখিয়ে
     having shown"

     "I have shown"   dekhiechi   দেখিয়েছি

     alternative objective   -e   -তে
     case ending

     "you (objective)"   tomae   তোমায়

B. <u>Have I shown you the red</u>   B. সে দিন যে লাল বেনারসীটা মিনুর
<u>Benares śaṛi which Minu's</u>   মাসী পাঠিয়েছে সেটা কি তোমায়
<u>aunt sent the other day?</u>   দেখিয়েছি ।

<u>śe kin ' je lal benarośiṭa ' minur</u>
<u>maśi ' paṭhieche ' śeṭa ki ' tomae</u>
<u>dekhiechi "</u>

5   "day before yesterday"   porśu   পরশু

superlative degree, "best, most of all", see Grammar, 3.

"is liked by her"

śɔb cee সব চেয়ে

or pɔchonᴏo ওর পছন্দ

__A.__ __Minu herself showed it to me day before yesterday; Minu said she likes that śari best of all.__

__A.__ পরশু মিনু নিজেই আমাকে দেখিয়েছে মিনু বললে এ শাড়ীটা ওর সবচেয়ে পছন্দ ।

__porśu ' minu nijei ' amake dekhieche " minu bolle ' oi śarita or śɔb cee pɔchondo "__

6. verb stem, "flatter, become (as clothes)"

mana- মানা—

__B.__ __Do you think that the śari will become her?__

তোমার কি মনে হয় শাড়ীটা ওকে মানাবে ?

__tomar ki mone hɔe ' śarita oke ' manabe "__

7. verb stem, "dress"

conditional conjunctive "if you dress"

verb stem, "see, appear"

"you will cause to appear"

"rose-colored"

loan word, "veil"

pɔra- পরা—
pɔrale পরালে

dæch- দেখ—
dækhabe দেখাবে
golapi গোলাপী
bhel ভেল

__A.__ __If you dress her in that, you will make her appear most beautiful; if there were a rose-colored veil with it, it would be even better.__

__A.__ ওটা পরালে ওকে খুব সুন্দর দেখাবে এর সঙ্গে একটা গোলাপী ভেল হলে আরো ভালো হয় ।

__ota pɔrale ' oke khub śundor dækhabe " er śɔnge ' ækta golapi bhel hole ' aro bhalo hɔe "__

8. informal address, used only between intimates; see Grammar, 4.

pipes and drums played at weddings

verb stem, "bring"

causative verb stem "cause to bring"

go গো

nɔhobɔt নহবত

an- আন—
ana- আনা—

B. Yes. You are having the
   instruments brought,
   aren't you?

B. হাঁগো , নহবত আনাচ্ছো না?

hãgo " nɔhobɔt ' anaccho na "

9. "husband's eldest
   brother"   bɔṭṭhakur   বটঠাকুর

   causative verbal noun,   anano   আনানো
   "causing to bring"

   noun, "consent"   raji   রাজী

   causative verb stem,   kɔra-   করা-
   "cause to do"

   "persuade"   raji kɔra-   রাজী করা-

A. (husband's eldest brother) A. বটঠাকুর আর ঠাকুরপো দুজনেরই ইচ্ছে
   and (husband's younger   নহবত আনানোর কিন্তু ওকে কিছুতেই রাজী
   brother) both want to   করানো যাচ্ছেনা ।
   have the instruments
   brought, but he (i.e.,
   speaker's husband) cannot   bɔṭṭhakur ar ṭhakurpo ' dujoneri
   be persuaded at all.   icche ' nɔhobɔt ananor ' kintu oke
                                kichutei ' raji kɔrano ' jacche na

10. "seventy"   śottor   সত্তর

    "eighty"   aśi   আশী

    "bridegroom"   bɔr   বর

    "trip, pilgrimage"   jattra   যাত্রা

    "traveller"   jattri   যাত্রী

    compound noun, "bride-   bɔrjattri   বরযাত্রী
    groom's companions"

    verb stem, "sit"   bɔś-   বস-

    causative verb stem,   bɔśa-   বসা-
    "seat, cause to sit"

B. I see. I hear that about   B. আচ্ছা , শুনছি প্রায় সত্তর আশীজন
   seventy or eighty people   বরযাত্রী আসছে , তা ওদের বসাচ্ছো
   are coming in the groom's   কোথায় ?
   party; where are you going
   to put them?   accha " śunchi ' prae śottor
                                aśijon bɔrjattri asche " ta oder
                                bɔśaccho kothae "

11. diminutive suffix   -ṭuku   -টুকু

    "such a little"   æṭoṭuku   এটুকু

    "both ... and ... "   ba ... ba ...   বা... বা ...

    noun, "son-in-law"   jamai   জামাই

compound noun, "daughter and son-in-law"   meejamai মেয়েজামাই

verb stem, "rest, lie down"   śo- শো–

causative verb stem, "cause to rest"   śoa- শোয়া–

A. <u>I'm also wondering about that -- both where in this little house I'm going to put the groom's party, and where I'm going to have the bride and groom rest.</u>

A. আমিও তাই ভাবছি — এই এতটুকু বাড়ীতে কোথায় বা বরযাত্রীদের বসাবো আর কোথায় বা মেয়েজামাইকে শোয়াবো ।

<u>amio tai bhabchi ' ei ætoṭuku barite ' kothae ba ' bɔrjattrider bɔsabo ' ar kothae ba ' meejamaike śoabo "</u>

12. "apart from that"   ta chaṛa তা ছাড়া

"young"   koci কচি

noun, "sleep"   ghum ঘুম

verb stem, "lay (something) down"   paṛ- পাড়–

causative, "cause to lay down, put to sleep"   paṛa- পাড়া–

causative, "cause to go to sleep, put to sleep"; see Grammar, 2.3.1.   ghum paṛa- ঘুম পাড়া–

"quiet, private"   niribili নিরিবিলি

B. <u>Apart from that, it would be a good thing if there were a secluded room in your house for putting the many little children to sleep.</u>

B. তা ছাড়া , তোমাদের বাড়ীতে তো অনেকগুলো কচি বাচ্চা , তাদের ঘুম পাড়াবার জন্যও একটা নিরিবিলি ঘর হলে ভাল হয় ।

<u>ta chaṛa ' tomader barite to ' ɔnekgulo koci bacca ' tader ghum paṛabar jonneo ' ækṭa niribili ghɔr hole ' bhalo hɔe "</u>

13. verb stem, "arrange, put in order"   gocha- গোছা–

"what can be done"   ki kɔra jae কি করা যায়

572

A. You're right. If you could come one day, we both could arrange and prepare the rooms and see what could be done where.

A. ঠিক বলেছো । তুমি যদি একদিন আসতে পারতে তা হলে দুজনে ঘরগুলো সাজিয়ে গুছিয়ে দেখতে পারতাম কোথায় কি করা যায় ।

thik bolecho " tumi jodi ' ækdin aśte parte ' ta hole ' dujone ghɔrgulo śajie guchie ' dekhte partam ' kothae ' ki kɔra jae "

14. "with my help, by means of me"

verb stem, "laugh"

"cause to laugh"

"let it be"

amake die   আমাকে দিয়ে

haś-   হাস-

haśa-   হাসা-

ja hok   যা হোক

B. You will arrange the house with my help. That makes me laugh.

B. আমাকে দিয়ে ঘর গুছোবে । তুমি হাসালে যা হোক ।

amake die ' ghɔr guchobe " tumi haśale ' ja hok "

15. post-position, "from" (a person); see Grammar, 5.

"insignificant"

noun, "help"

kach theke   কাছ থেকে

śamanno   সামান্য

śahajjo   সাহায্য

A. Why? Can't I get even this trifling little help from you?

A. কেন ? তোমার কাছ থেকে কি আমি এই সামান্য সাহায্যটুকু পেতে পারি না ?

kæno " tomar kach theke ki ' ami ei śamanno śahajjotuku ' pete pari na "

16. expression of reproach

"neat, fastidious"

"untidy, sloppy"

"appropriate"

verb stem, "increase"

"(to) overrate (someone)" -- lit. "increase the price of"

chi chi   ছি ছি

gochal   গোছাল

ɔgochal   অগোছাল

upojukto   উপযুক্ত

baɽa-   বাড়া-

dam baɽie de-   দাম বাড়িয়ে দে-

B. Come now. It's not that.
You overrate me, thinking
it appropriate for a sloppy person like me to
arrange the house.

B. হি , হি , তা নয় । আমার মত অগোছাল
লোককে ঘর সাজানোর উপযুক্ত ভেবে তুমি
আমার দাম বাড়িয়ে দিলে ।

chi chi ' ta nɔe " amar mɔto
ɔgochal lokke ' ghar sajanor
upojukto bhebe ' tumi amar '
dam barie dile "

17.   noun, "joke"   ṭhaṭṭa   ঠাট্টা

      verb stem, "cry, weep"   kād-   কাঁদ-

      causative, "cause to cry"   kāda-   কাঁদা-

A. It's not a joke; tell me
when you are coming. But
if it upsets the baby,
don't come.

A. ঠাট্টা নয় , কখন আসছো বলো । তবে
ছেলে কাঁদিয়ে এসো না ।

ṭhaṭṭa nɔe " kɔkhon aścho bɔlo "
tɔbe chele kādie ' eśo na "

18.   colloquial form, "night"   rattir   রাত্তির

      verb stem, "eat"   kha-   খা-

      causative stem, "feed"   khaoa-   খাওয়া-

      causative PAP, "having fed"   khaie   খাইয়ে

      compound stem, "cause   khaie de- খাইয়ে দে-
      to be fed"

      "while listening"; see   śunte śunte   শুনতে শুনতে
      Grammar, 6.

B. I can go tonight even;
when I have the baby fed,
he falls asleep while
listening to a story
from his father.

B. আজ রাত্তিরেই খেতে পারি , ছেলেটাকে
খাইয়ে দিলে ওর বাবার কাছে গল্প শুনতে
শুনতে ঘুমিয়ে পড়ে ।

aj rattirei jete pari "
cheleṭake khaie dile ' or babar
kache ' gɔlpo śunte śunte ghumie
pɔre "

      noun, "bother, nuisance"   jhamela   ঝামেলা

      causative verb stem,   neoa-   নেওয়া-
      "cause to take"

      "will have to cause to   neoate hɔbe   নেওয়াতে হবে
      take"; see Grammar, 7.

      verb stem, "reach"   poŭcho-, poŭcha-   পৌঁছো- পৌঁছা-

      compound verb, "cause   poŭche de-   পৌঁছে দে-
      to reach"

"will have to cause to reach"   poŭche dite hɔbe পৌঁছে দিতে হবে

B. The bother will be only this, that you will have to have someone take me and bring me back (i.e., "cause me to reach home").

B. ঝামেলা শুধু এই যে তোমাকে কাউকে দিয়ে আমাকে নেওয়াতে হবে আর পৌঁছে দিতে হবে ।

jhamela śudhu ei ' je tomake ' kauke die ' amake neoate hɔbe ' ar poŭche dite hɔbe "

19. A. We'll talk about taking you home later; I'm wondering about who will bring you.

A. পৌঁছে দেবার কথা পরে হবে , কাকে দিয়ে তোমায় আনাই তাই ভাবছি ।

poŭche debar kɔtha ' pɔre hɔbe " kake die ' tomae anai ' tai bhabchi "

Lesson 22, part 2. Grammar.

1. Causative verbs.

1.1. It will have been noted that the causative stem is formed by the addition of /-a-/ to consonant-final stems, and /-oa-/ to vowel-finals. Thus:

Consonant stem: pɔr- "wear"   Causative: pɔra- "cause to wear, dress"

pɔṛ- "read"   pɔṛa- "cause to read, teach"

Vowel stem: kha- "eat"   Causative: khaoa- "cause to eat, feed"

ja- "go"   jaoa- "cause to go"

1.2. The causative verbal noun is formed by the addition of /-no/ to the stem + /a/ or /oa/ complex, thus:

dækha-	"show"	dækhano	"showing"
ana-	"bring"	anano	"bringing"
paoa-	"cause to get"	paoano	"causing to get"

1.2.1. The verbal noun suffix /-ba-/, used in the genitive, is also affixed to the stem /a/ or /oa/:

pɔra-	"dress"	pɔrabar	"of dressing"
khaoa-	"feed"	khaoabar	"of feeding"

1.2.2. The case endings are affixed to the /-a-/, /-oa-/, or /-ba-/ suffixes, as in other types of verbal nouns.

1.2.3. Tense suffixes for the simple tenses **and conditional** conjunctive suffix are added to the low stem + causative **suffix** complex.

dækhabo	"I will show", etc.
bɔśalum	"I caused to sit", etc.
kɔracchi	"I am causing to do", etc.
jaoacchilum	"I was causing to go", etc.
khaoale	"If (I) feed"

1.3. Tenses formed on the base of the PAP (present completive, past completive), the PAP itself, and the future imperative are somewhat different.

1.3.1. The PAP is formed by the <u>high stem</u> of consonant-stem verbs, except where the stem-vowel is /a/, plus the suffix /-i-/ plus the PAP ending /-e/:

kena-	"cause to buy"	kinie	"having caused to buy"
kɔra-	"cause to do"	korie	"having caused to do"

1.3.2. The PAP of consonant-final stems where the stem-vowel is /a/ and of vowel-final stems preserves the low stem, and adds the suffix /-i-/ and the PAP ending /-e/:

haśa-	"cause to laugh"	haśie	"having caused to laugh"
paoa-	"cause to get"	paie	"having caused to get"

1.3.3. The stems /de-/ and /ne-/ **form** a separate class, taking high stems /di-/ and /ni-/:

deoa	"cause to give"	diie	"having caused to give"

1.3.4. The verb formations based on the PAP add the regular tense and personal ending complex to this causative PAP:

koriechi	"I have caused to do"
khaiechi	"I have fed"

1.3.5. The future imperative causitive adds the imperative ending /-o/
to the high stem + /i/ complex:

ośio	"seat (him)"
diio	"give (it)"

2. Non-causative derivative stems:

2.1. There is a class of verbs in Bengali which is derived from noun
stems; the shape of the stem-forms of these verbs is CVCa-, or, sometimes
in the colloquial, CVCo-. These are similar to causative stems in shape,
but do not have causative meaning. Some of them we have already met,
for example:

Noun	Gloss	Verb Stem	Gloss
ghum	sleep	ghumo-, ghuma-	(to) sleep
douɽ	run	douɽo-, douɽa-	(to) run

2.2. This class of verbs has several peculiar characterisitics.

2.2.1. The non-finite PAP may be formed from either the CVCo- or CVC-
stem:

śamlie or śamle	"having restrained"
poŭchie or poŭche	"having reached"

The stem /ghumo-/ forms a subclass; only /ghumie/ occurs in PAP.

2.2.2. /poŭcho-/ presents the following three possibilities of causative formation:

2.2.2.1. PAP + causative auxiliary:

poŭche deoa-	"cause to reach"
take poŭche diiechi	"I caused him to reach"

2.2.2.2. Causative PAP + suffixes, poŭchie + chi, etc.:

take poŭchiechi	"I caused him to reach"

2.2.2.3. Causative PAP + non-causative auxiliary:

pouchie + de-	"cause to reach"
take poŭchie diechi	"I caused him to reach"

2.2.2.4. The formation in 2.2.2.1. occurs in one type of idiolect and those in 2.2.2.2. and 2.2.2.3. occur free-variantly in other types of idiolects.

2.2.2.5. Forms such as:

śamla-	"restrain"
hatra-	"grope"
śatra-	"swim"
kamra-	"bite"

though of different canonical shape, class with /poŭcho-/, as above.

2.3. The forms /douro-/ and /ghumo-/ also form a separate class presenting the following possibilities of causative formation:

2.3.1. Noun stem + causative auxiliary, /kɔra-/, /ana-/, /para-/, etc.

dour kɔra-	"cause to run"
dour deoa-	"cause to run"
take dour koriechi	"I caused him to run"
take dour diiechi	"I caused him to run"
ghum paro-	"cause to sleep"
take ghum pariechi	"I caused him to sleep"

2.3.2. Causative PAP + suffixes = dourie + chi, etc.

take douriechi	"I caused him to run"

2.3.3. However, the form /ghumiechi/, though it occurs, has non-causative semantic value.

3. Comparative and superlative degrees of modifiers:

3.1. The comparative degree is formed by the use of the connective /cee/, "than" and the adjective /aro/, "more". Note that that to which the subject is being compared stands first in the clause or sentence:

amar cee'śe lɔmba"	He is taller than I.
amar cee'śe aro lɔmba"	He is even taller than I.

3.2. The superlative degree is indicated by the use of /śɔb cee/, "than all".

378

śe'śɔb cee'lɔmba	He is tallest (i.e., he is taller than everyone).
amader chattro-chattrira' śɔb cee bhalo"	Our students are the best (of all).

4. The form /go/.

/go/ is a form of address, or, if you prefer, a vocative particle, which is used between close friends or intimates in informal situations. A husband might use the form in addressing his wife, for example, or a wife her husband. It is not a form which a foreigner can often use.

5. The form /kach theke/.

"From (a person)" is always expressed by /kach theke/:

ami'tar kach theke'śunechi"	I have heard it from him.
ami'tar kach theke'peechi"	I have gotten it from him.

There is another possible use. /kach/ means "near"; thus the expression /ʈebiler kache theke/, "from near the table", is possible.

6. Reduplicated infinitive, as in sentence 18.

A reduplicated infinitive gives the meaning "while (doing something)":

bæɽate bæɽate	while wandering around
colte colte	while going
bhabte bhabte	while thinking (reflecting)

7. The infinitive plus a third person form of the verb /hɔ-/ has the force of "have/has to"; note the case inflection of the pronoun which in the English sentence is the subject.

tomake amae'eʈa paʈhate hɔe"	You have to send it to me.
amake'ækhon baɽi'jete hɔbe"	I have to go home now.

Lesson 22, part 3. Patterns.

1. Pattern: sentence 1.

a. I heard that you have made arrangements to decorate the room.
b. I heard that you have made arrangements to feed me tonight.
c. I heard that you have made arrangements to put the children to sleep here.

d. I heard that you have made **arrangements to have** the food brought from home.

e. I heard that you have made **arrangements** to show your pictures to me.

2. Pattern: sentence 2.

a. Yes, I have had many kinds of colors and cloths brought to decorate the room.

b. Yes, I have had many kinds of food brought to feed you tonight.

c. Yes, I have had many rooms arranged to put the children to sleep.

d. Yes, I have had arrangements made to have the food brought from there.

e. Yes, I have had many pictures brought to show to you.

3. Pattern: sentence 3.

a. In which colors will you decorate the room on the night of the celebration?

b. In which sari will you dress Lila on the night of the puja?

c. In which rooms will you put the children to sleep tonight?

d. In which rooms will we feed all the people tonight?

e. In which places will you show me the pictures?

4. Pattern: sentence 4.

a. Have I shown you the red cloth which my sister sent me the other day?

b. Have I shown you the new Benares sari which I had (i.e., caused to be) bought the other day?

c. Have I shown you the south rooms, which I had decorated the other day?

d. Have I shown you the rooms which I had arranged the other day?

e. Have I shown you this picture, which I had brought from Calcutta the other day?

5. Pattern: sentence 5.

a. You showed it to me yourself day before yesterday; I like that cloth best of all.

b. Lila showed it to me yesterday; I like it better than this one.

c. Ram showed them to me this morning; I like them better than these rooms.

d. You showed them to me yourself yesterday; I like them best of all.

e. You have not shown me that one; I like it best of all.

6. Pattern: sentence 7.

a. Yes, if I decorate the room in that color, I will make it appear very beautiful.

b. Yes, if I dress her in that, I will make her appear very beautiful.

c. Yes, if we put the children to sleep in there, it will be very good.

d. Yes, if we feed the people in these rooms, it will be very convenient.

e. Yes. If I showed you my new pictures, you would like them even better.

7. Pattern: sentence 8.

a. You are having lamps and such brought, aren't you?

b. You are having food and such brought, aren't you?

c. You are having beds and such brought, aren't you?

d. You are having mats and such brought, aren't you?

e. You are having the pictures brought, aren't you?

8. Pattern: sentence 9.

a. He wants to have them brought, but I cannot be persuaded at all.

b. I want to have the food brought from Calcutta, but he cannot be persuaded at all.

c. I want to have new beds brought, but he cannot be persuaded at all.

d. We want to have them brought, and he is being persuaded.

e. I want to have them sold, but the painter cannot be persuaded at all.

9. Pattern: sentence 10.

a. I hear that fifty or sixty guests are coming. Where are you going to put them all?

b. I hear that hundreds and hundreds of people are coming from the city; where are you going to put them all?

c. I hear that many children are coming; will you put them all to sleep in there?

d. I hear that thirty or forty people are coming; will you feed them all in here?

e. I hear that many people are coming to see the pictures; will you show all the pictures to them?

10. Pattern: sentence 11.

    a. I'm wondering both where to seat them all and how to feed them.
    b. I'm wondering both where to seat them all and where to have have them rest.
    c. I'm wondering both where to put them to sleep and how to feed them.
    d. I'm wondering both where to feed them and where to seat them.
    e. I'm wondering both how and where to show the pictures to them.

11. Pattern: sentence 13, 14.

    a. If I could come one day, we both could arrange the rooms.
    b. If I could come one day, we both could see what could be done where.
    c. If I could come one day, you could arrange the room through me.
    d. If I could come one day, you could get a little help from me.
    e. Let it go. If I could come one day, we both could arrange the rooms for showing the pictures.

12. Pattern: sentence 16.

    a. I cannot keep from laughing; you overrate me, thinking it appropriate for me to arrange the rooms.
    b. I cannot keep from laughing; you overrate me, thinking that I could give you even a little help.
    c. I cannot keep from laughing; you overrate yourself, thinking that a person like you could help me arrange the room.
    d. I could not help laughing; you overrate me, thinking it appropriate for a person like me to arrange the rooms.
    e. I could not help laughing, when I heard that two sloppy people like us would arrange the rooms.

13. Pattern: sentence 18.

    a. Come now. It's not that. But I will have to have someone bring you and take you back.
    b. It's not a joke. I will have someone bring you here and take you back.
    c. It's not a joke. But it will be a bother to you, that you will have to have someone bring me and take me back.
    d. Come now. We'll talk later about taking me home; but you will have to have someone bring me here.
    e. Come now. We'll talk about arranging the rooms later. Now we will have to talk about who will bring me here and take me back.

Lesson 22, part 3. Sentence Drills.

Drill 1

--Have you fed the baby?

--Yes, I fed him an hour ago.

--And have you dressed him?

--Yes, I have dressed him in his new clothes.

--Has he been good today?

--Yes, he has slept most of the day. Some people came this afternoon and tried to make him laugh.

--Why do people always make babies laugh or dance?

--I don't know. I decorated his room today with two new pictures and some flowers.

--Have you shown Nina the new decorations?

--Yes. She doesn't like them.

--Why don't you make her feed the baby once in a while. She is old enough.

--I made her feed the baby today. She didn't like it.

--What does she like to do?

--She likes to make the baby laugh and dance. She dressed him in my new sari today.

--I've been standing all day long. I think I'll go to sleep.

Drill 2

--Why are you lifting that chair? It's too heavy for you.

--I'm not lifting it. I'm only trying to move it over there.

--Let me move it for you. You rest for a while.

--All right. I bent the leg of it a little when I was trying to move it.

--Show me the place. I'll make it right.

--There is where I bent it. Can you fix it?

--Yes, I'll fix it right away. Has the dog been sleeping all day?

--No, he bit the postman this morning.

--Is he all right now?

--No. When the dog bit him the postman jumped and fell down the stairs.

--I'm not talking about the postman. Is the dog all right?

--Yes, he's all right.

Lesson 22, part 5. Vocabulary.

khoka	baby	ghum-, ghuma-,	sleep
koci chele	baby	otha-	lift
bacca chele		tola-	
sĭri	stairs	nora-	move (wiggle, shake)
pion	postman	śora-	move (push)
kukur	dog	bæka-	bend
jothesţo	enough	kamŗa-	bite
kokhono kokhono	once in a while	lapha-	jump
		lagano-	(to) fix
		mæramot kora-	(to) repair
		ceśţa kora-	(to) try